Dedication

To the undergraduate group piano students of the University of Texas at Austin—I really do believe in your ability to succeed. Always bring some joy to your music making whether on your own instrument or voice or *even on the piano*!

To my "groupies," the class piano graduate teaching assistants for the 2000–2001 academic year—Alexandre Dossin, Naoki Hakutani, Alejandro Hernandez, Owen Lovell, Paola Perin, Kevin Richmond, and Mini Zhang—thank you for your patience this year and for your helpful input at revision time.

PDM

Piano for the Developing Musician

Fifth Edition

Martha Hilley
The University of Texas at Austin

Lynn Freeman Olson

Australia • Canada • Mexico • Singapore • Spain
United Kingdom • United States

Editorial Director for the Humanities: Clark G. Baxter
Assistant Editor: Jennifer Ellis
Editorial Assistant: Jonathan Katz
Executive Marketing Manager: Diane McOscar
Marketing Assistant: Kasia Zagorski
Project Manager: Dianne Jensis Toop
Print/Media Buyer: Karen Hunt
Permissions Manager: Robert Kauser
Production Service: A-R Editions, Inc.
Copy Editor: A-R Editions, Inc.
Cover Designer: Carole Lawson
Cover Image: The Metropolitan Museum of Art, Frank Lloyd Wright, window triptych from the Avery Coonly Playhouse. Purchase, Edward C. Moore, Jr. Gift and Edgar J. Kaufman Charitable Foundation Gift. 1967 (67 213 1-3)
Cover Printer: Malloy Lithographing, Inc.
Compositor: A-R Editions, Inc.
Printer: Malloy Lithographing, Inc.

Printed in the United States of America
2 3 4 5 6 7 05 04 03 02

For permission to use material from this text, contact us by
Web: http://www.thomsonrights.com
Fax: 1-800-730-2215
Phone: 1-800-730-2214

Wadsworth/Thomson Learning
10 Davis Drive
Belmont, CA 94002-3098
USA

ISBN 0-534-51778-1

For more information about our products, contact us:
Thomson Learning Academic Resource Center
1-800-423-0563
http://www.wadsworth.com

International Headquarters
Thomson Learning
International Division
290 Harbor Drive, 2nd Floor
Stamford, CT 06902-7477
USA

UK/Europe/Middle East/South Africa
Thomson Learning
Berkshire House
168-173 High Holborn
London WC1V 7AA
United Kingdom

Asia
Thomson Learning
60 Albert Street, #15-01
Albert Complex
Singapore 189969

Canada
Nelson Thomson Learning
1120 Birchmount Road
Toronto, Ontario M1K 5G4
Canada

Contents

2. Pentascales

3. Root Position Triads

RELATED SKILLS AND ACTIVITIES

SUBSEQUENT REPERTOIRE

4. Extended Use of Intervals, Pentascales, and Triads/ Dominant Seventh

EXEMPLARY REPERTOIRE

TOPICS TO EXPLORE AND DISCUSS

RELATED SKILLS AND ACTIVITIES

7. White-Key Major Scale Fingerings/Blues Pentascale and the 12-Bar Blues

8. White-Key Minor Scale Fingerings/ Diatonic Harmonies in Minor

SUBSEQUENT REPERTOIRE

9. The ii–V7–I Progression

EXEMPLARY REPERTOIRE

TOPICS TO EXPLORE AND DISCUSS

RELATED SKILLS AND ACTIVITIES

SUBSEQUENT REPERTOIRE

10. Secondary Dominants/Styles of Accompanying

11. Harmonic Implications of Common Modes

TOPICS TO EXPLORE AND DISCUSS

RELATED SKILLS AND ACTIVITIES

SUBSEQUENT REPERTOIRE

12. Diatonic Seventh Chords in Major and Minor/ Secondary Seventh Chords

EXEMPLARY REPERTOIRE

TOPICS TO EXPLORE AND DISCUSS

RELATED SKILLS AND ACTIVITIES

SUBSEQUENT REPERTOIRE

13. Altered/Borrowed Triads

EXEMPLARY REPERTOIRE

TOPICS TO EXPLORE AND DISCUSS

RELATED SKILLS AND ACTIVITIES

SUBSEQUENT REPERTOIRE

14. Altered Seventh Chords/Extended Harmonies (Ninth, Thirteenth)

EXEMPLARY REPERTOIRE

TOPICS TO EXPLORE AND DISCUSS

RELATED SKILLS AND ACTIVITIES

SUBSEQUENT REPERTOIRE

Preface

Piano for the Developing Musician, fifth edition, has been both joy and challenge. It is always a joy to have the chance to try to make things better, easier to comprehend, more user friendly, and more relevant. It is also always a challenge to find and/or create the materials that will enable you to reach your goals. As with the Comprehensive Edition, this edition is in a single volume. I have heard from many who said "more shorter examples." This need has been addressed. Together with the text, the on-line Instructor's Manual and the PDM Web Site, teachers and students will find more than enough materials for the four-semester sequence.

You will find that the skill areas are more gradually developed. In many instances, implementation of a skill is now being delayed until the chapter *after* the concept is introduced. If the faster pace of previous editions is to your liking, please use material from the Instructor's Manual or the PDM Web Site. In each area spiral learning builds on what students know. You will find more emphasis on two-handed accompaniment styles of harmonization in the early chapters. This allows the students to become more quickly familiar with basic diatonic harmonies before being presented with the challenge of playing melody and harmony hands-together.

A full integration of the resources of the Web allows the computer to act as a "practice supervisor." You will notice icons ( ) directing you to extensive use of the PDM Web Site for additional content and pedagogical suggestions for practice. Additional plug-ins may have to be downloaded if not already included in your Netscape and/or Internet Explorer folders (latest version of Shockwave by Macromedia and QuickTime). We suggest Netscape 4.7 and Internet Explorer 5.0 minimum.

The Preliminary Chapter should be used to help those students with no keyboard background. The basic PDM chapter outline holds true. Each chapter is divided into the following sections:

EXEMPLARY REPERTOIRE

A carefully chosen compositional work opens each chapter and forms the basis for discovery of the pedagogical goals to come.

TOPICS TO EXPLORE AND DISCUSS

Selected names and terms are suggested for further study. Use this section to integrate music history and performance practices into the piano classroom. Elaboration appears in the on-line Instructor's Manual.

RELATED SKILLS AND ACTIVITIES

Technique—A series of drills and etudes stress finger and hand development, independence and coordination.

Reading—Compositions and excerpts address the challenge of reading and sight-playing music at the keyboard. A variety of styles and keys are used as are a variety of score configurations and clefs. Be certain to take advantage of the additional reading materials for each chapter and/or study suggestions as provided on the PDM Web Site.

Keyboard Theory—In many instances the heart of the chapter, drills and exercises stress a full understanding of the subject matter. Check out the Web Site for extra help with much of the keyboard theory content.

Harmonization—Melodies from folk and other composed sources, as well as original melodies, have been extended in number. Suggested accompaniment styles have been provided for the majority.

Transposition—This skill of musicianship and application of theoretical understanding is practiced through regular execution. As requested, you will notice a greater number of shorter exercises.

Improvisation—The ability to express oneself freely at the keyboard grows from an understanding of the melodic and harmonic components of music.

Composition—Brief compositional assignments act to reinforce repertoire as well as theory. Examples of student work can be seen on the PDM Web Site.

Ensemble—Compositions from original and transcribed sources give equal emphasis to the duet repertoire and multi-keyboard scores.

Subsequent Repertoire—Additional collections of keyboard literature, many with brief study suggestions, offer pedagogical reinforcement and the opportunity to go further with an idea.

It is an exciting time to a part of higher education and the study of music. We happen to be using the piano keyboard as our method of transportation through the ever-changing world of functional skills and musical understanding. A full integration of the Web allows the computer to act as a Practice Supervisor. From the PDM Web Site, instructors and students can access web-based tutorials or find additional practice drills, exercises and compositions. E*njoy*!

Acknowledgments

I have been in this business of group piano instruction for over thirty years. That alone is pretty scary! What would be even scarier would be if I had come through those years without the many wonderful students asking "why" or "what if." The past few years have given me the opportunity to work with some graduate students who have constantly pushed me "outside the box" through their curiosity about technology and its benefits to basic piano pedagogy. A very, very special thank you to William Chapman Nyaho, Lucia Unrau, Mary Nelson Tollefson, Cynthia and Michael Benson, Christina Beeler, Janice Buckner, Carlyn Morenus, Kathy Winston, Sandra Ramawy, Paola Perin, Allison Hudak and Kevin Richmond. You guys have always kept me on my toes!

I give my sincere thanks to the reviewers of this edition. This was a considerable time commitment and you are all busy folk—Joan Reist, University of Nebraska–Lincoln; Susanna Garcia, University of Louisiana at Lafayette; David Cartledge, Indiana University; Nancy Matesky, Shoreline Community College. What an honor it has been to have Abigail Baxter as my editorial support. Revisions will never again go as smoothly without you on board. What a treat it has been to get to work with Bonnie Balke at A-R Editions. You were "the rock!" And again, thank you to Larry Harms (RolandCorp US) as well as Britt Cawthon and Ron Edelman (Capital Music Center). A special acknowledgment to David Hainsworth, Systems Analyst, UT Austin School of Music, for your patience with all of my questions and frustrations. The Web Site wouldn't exist without your expertise.

Martha Hilley

Preliminary Chapter

PIANO FOR THE DEVELOPING MUSICIAN assumes some previous musical knowledge. Not every music major, however, has rudimentary skills. To make it possible to begin Chapter 1 in a class setting, we offer some "entrance level" review here.

COMMON METER SIGNATURES

2/4 3/4 4/4 6/4 3/8 6/8 2/2

The top number indicates total basic pulses per measure. The bottom number indicates what type of note will receive one pulse (beat).

TABLE OF COMMON NOTE VALUES

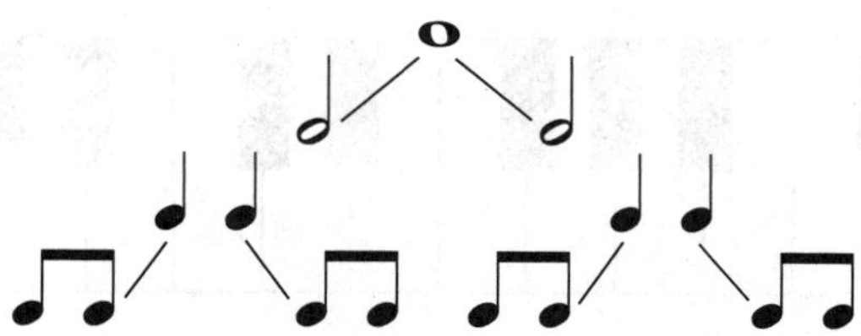

TABLE OF COMMON REST VALUES*

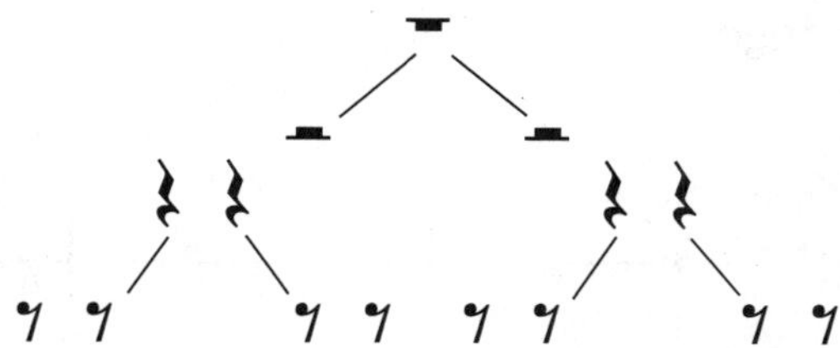

* In many editions a whole rest is used to indicate a measure of silence, regardless of the meter.

KEYS AND NOTE NAMES

1. As you know, the musical alphabet involves seven letter names. As a drill, say the given letter name and then recite the missing ones in order. If the noteheads move upward, go forward in the alphabet; if the noteheads move downward, go in reverse. Recite in rhythm.

a. ♩ = 60

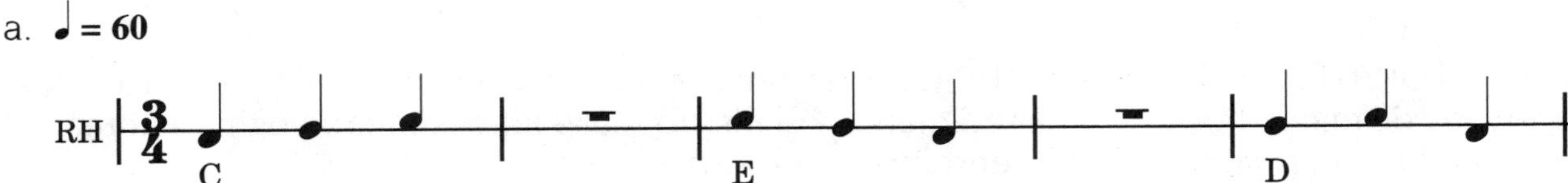

b. ♩ = 60

2. White keys relate directly to the musical alphabet. What visual cues quickly help you identify with the names of the white keys?

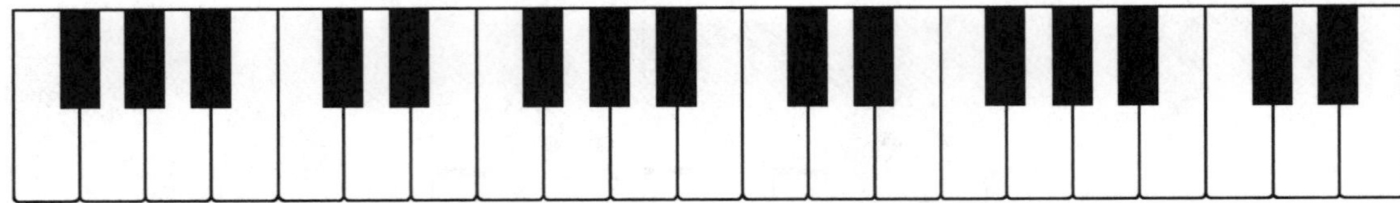

3. Now play the naming drills in item 1 above. Use a pointer finger, anywhere on the keyboard. Continue to *name while you play*.

4. Simultaneously play and name these similar exercises. Occasionally change hands but continue to use only a pointer finger.

a.

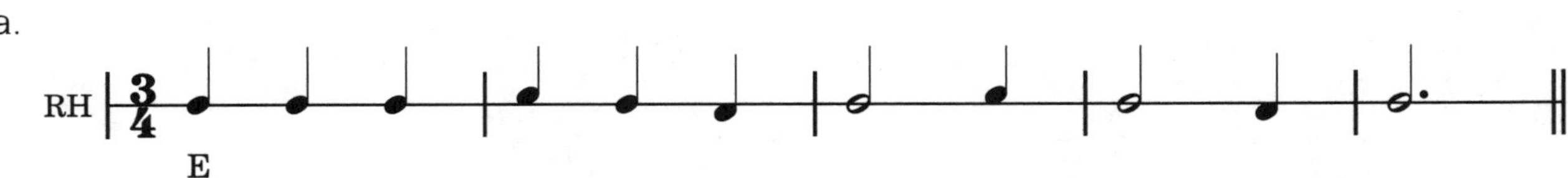

b.

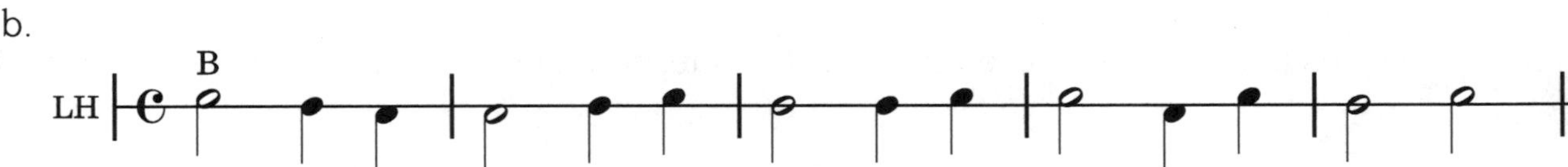

c.

RH 3/4

A

RH 5/4

F

Go to the PDM Web site for additional examples.

5. In keyboard work, fingers are numbered like this:

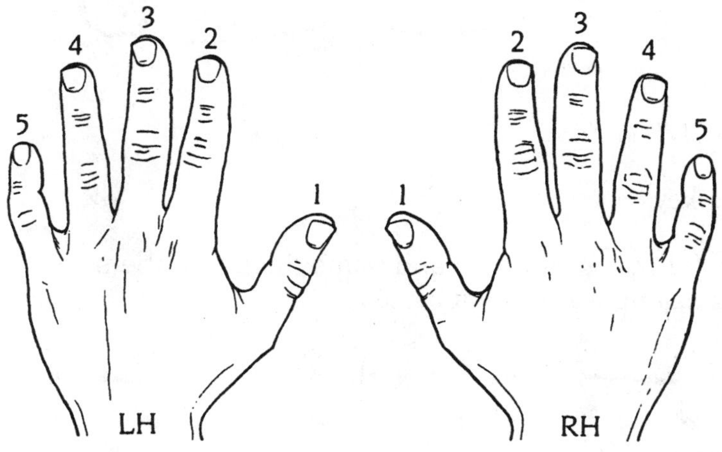

You can see that if you have a three-note pattern of adjacent keys to play, you have three different finger groups to choose from (adjacent keys are generally played by adjacent fingers).

RH: 1 2 3 (or 3 2 1); 2 3 4 (or 4 3 2); 3 4 5 (or 5 4 3).

LH: 3 2 1 (or 1 2 3); etc.

What will be true of four adjacent keys? Five adjacent keys?

GOOD HAND SHAPE

Let your arms hang at your sides. Notice how the fingers are slightly curved at the middle joint. This is a natural, unforced, relaxed hand position. Place both hands on a flat surface in front of you. Maintain the natural shape of your hand. Notice the slightly "rounded" condition of your fingers and overall hand shape; this is the most natural and best position for your hands in playing the piano.

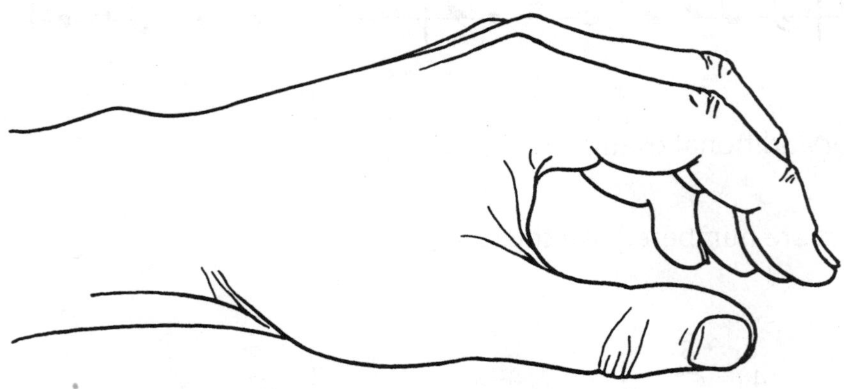

FINGER PATTERNS AND NOTES

1. Using all white keys,
    - play the following example and name finger numbers
    - play the example and name notes

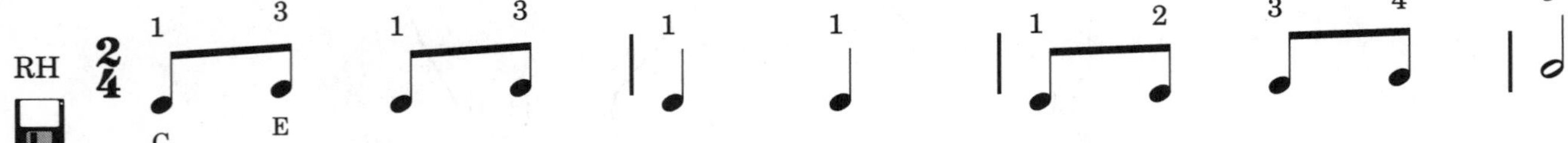

2. Play the following examples and name fingers. Then play and name notes.

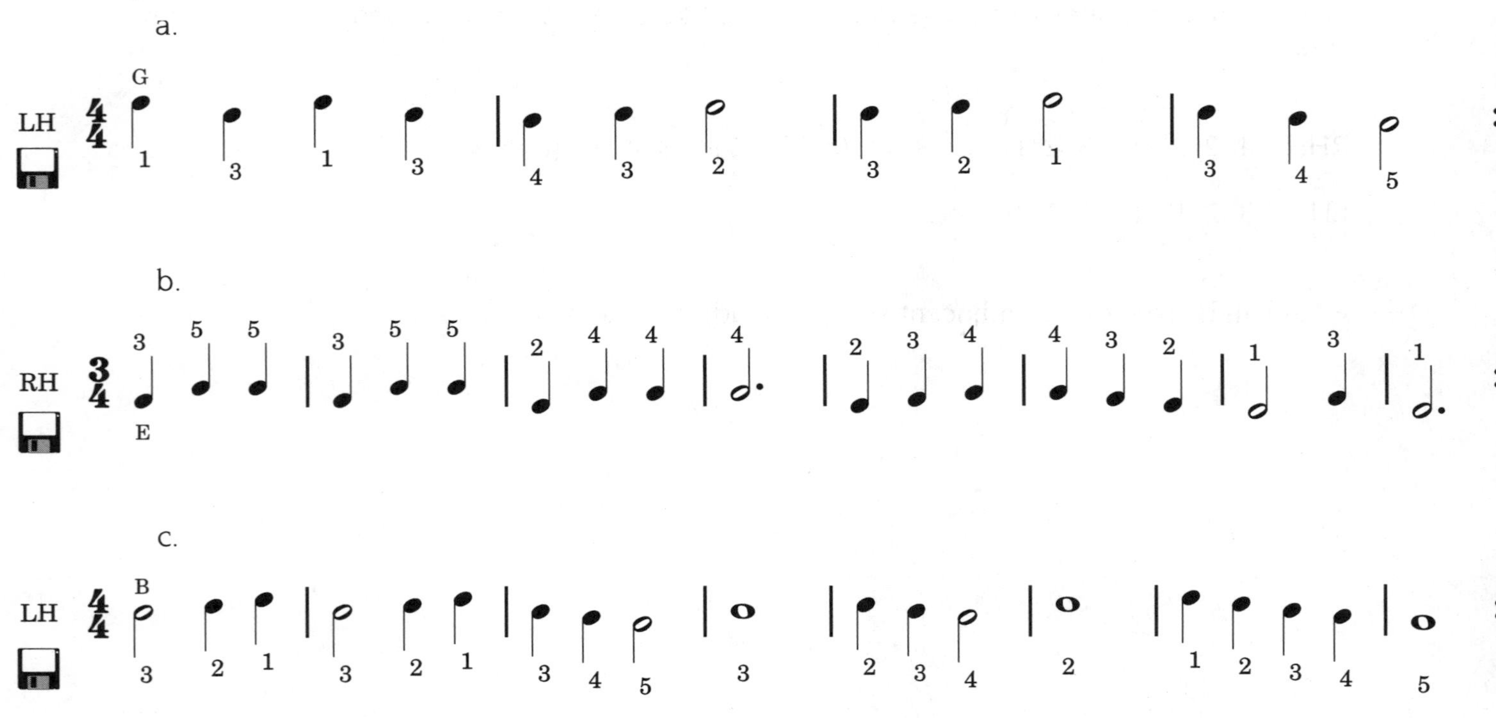

When you played 1–3, you skipped a white key. In keyboard positions using adjacent keys, to skip a finger is to skip a key and a note name.

THE STAFF AS RELATED TO THE KEYBOARD

1. The majority of keyboard music appears on a double staff joined by a brace. This arrangement accommodates the two hands.

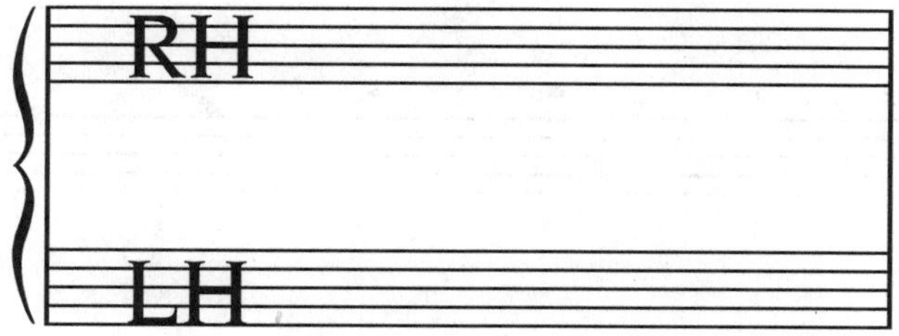

2. Play the following "five finger" melodies.

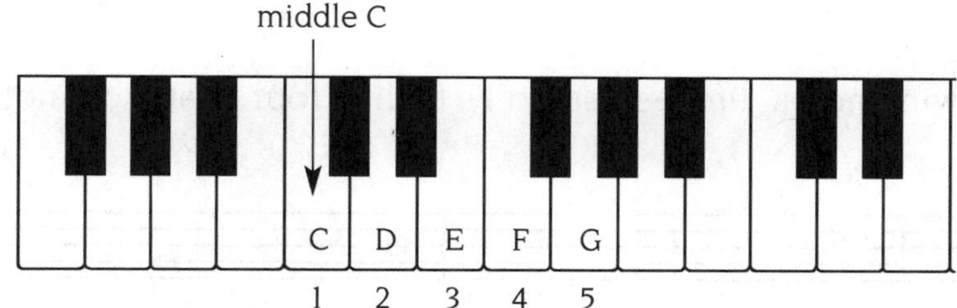

a.

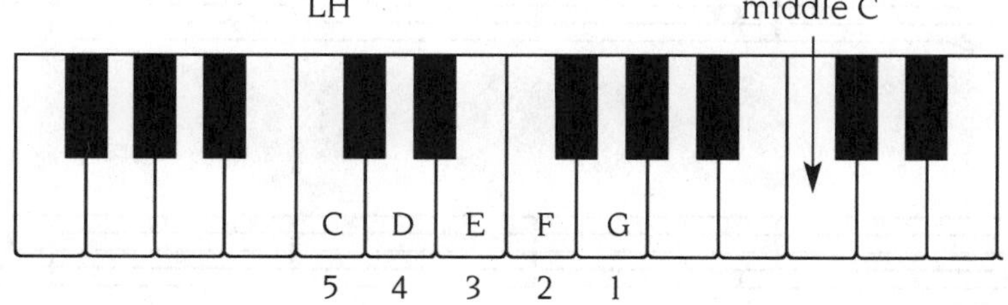

b.

1 3

c.

3 5

d. Determine position before playing.

5

3. Verbally name the following notes. Proceed steadily, feeling four beats to a note. Think treble clef.

Name the same notes again, this time allowing only three beats per note. If you have no trouble doing this, turn your book upside down and do it once again. Think treble clef the first time and bass clef on the repeat.

Go to the PDM Web site for additional "random whole note reading."

4. Return to the notes in item 3. *Play* each note, four beats to a note. This time think bass clef. Place a mark by the notes on which you hesitate. Practice the ones you marked.

   If you have no trouble with four beats to a note, repeat the exercise using two beats for each note.

5. The end goal for item 3 will be to *play* through twice, ***one beat to a note***, treble clef first time and bass clef on the repeat. Tempo should be approximately one beat = 60.

6. Keyboard music most often employs the *Grand Staff*, a combination of a *Treble Staff* (G clef) in the upper position and a *Bass Staff* (F clef) in the lower position.

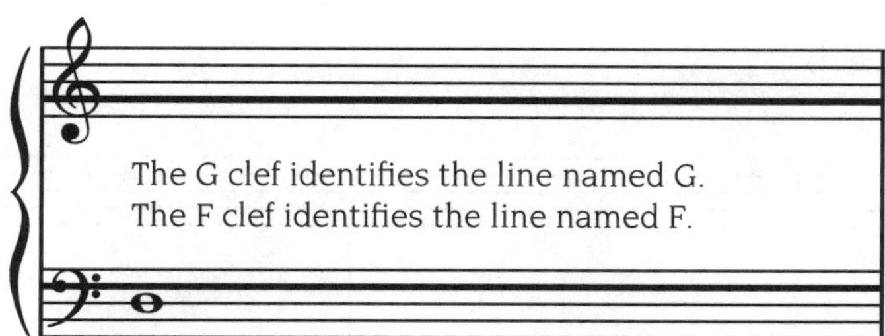

The G and the F represent specific keys close to the center of the keyboard, thus establishing the following permanent relationship. Notice that, on the staff, adjacent notes move from line to space, space to line.

7. Play the following, all based on five-finger patterns. Notice the direction of upward, downward, and repeating.

a.

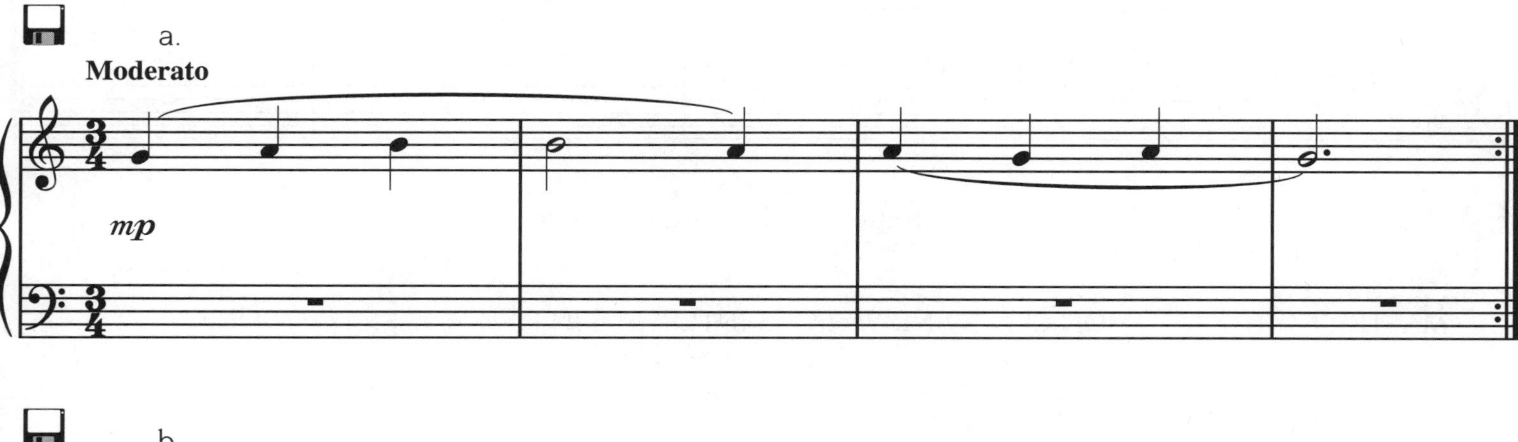

b.

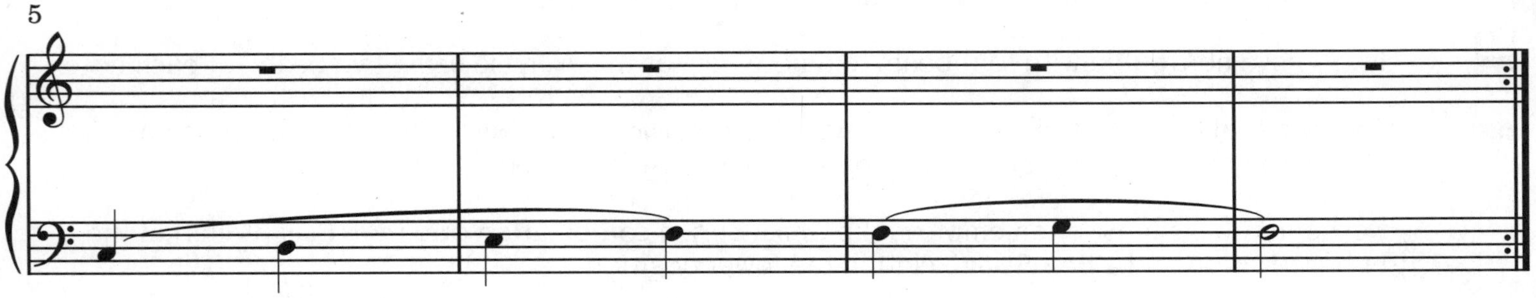

5

c.

Allegro

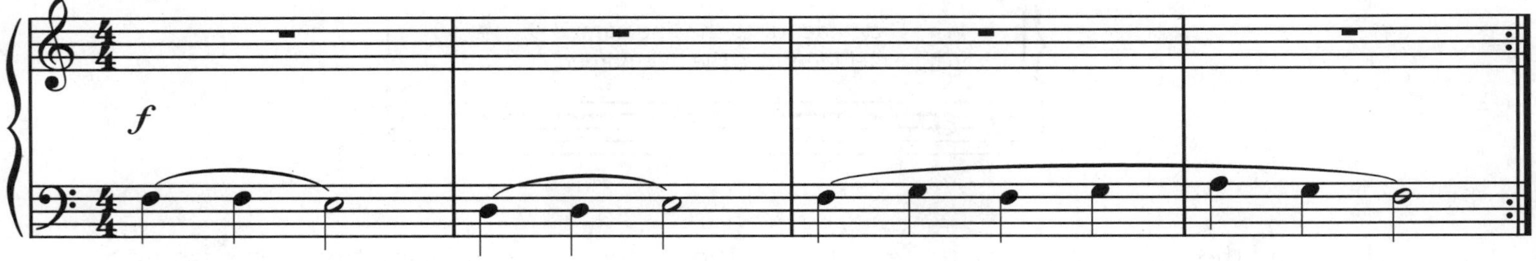

f

d.

Andantino

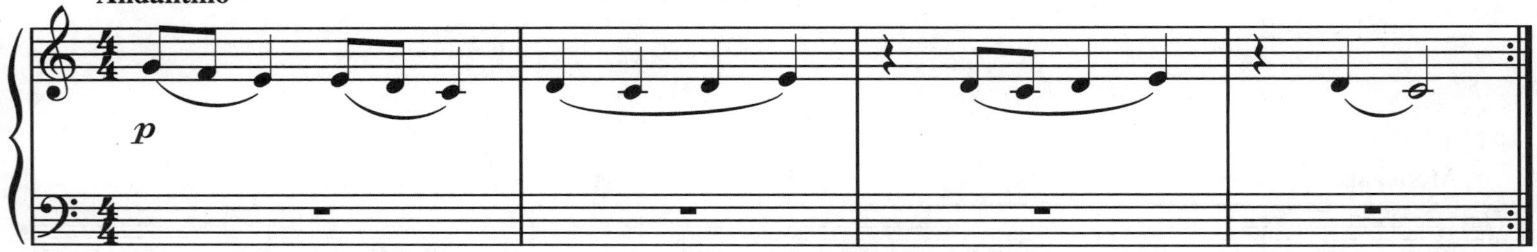

p

Go to the PDM Web site for more examples in alternate five-finger patterns.

MASTERING THE COMMON CLEFS AND VARIOUS INTERVALS IN FIVE-FINGER POSITIONS

1. To focus on individual clefs (as well as to save space), we will now show only one staff. However, you will always know which hand to use.

   Before playing each example, scan for fingering range. Recall the principles of fingering discussed earlier, then decide which fingers to use. The following begin on either Treble G or Bass F.

a.

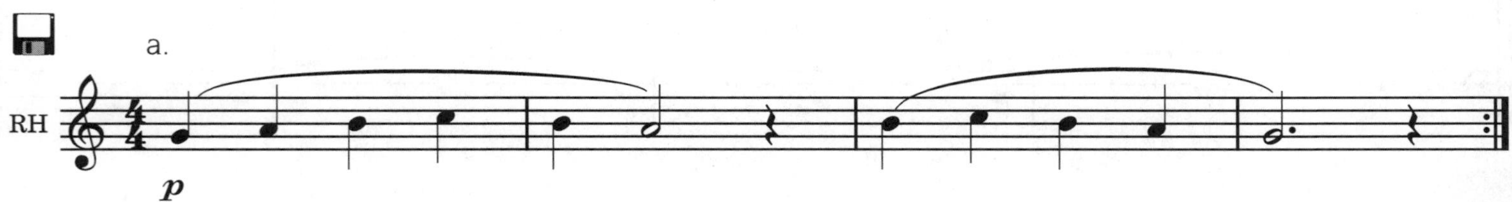

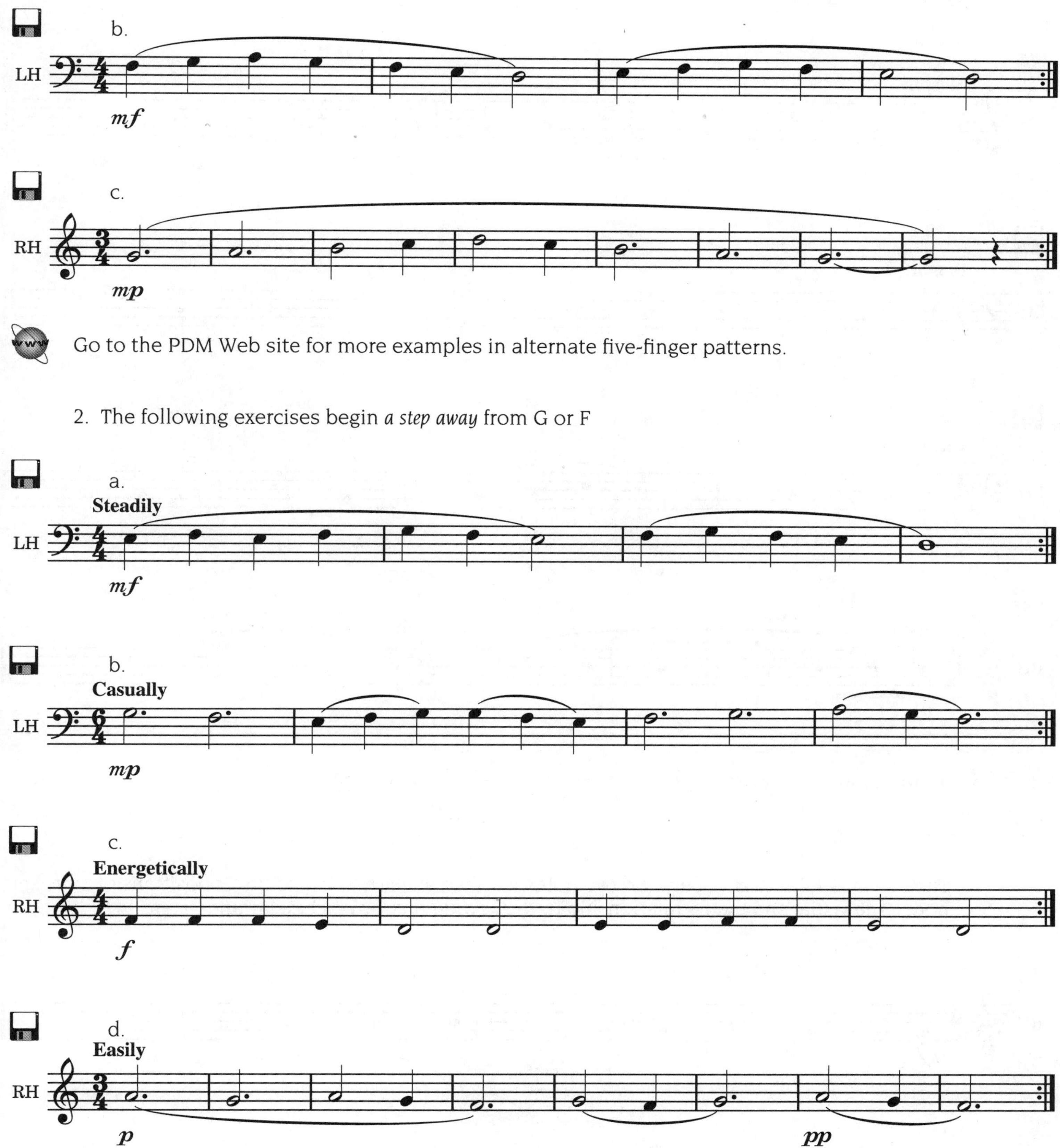

Go to the PDM Web site for more examples in alternate five-finger patterns.

2. The following exercises begin *a step away* from G or F

Go to the PDM Web site for more examples in alternate five-finger patterns..

3. The following begin *a skip away* from G or F.

a.

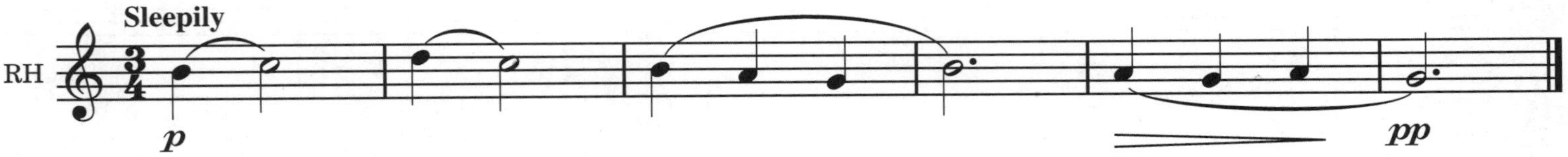

Sleepily

RH

p *pp*

b.

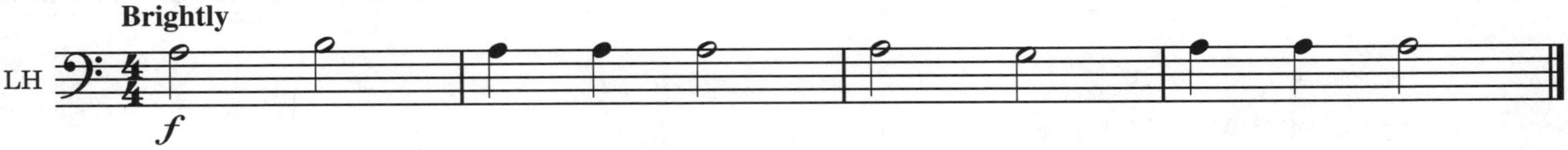

Brightly

LH

f

c.

Carefully

LH

mp

d.

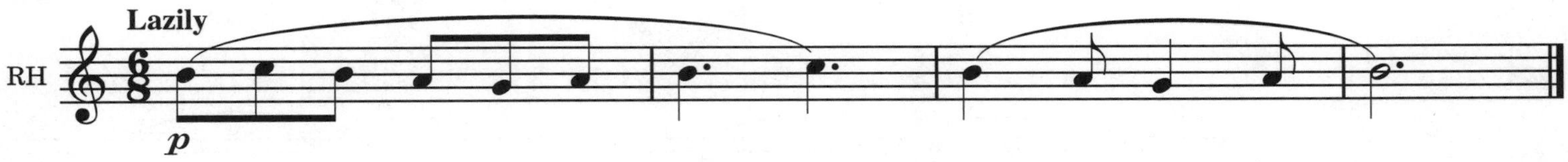

Lazily

RH

p

Go to the PDM web site for additional examples using alternate clefs.

4. The distance relationship between two notes is called an *interval*. In five-finger positions of adjacent notes, the visual and tactile relationship to the keyboard is very clear. Play and listen:

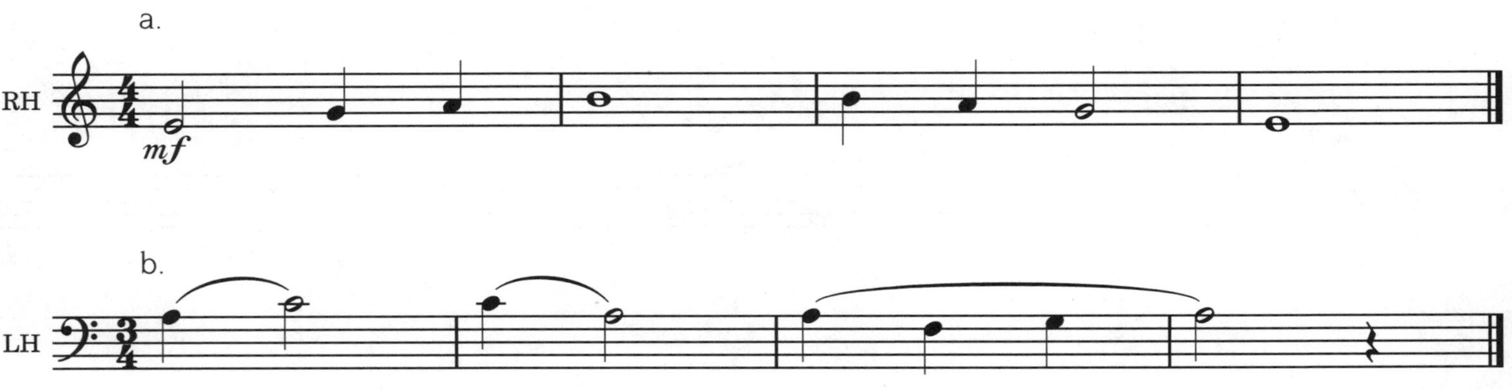

5. Play the following single-staff examples after determining fingering and scanning the intervals. Notice that some examples begin *on the clef line*, whereas others do not.

a.

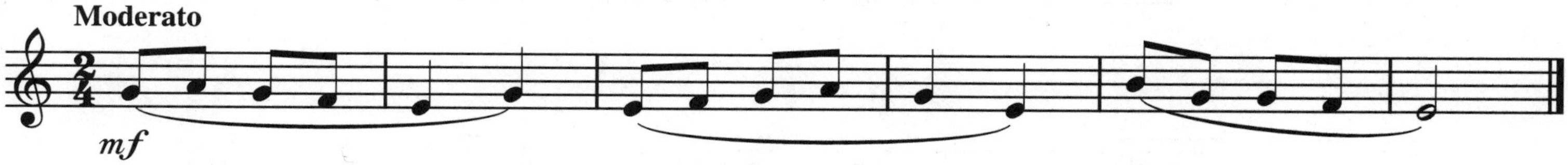

Moderato
mf

b.

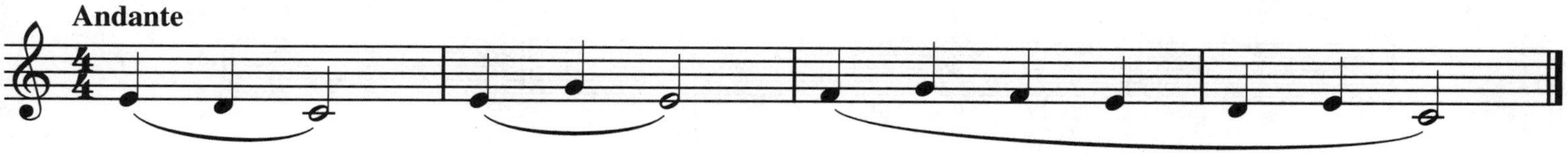

Andante

c.

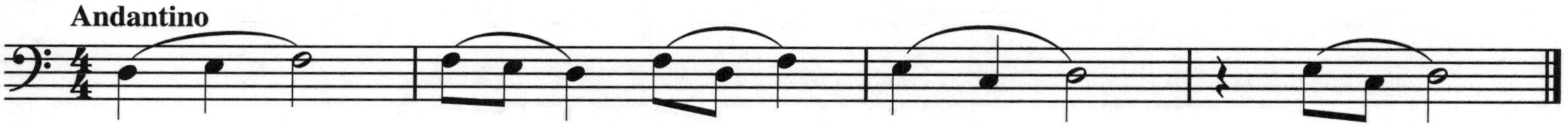

Andantino

d.

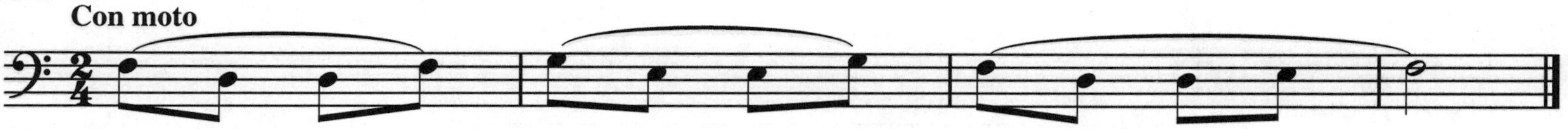

Con moto

Go to the PDM Web site for additional examples using alternate clefs.

6. Within a five-finger position, various intervals can be used. They are named for their total compass:

2nd
3rd
4th
5th
3rd
5th
4th
2nd

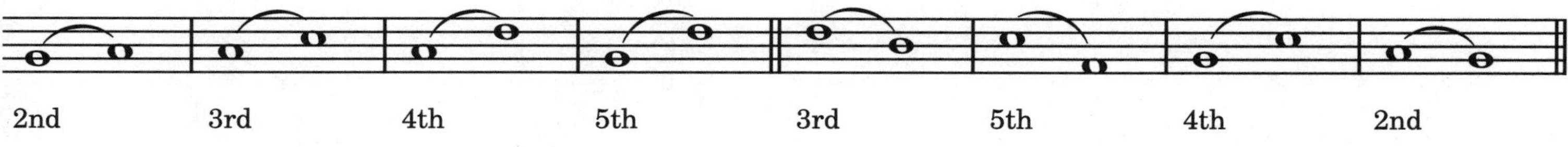

As you can see, 3rds and 5ths appear on two lines or two spaces; 2nds and 4ths appear on a space and a line. Intervals also may appear in "blocked" fashion, the tones to be sounded simultaneously.

3rd
4th
2nd

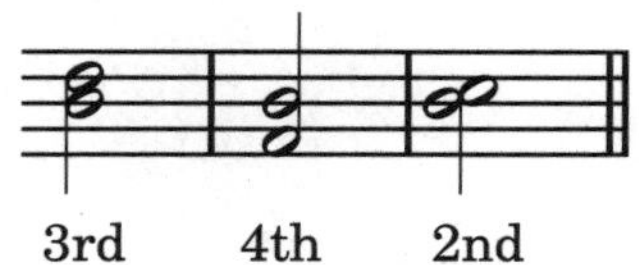

7. Name the intervals shown in each measure:

8. In five-finger positions, a 4th is played by skipping two fingers; a 5th will use only fingers 1 and 5.

9. Play these reading drills after scanning quickly for fingering range and interval patterns.

Begin on G or F.

a.

Cheerfully

mf

b.

Robustly

f

c.

Liltingly

mp

5

d.

Sorrowfully

p

pp

Go to the PDM Web site for additional examples using alternate clefs.

10. Begin an interval *away* from G or F.

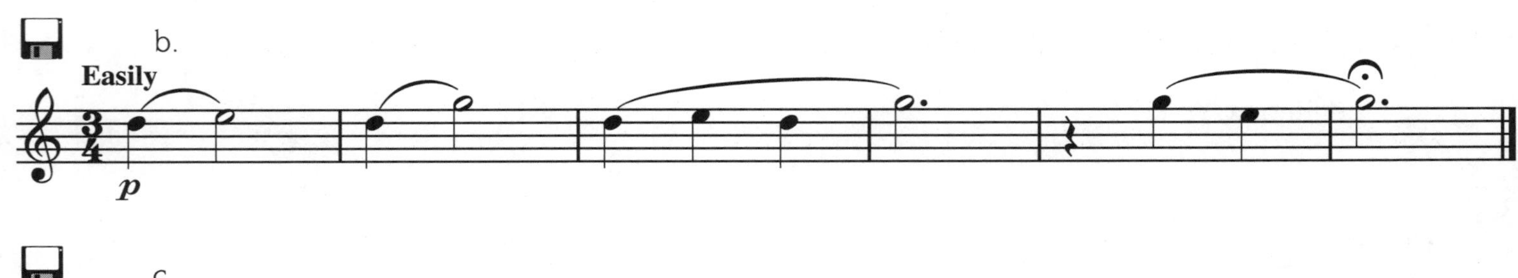

Go to the PDM Web site for additional examples using alternate clefs.

ADDING SHARPS AND FLATS TO FIVE-FINGER POSITIONS

1. Because sharps and flats most often use black keys, a different keyboard "feel" results. The hand adjusts on the keyboard, forming a natural shape to accommodate the black key or keys.

   On the keyboard, a *sharp* indicates a move to the very next key *upward*, black or white; a *flat* indicates a move to the very next key *downward*, black or white.

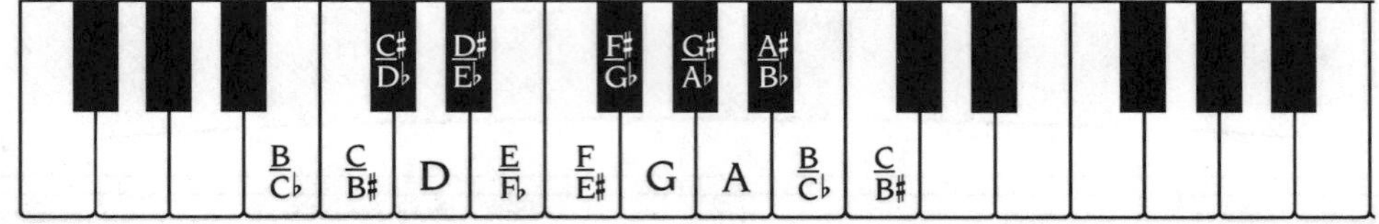

2. Play the following examples using sharps and flats.

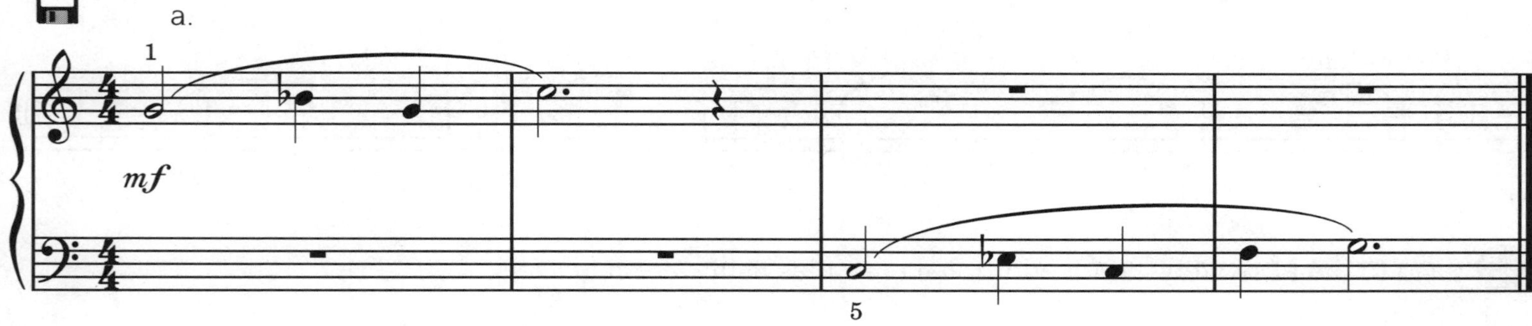

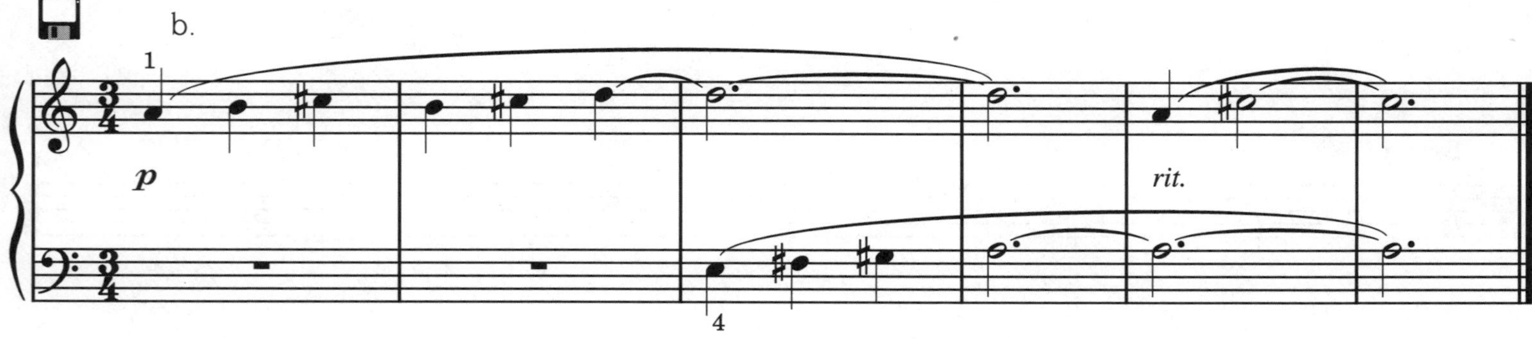

Go to the PDM Web site for more examples in alternate five-finger patterns.

OTHER USEFUL STAFF LOCATORS

1. In addition to the clef lines for G and F, it is helpful to memorize certain other "landmark" notes and know where they are on the keyboard. Learn these notes and related keys.

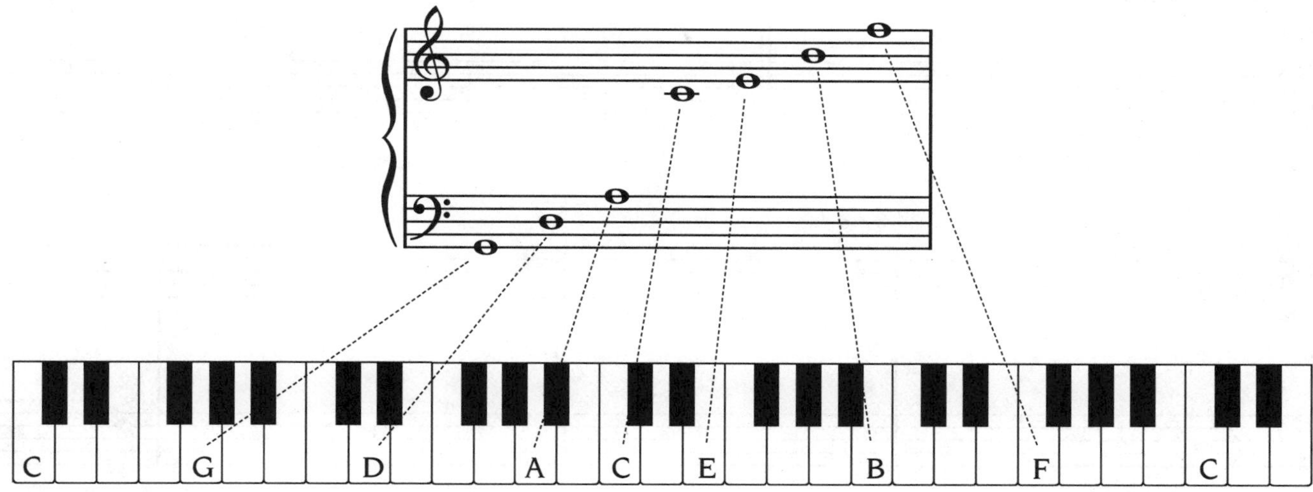

2. Each of these brief examples begins on one of the staff locators. Remember to check for fingering range, then play. You may pause and get your bearings at each double bar.

e.
f.
g.
h.
i.
j.

OTHER HAND POSITIONS

1. In keyboard music, the hands often expand to cover positions larger than five keys. As you go on, you will gain a tactile sense of many such expansions (as well as contractions). One common expansion covers a 6th:

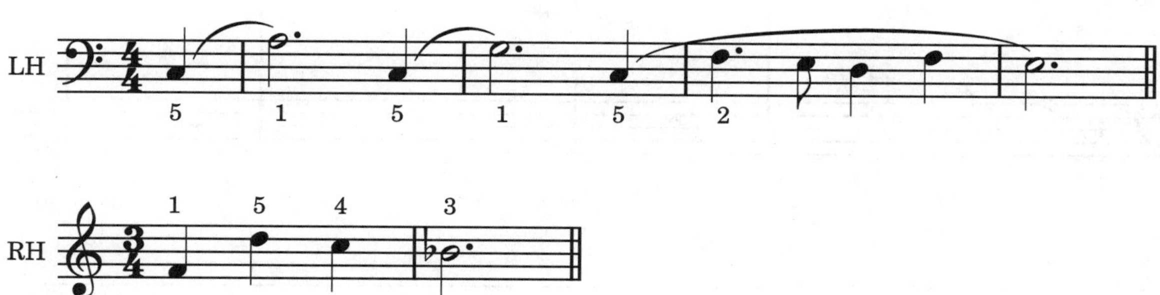

2. Notes too high or too low for the five-line staves appear on small *leger lines* or in their spaces.

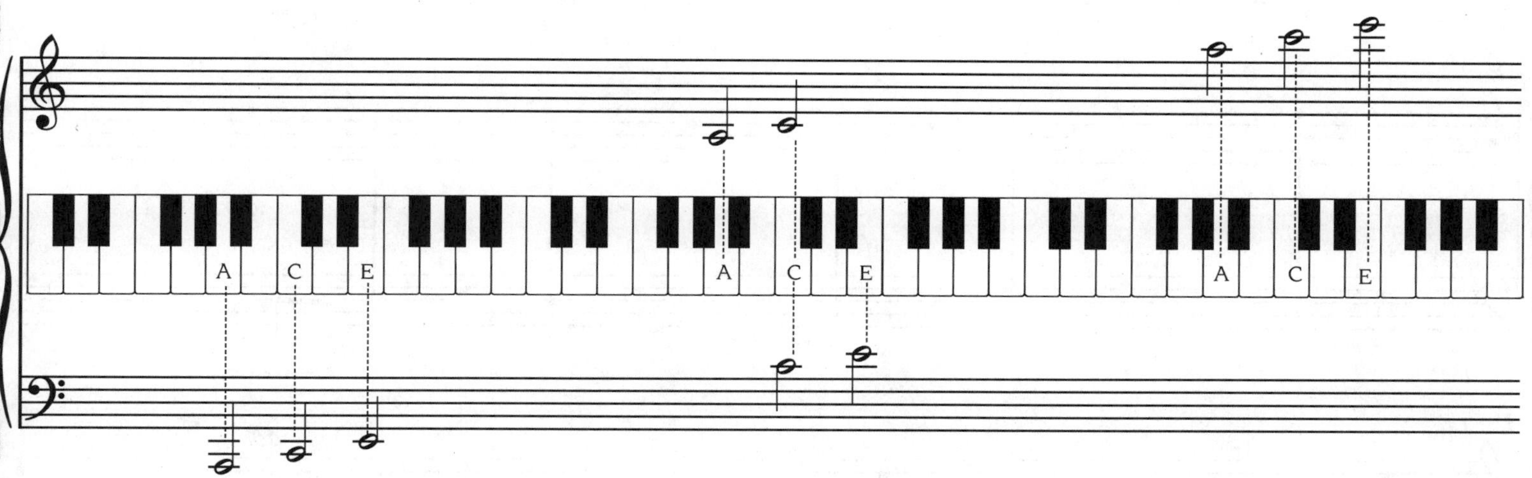

Play and name the keys and notes you see above, just to fix them in your ears and mind as a keyboard/staff relationship. Remember the RH/LH rule.

3. Notice the range of each measure of music. During the open measures, locate the next position.

KEY SIGNATURES

1. Key signatures can be viewed as lists of flats or sharps occurring throughout the example, section, or composition and affecting all notes of the same name no matter where they appear on the staff.

a. How many different positions occur in this example? Check the PDM Web site to confirm your answer and see additional examples.

b. This is a study in "5ths and 4ths." Prepare carefully for the hands-together ending.

2. Key signatures, of course, are much more than lists; they help summarize and remind us of tonalities.

- In major sharp signatures, the last sharp (farthest to the right) is a half step below the *key name*.

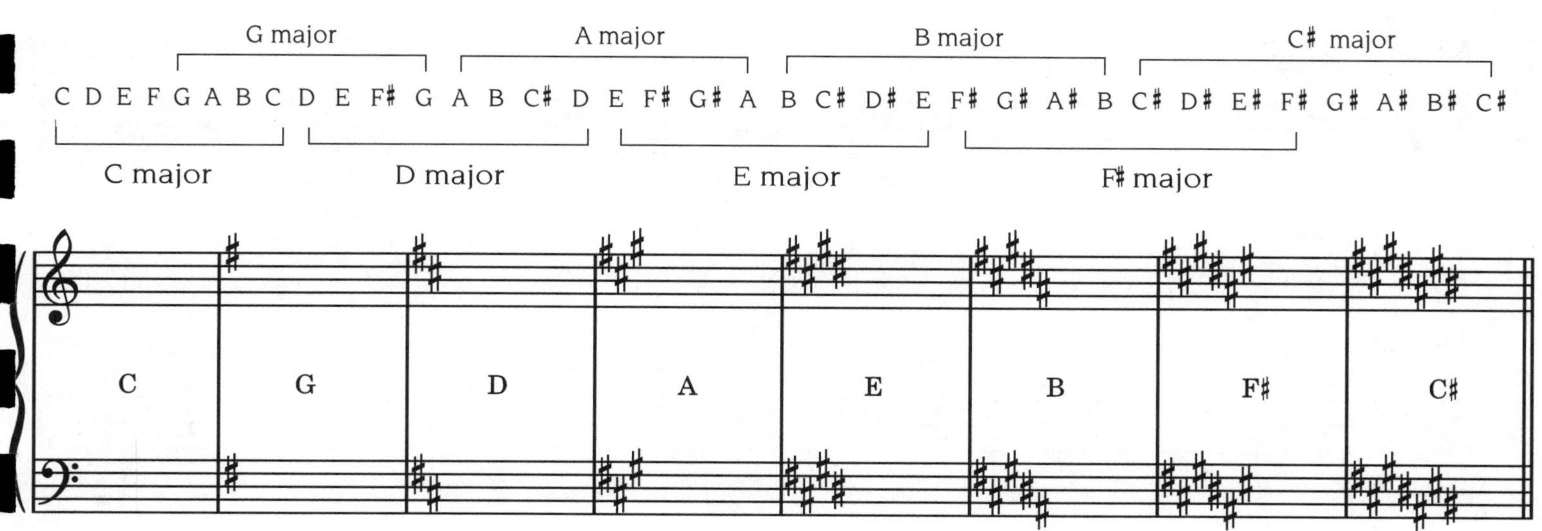

- In major flat signatures, the next-to-last flat names the key (F major has one flat).

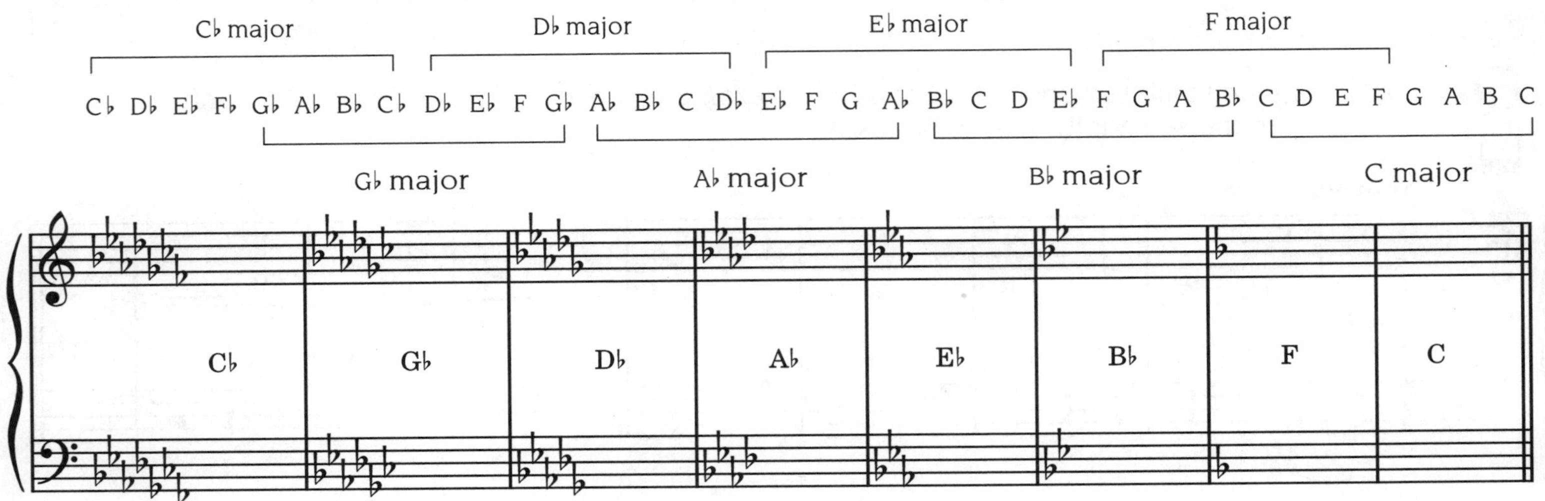

SUGGESTIONS FOR GOOD READING

1. As quickly and as much as possible, eyes should be off the keys and focusing on the notes.
2. Sit at the center of the keyboard and maintain this position no matter how low or high the music goes. This way, you will gain a physical memory for key location without looking too much at the keys.
3. Scan all music for fingering range, position changes, intervals, sharps, and/or flats.
4. Train yourself to see groups of notes rather than just one note at a time. The circles in the following indicate some natural groupings. What makes each one "natural"? (Sometimes a parallel or related feature between patterns makes a kind of "natural" reading symmetry.)

   Play each example after planning fingering:

c.

Vivace

f

d.

Moderato

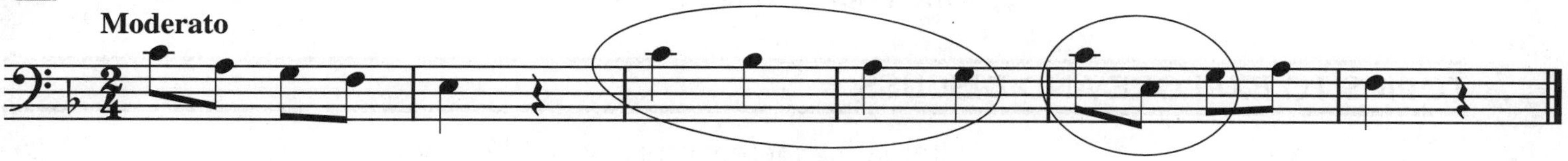

e.

Allegretto

mp

f.

Allegro

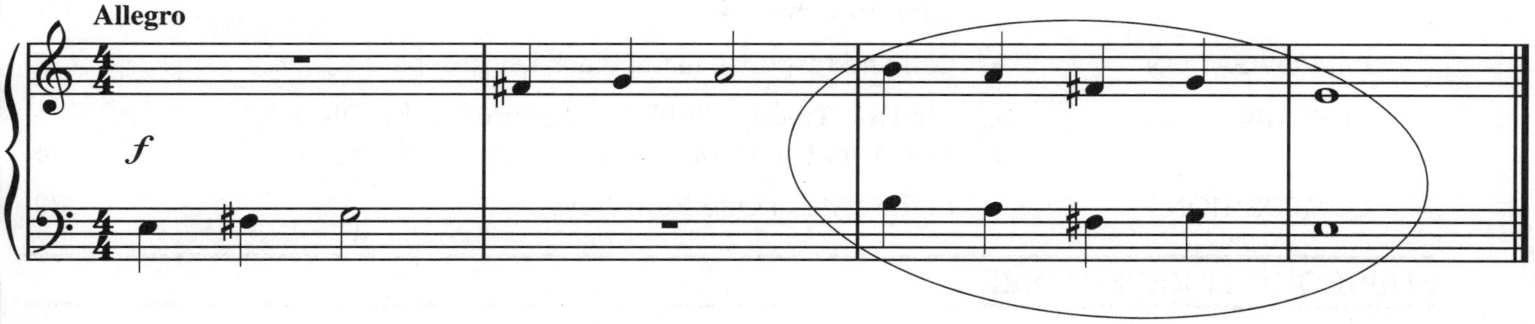

f

g.

Eagerly

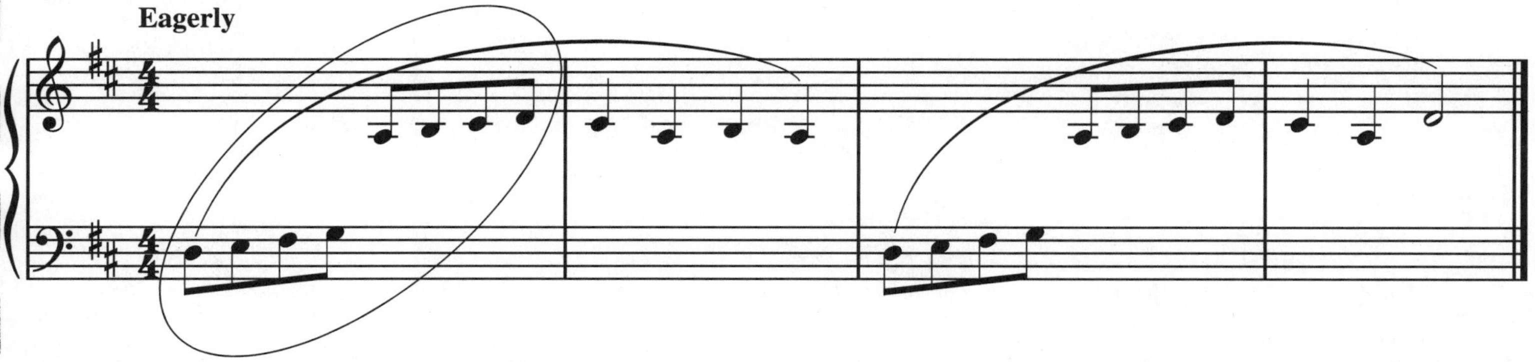

Go to the PDM Web site for more examples in alternate five-finger patterns. There are also suggested tempi with voice-over counting.

1.

EXEMPLARY REPERTOIRE

TOPICS TO EXPLORE AND DISCUSS

RELATED SKILLS AND ACTIVITIES

SUBSEQUENT REPERTOIRE

Intervals

EXEMPLARY REPERTOIRE — **One Four Seven** Lynn Freeman Olson

INQUIRY

1. Scan *One Four Seven*. Observe:
   - actual number of measures to be learned
   - pattern of intervallic change
2. Determine logical fingering.
3. Given the meter, determine a tempo.
4. Given the overall character, determine dynamics.
5. What does the title mean?

PERFORMANCE

1. Block the right- and left-hand intervals, hands together, restriking only when the intervals change.

2. With both hands, tap the rhythms of the piece on top of the piano.
3. Play right-hand intervals while tapping left-hand rhythms on top of the piano.
4. Play as written.

One Four Seven

LYNN FREEMAN OLSON

TOPICS TO EXPLORE AND DISCUSS

- Alternating meters versus variable meters
- Intervals: melodic and harmonic

RELATED SKILLS AND ACTIVITIES

TECHNIQUE

1. The following exercises use harmonic and melodic intervals. Determine a logical fingering for each example before playing.

a.

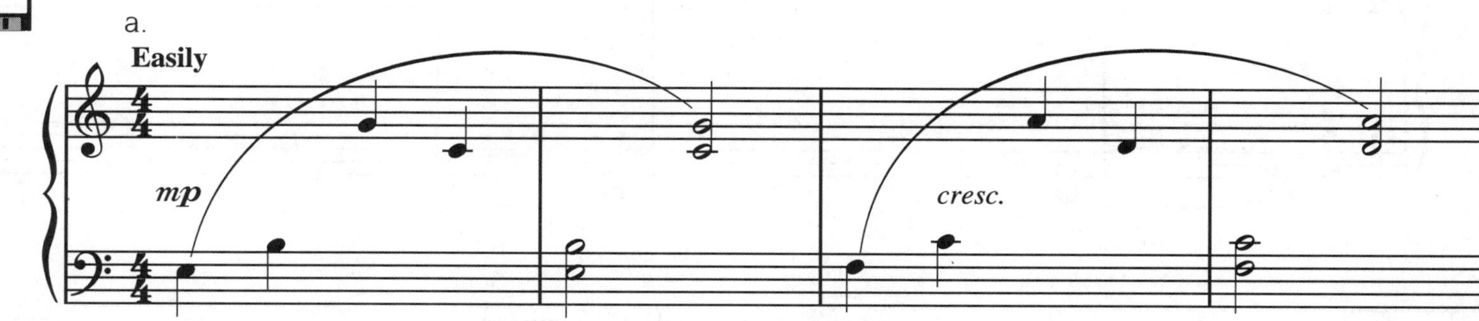

b.

c.
Alla marcia
LH
f
5
d.
Andantino
pp
5
e.
Andante
p
5

Go to the PDM Web site for additional examples using alternate keys and clefs.

READING

1. *Intervallic reading*. With hand in lap, think:

- interval
- keyboard location
- fingering

Then play with a measure of rest between each interval.

Go to the PDM Web site for additional intervallic reading.

2. *Rhythmic reading*. Tap the following while counting the beat.

a.

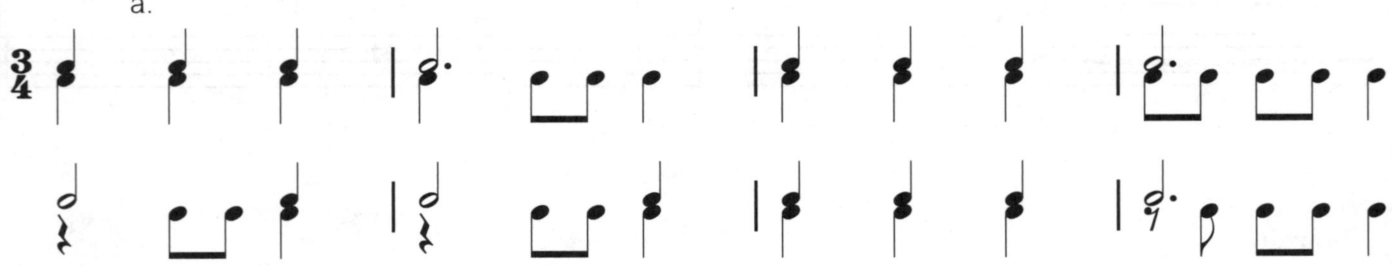

b.

c.

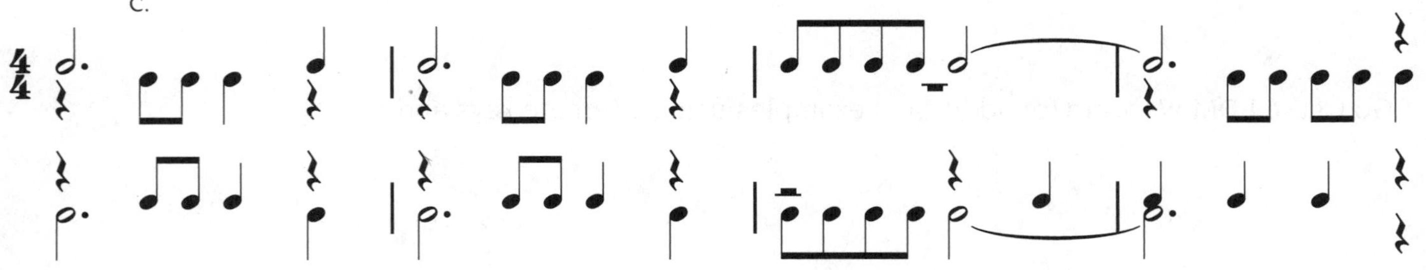

d.

e.

3. *Rhythmic ensemble*. In the $\frac{4}{4}$ rhythm chart, use the following physical motions for given note values:

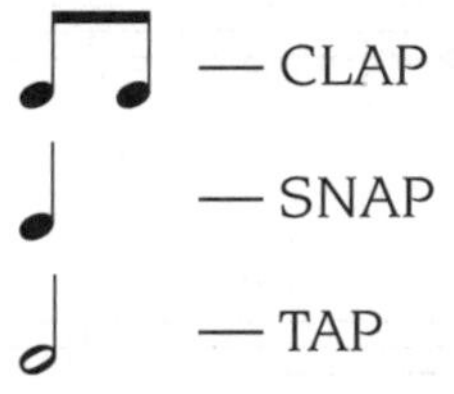

Count aloud as you perform only the quarter notes.

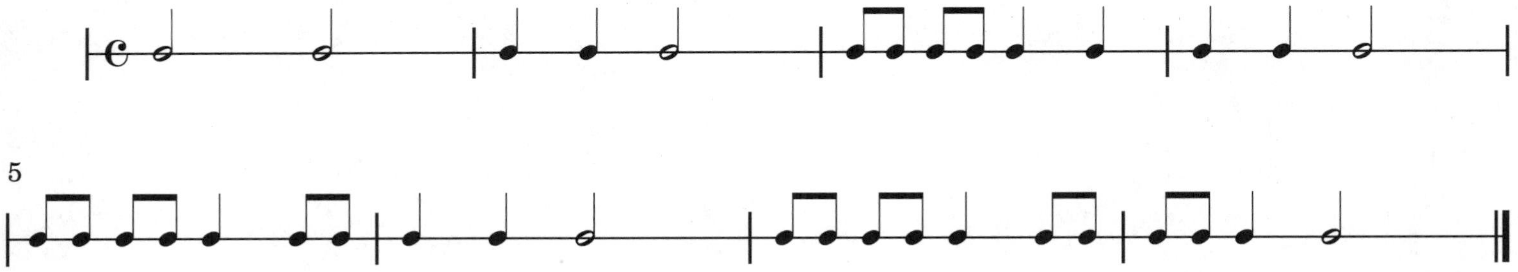

Count aloud as you perform only the half notes.

Count aloud as you perform only the eighth notes.

Form a rhythm ensemble by assigning certain note values to certain students. When you perform together, you will hear all the rhythms given.

4. You will find additional bass and treble clef note reading on the PDM Web site.

KEYBOARD THEORY

1. Play the indicated intervals above and below the following pitches. Use white keys only. Play one interval for each pitch.

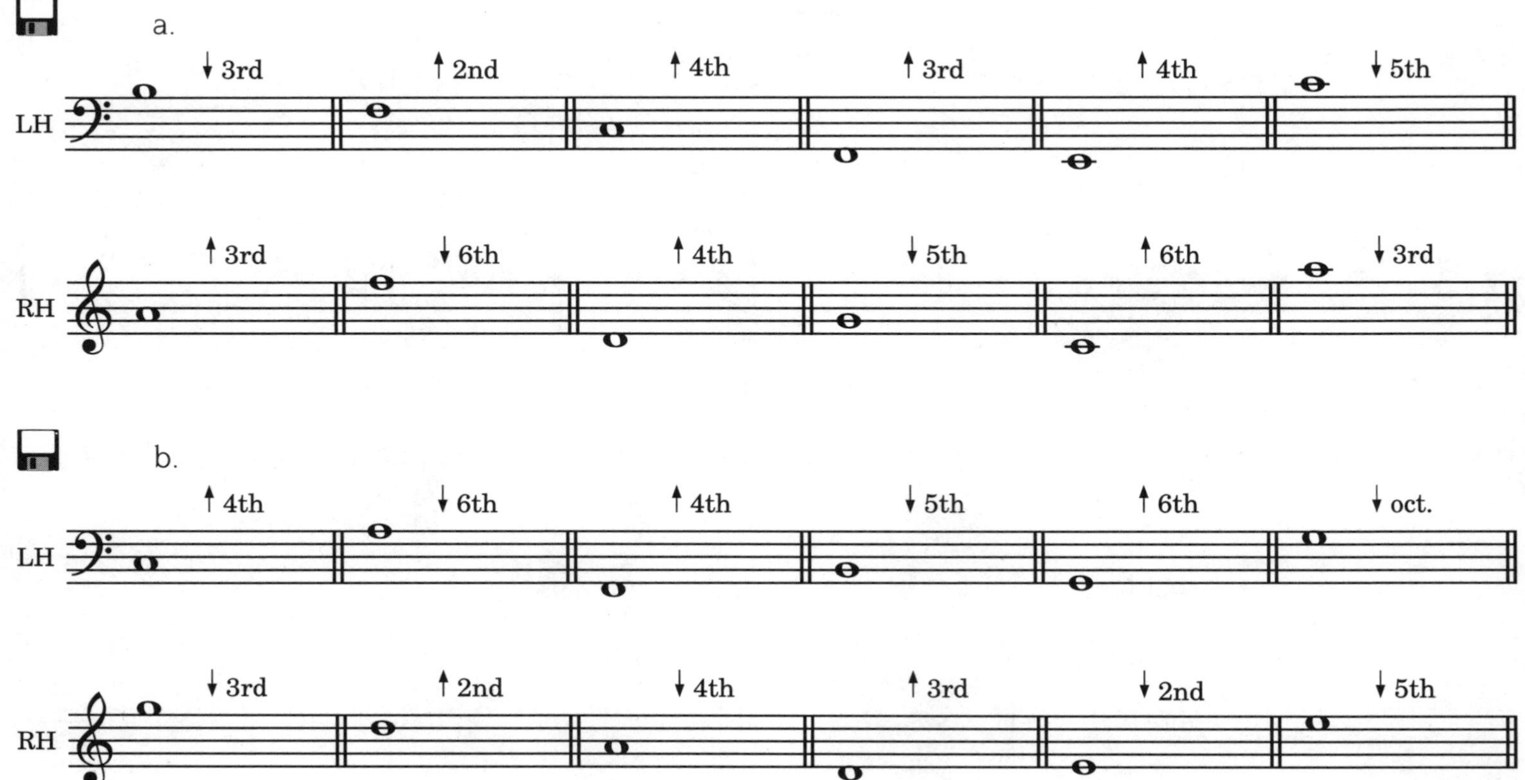

HARMONIZATION

1. Harmonize each of the following melodies with the 5th indicated in parentheses. Play the 5th blocked (in long or short values) and/or broken. Select an accompaniment style to enhance the mood.

a.

British

b.

American

Happily

mf–*p*

c.

British

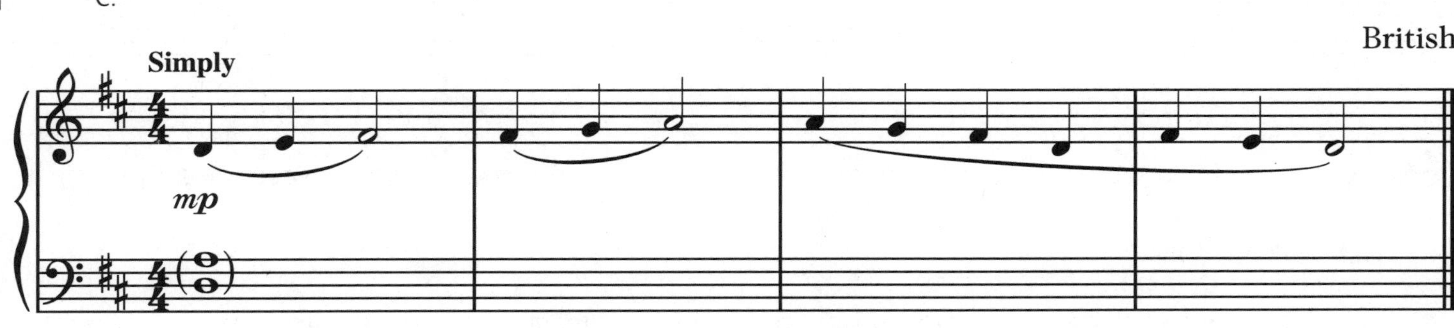

d.

American

e.

American

Go to the PDM Web site for additional harmonization examples with ostinato accompaniment.

TRANSPOSITION

1. Transpose each of the Harmonization examples to at least three other major keys.
2. Play *One Four Seven* with the first interval based on G, transposing the rest of the piece accordingly.

IMPROVISATION

1. Use the two- and three-black-key groups to play answers to your teacher's musical questions. These are improvised answers, not melodic echoes.

Student response:

5

9

13

17

Go to the PDM Web site for additional improvisation work.

ENSEMBLE

1. The following is a "spoken invention." Discuss as a class the musical meaning of the word *invention*. Perform as a three-part chant with clapping. Additional directions follow the score.

My Dog Treed a Rabbit

American
Arr. Lynn Freeman Olson

12

1 go roun' rab - bit. Gon - na milk my cow, gon - na

2 watch that crit - ter how he do that dog. Now go roun'

3 dog treed a rab - bit. Now watch that crit - ter sit - tin'

4

15

1 catch her by the tail; Gon - na milk her in the cof - fee pot, pour it in the pail. Now

2 rab - bit, Now go roun' rab - bit, Now

3 on that log, Now watch that crit - ter how he do that dog. Now

4

18

1 go roun' rab - bit, Now go roun' rab - bit.

2 go roun' rab - bit, *f* Now go roun' rab - bit.

3 go roun' rab - bit, *f* Now go roun' rab - bit.

4

Improvise on black keys to match the rhythm. "Rabbit" is always played on E♭ and G♭. The clapping part plays a bass ostinato throughout.

2. Play with the recorded disk example.

Hoo Doo

(In a Hollywood Bazaar)

LYNN FREEMAN OLSON

9
1
2
3
4
5
6
f
f
f
13
mf
p
mf

18
1
2
3
4
5
6
mp
p
mp
pp
p
mp
22
1
2
3
4
5
6
cresc.

COMPOSITION

Create a piece in the style of *One Four Seven* using variable meter. Refer to observations in the Inquiry section (page 23).

Trade compositions with your classmates and prepare for class performances.

SUBSEQUENT REPERTOIRE

1. *Seaview, After Turner* uses 5ths and tone clusters that cover the span of a 5th. Determine the pattern of motion throughout the piece from one position to another. What did you discover?

Notice the sign for pedal: *down* *hold* *up*

Go to the PDM Web site for additional reading suggestions.

Seaview, After Turner

LYNN FREEMAN OLSON

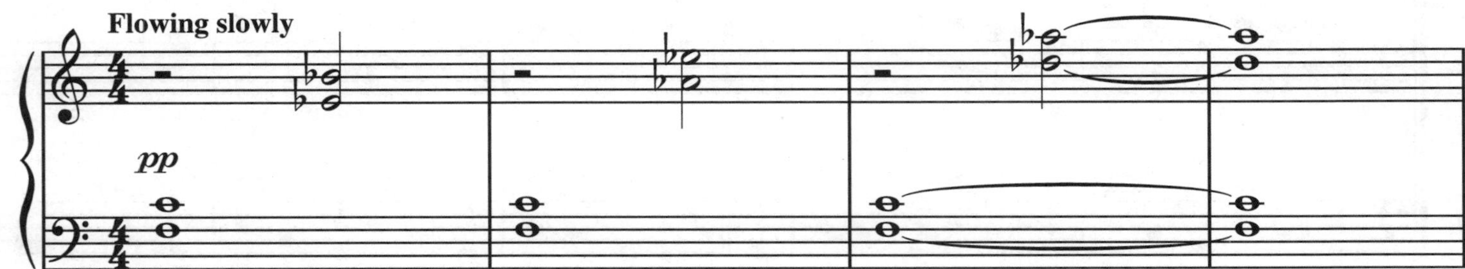

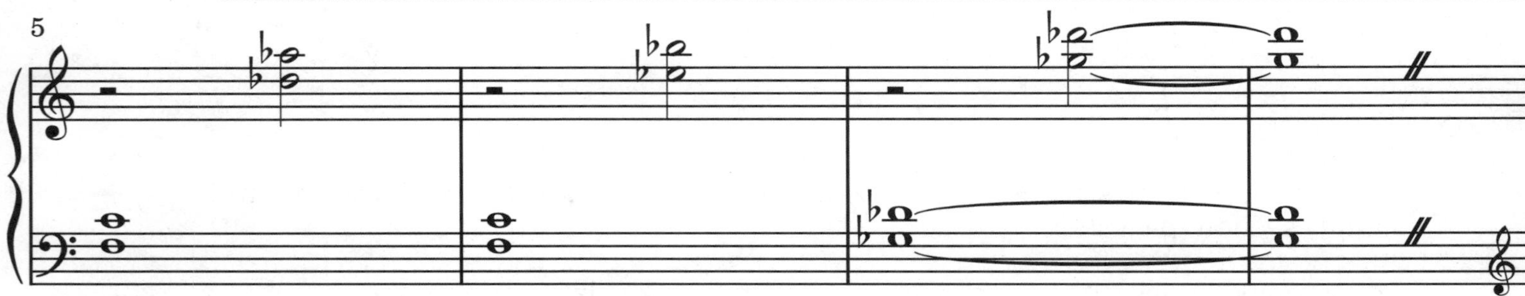

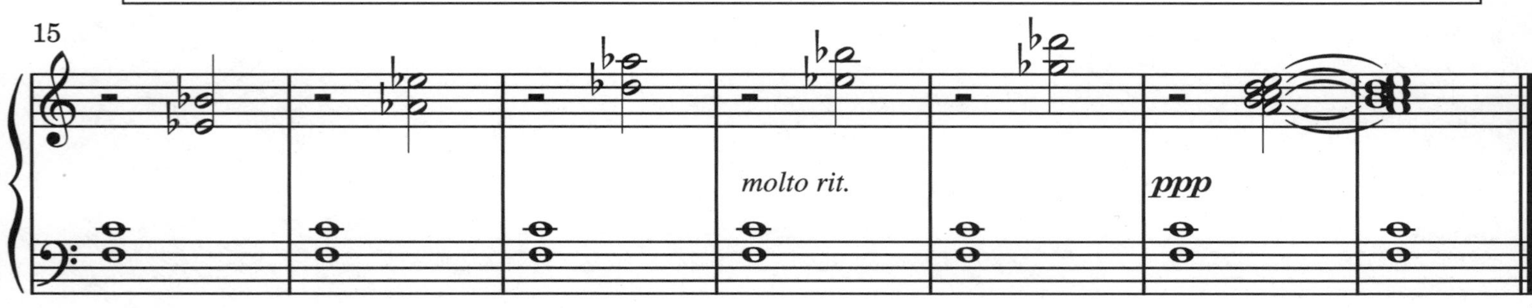

2. Block each interval position in *Saturday Smile*, keeping a steady beat.

Experiment to find a tempo that feels right for the piece. Then perform as written.

Go to the PDM Web site for additional reading suggestions.

Saturday Smile

LYNN FREEMAN OLSON

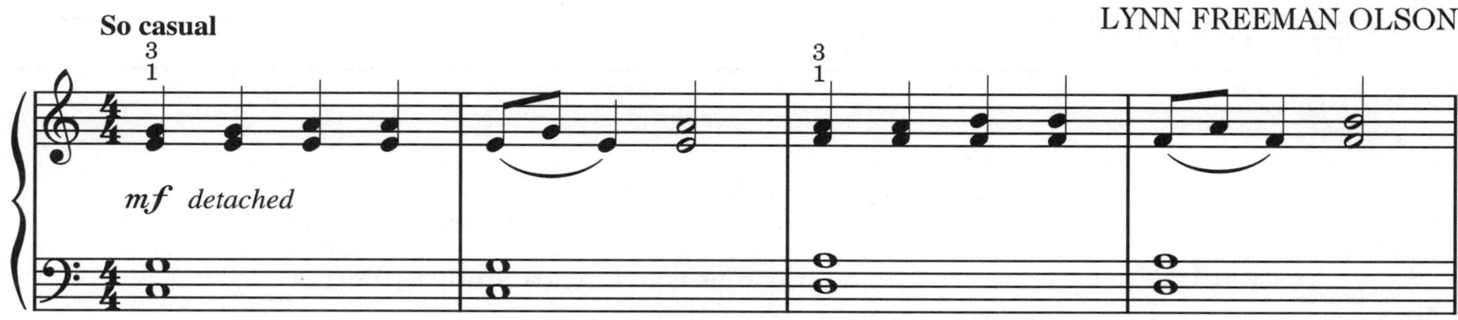

2.

EXEMPLARY REPERTOIRE

TOPICS TO EXPLORE AND DISCUSS

RELATED SKILLS AND ACTIVITIES

SUBSEQUENT REPERTOIRE

Pentascales

EXEMPLARY REPERTOIRE **Con Moto, Op. 117, No. 4** Cornelius Gurlitt

INQUIRY

1. Scan *Con Moto*. Observe:
   - type of motion between hands
   - melodic range
     — a pentascale is a pattern of five consecutive stepwise pitches
     — name the pitches of the pentascale used in *Con Moto*
   - repetition
   - first and second endings
     — expansions of range in second ending
2. Determine logical beginning fingerings.

PERFORMANCE

1. A *legato* sound is appropriate.
2. Use dynamic shading to emphasize the phrase structure.
3. As you play, describe the movement of the music (i.e., moves in, moves out, moves up, moves down).

Con Moto

(Original in C)

CORNELIUS GURLITT, Op. 117, No. 4
(1829–1901)

TOPICS TO EXPLORE AND DISCUSS

- Cornelius Gurlitt
- Béla Bartók
- Legato
- Sound: Describe the musical effects of parallel, contrary, and oblique motion.
  Describe the musical effect of one octave versus two octaves apart. What is the visual effect?

RELATED SKILLS AND ACTIVITIES

TECHNIQUE

1. The pentascale used in the Gurlitt *Con Moto* is major.

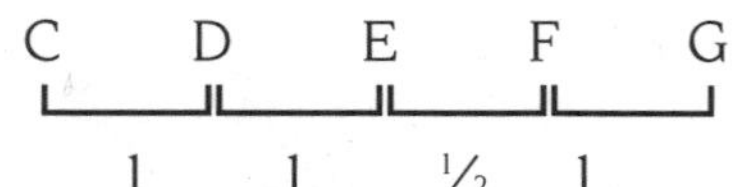

All major pentascales use the same pattern of whole and half steps.

The Italian *staccato* derives from a word meaning to "pull apart" or detach. In playing *staccato*, you do not punch the keys or jump away from them; you simply shorten each sound by releasing the key. You will feel your hand "release" easily. A dot above or below the notehead indicates staccato. Play each example.

a.

b.

A special sign is not always necessary to show a legato sound.

2. Perform the following legato major pentascale phrases.

a.

and so on, upward on every white-key pentascale pattern.

b.

and so on, downward, on every white-key major pentascale pattern.

Repeat:

- finger staccato, ***mp***
- wrist staccato, ***f***

Go to the PDM Web site for additional examples.

3. Play the 5th. Feel the shoulder, elbow, and wrist relax; then play the other notes with finger staccato.

a.

b.

4. *One-handed exercises.* Play with the nondominant hand; tap the beat with the other hand.

a.

b.

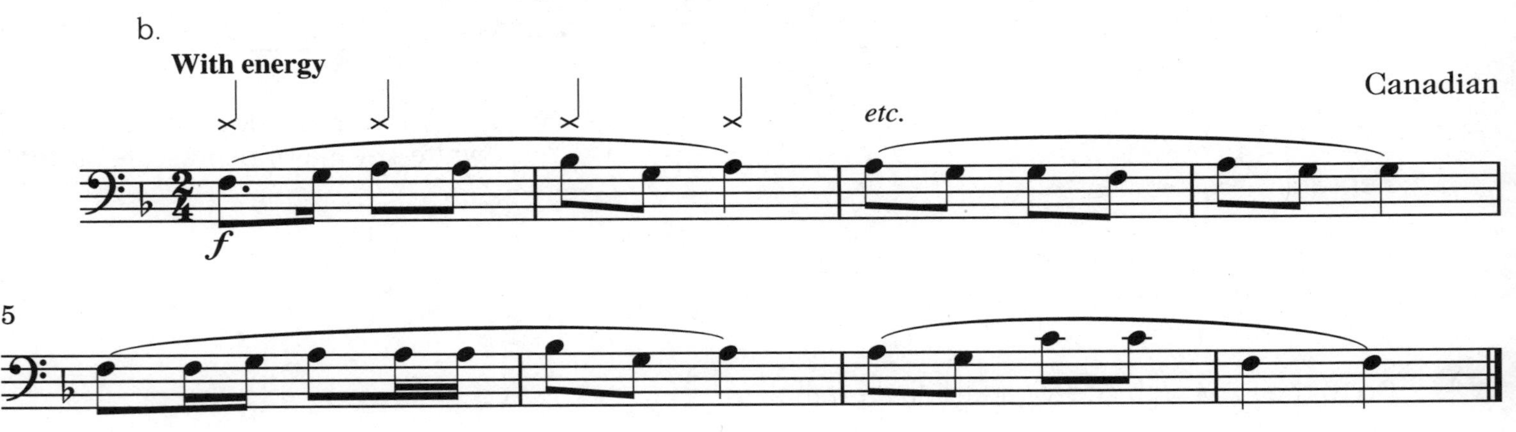

READING

1. Number the phrases of the Bartók *Legato Study*. Your teacher will call for random phrases.

Legato Study

from *The First Term at the Piano*

BÉLA BARTÓK
(1881–1945)

Moderato

f

5

9

2. Play the following unison melodies. Consider:

   - evenness of touch
   - phrasing
   - dynamics

a.

b.

Risentito

mf

c.

Scorrendo

f

d.

Not hurried

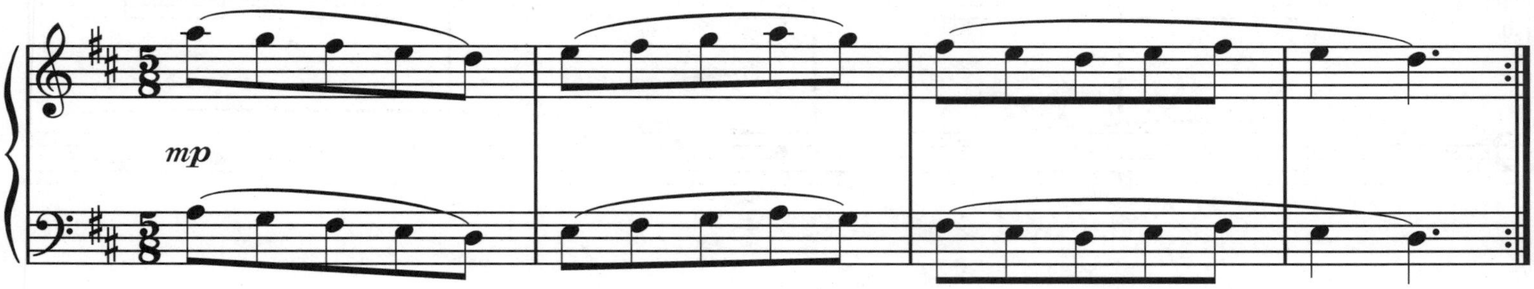

mp

3. The following examples were composed by group piano students.

a.

MARK MERTINS

b. JAMIE TAYLOR

c. JONATHAN FERGUSON

d. QUINN McCARTHY

Go to the PDM Web site for additional examples.

4. In the $\frac{4}{4}$ rhythm chart, use the following physical motions for given note values:

— TAP

— CLAP

— SNAP

Count aloud as you perform only the quarter notes.

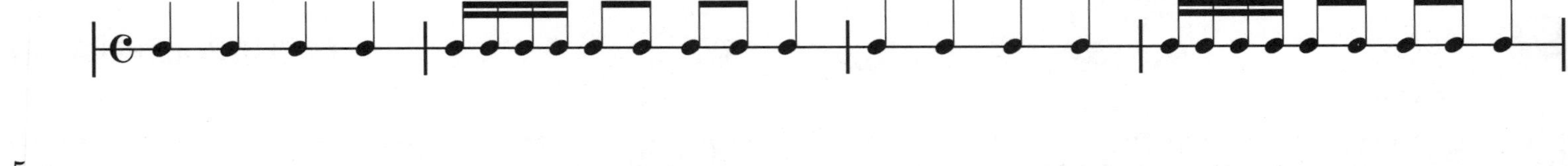

Count aloud as you perform only the sixteenth notes, then count aloud as you perform only the eighth notes,

Form a rhythm ensemble by assigning certain note values to certain students. When you perform together, you will hear all the rhythms given.

KEYBOARD THEORY

1. In a major pentascale, the bottom tone is called *tonic* (I) and the top tone *dominant* (V). Pentascale melodies may be accompanied by these single tones.

   Generally, when the melody is made mostly of tones 1, 3, and 5, accompany with the tonic (I); when the melody is made mostly of 2 and 4, accompany with the dominant (V). Your ear will always be the final test of appropriate accompaniment.

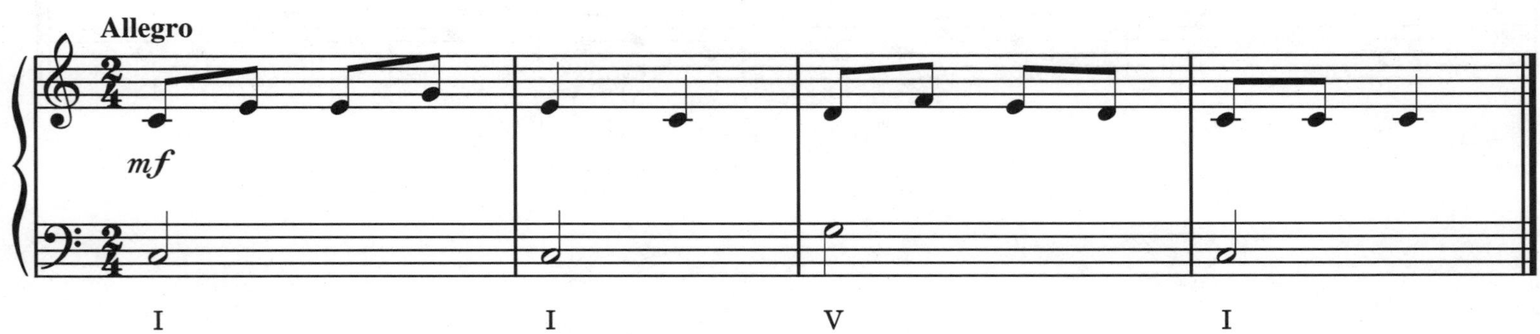

For right-hand melodies, you may choose to place the left hand in pentascale position as illustrated. We also encourage the frequent use of dominant *below* tonic. This is easy when you place your left-hand thumb on a white-key tonic.

Go to the PDM Web site for additional exercises using tonic and dominant tones of major keys.

HARMONIZATION

1. Return to the harmonization items in Chapter 1 (pp. 31–32). Use tonic and dominant tones to harmonize these melodies.

2. Accompany the following melodies with tonic and dominant tones. Try both the "dominant above" and the "dominant below" left-hand positions. Place Roman numerals under each melody with an arrow designation for the dominant (↓ or ↑).

d.

e. American

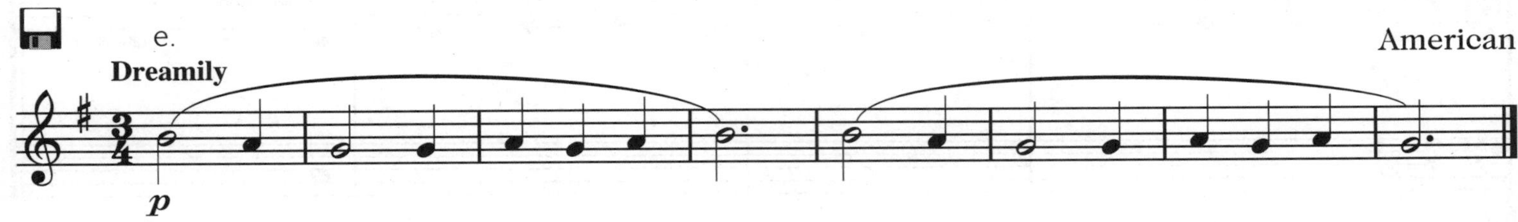

Go to the PDM Web site for additional examples.

TRANSPOSITION

1. Transpose each melody and tonic/dominant accompaniment from item 1 in Harmonization on page 51 to two other major pentascales.

3. Transpose the following to C, F, and E major.

Quiet Conversation

LYNN FREEMAN OLSON

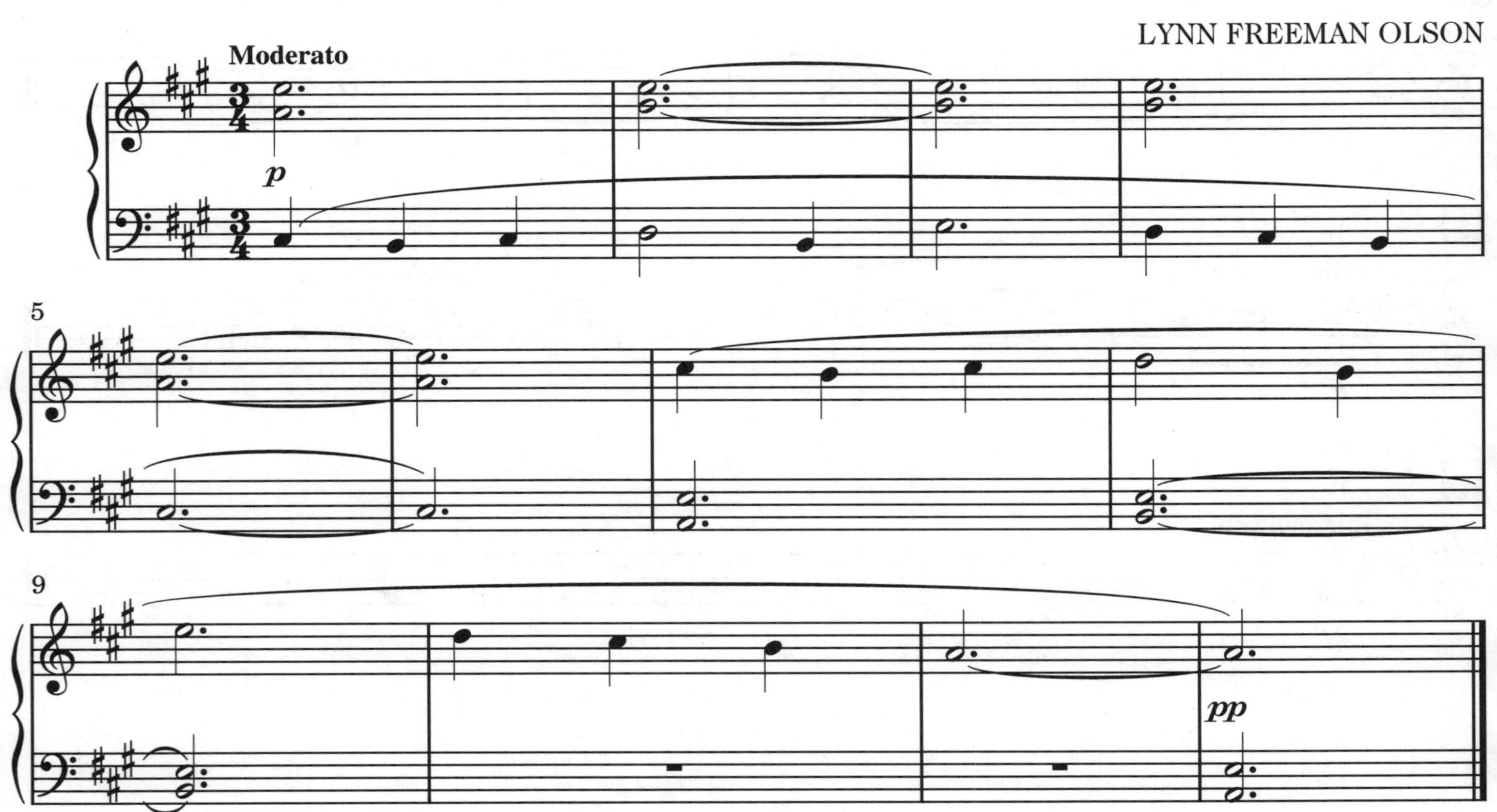

Go to the PDM Web site for additional examples.

IMPROVISATION

1. Using the rhythms of item 4 (page 50), improvise melodically within a major pentascale.

ENSEMBLE

1. Pay careful attention to articulation.

Li'l Liza Jane

Arr. Martha Hilley

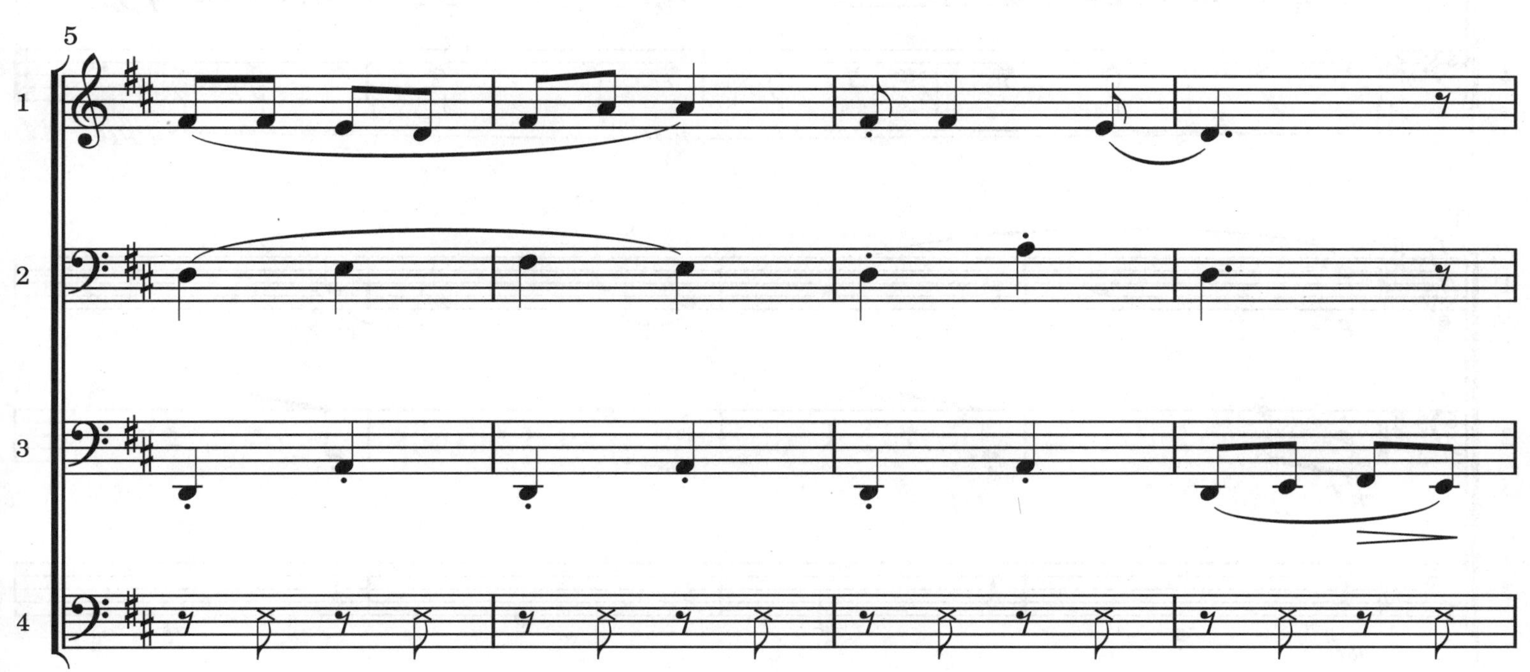

9
1
2
3
4
mp
p
p
p
13
Fine
mf
pp
mp
mp
ppp
mp
ppp
17
f
mf
mf
Clap
mf

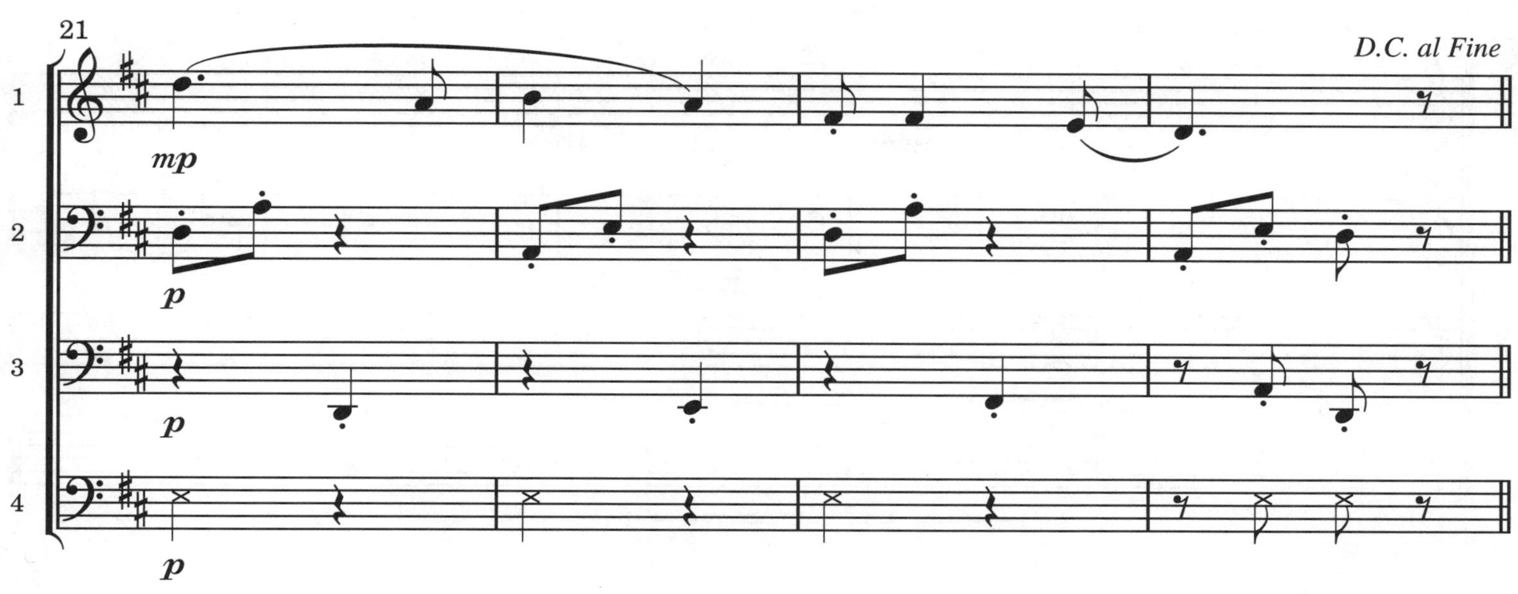

2. Perform twice without stopping. Switch parts the second time through.

Lullaby
(adapted)

LOUIS KÖHLER
(1820–1886)

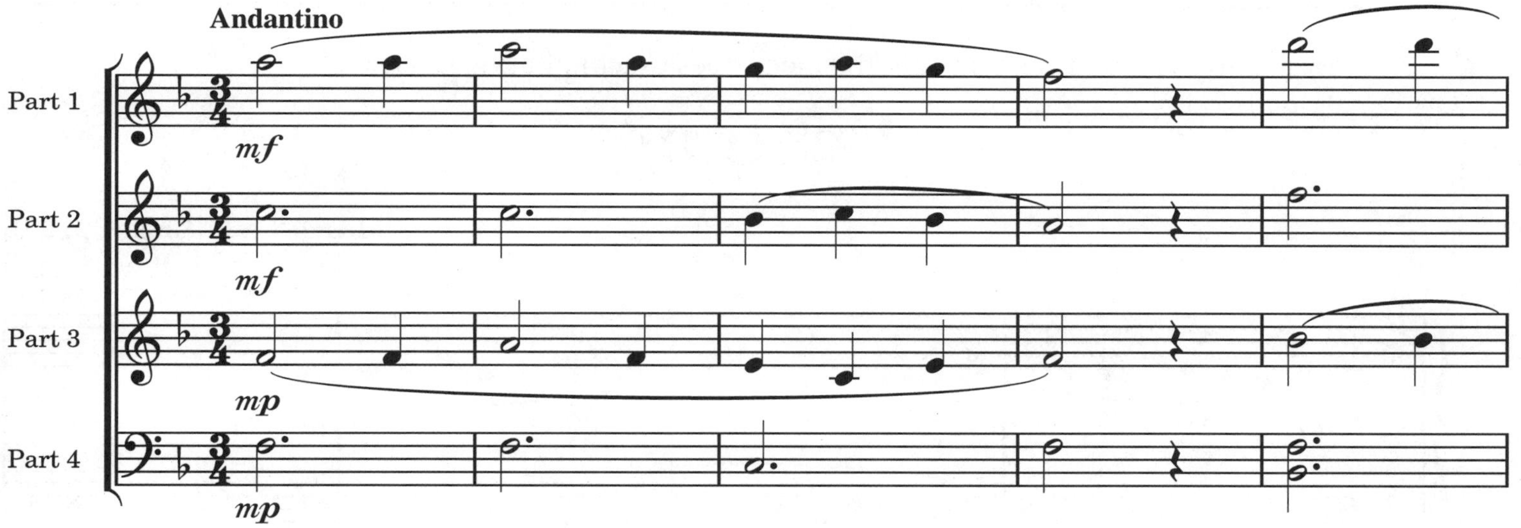

Andantino

Part 1 *mf*

Part 2 *mf*

Part 3 *mp*

Part 4 *mp*

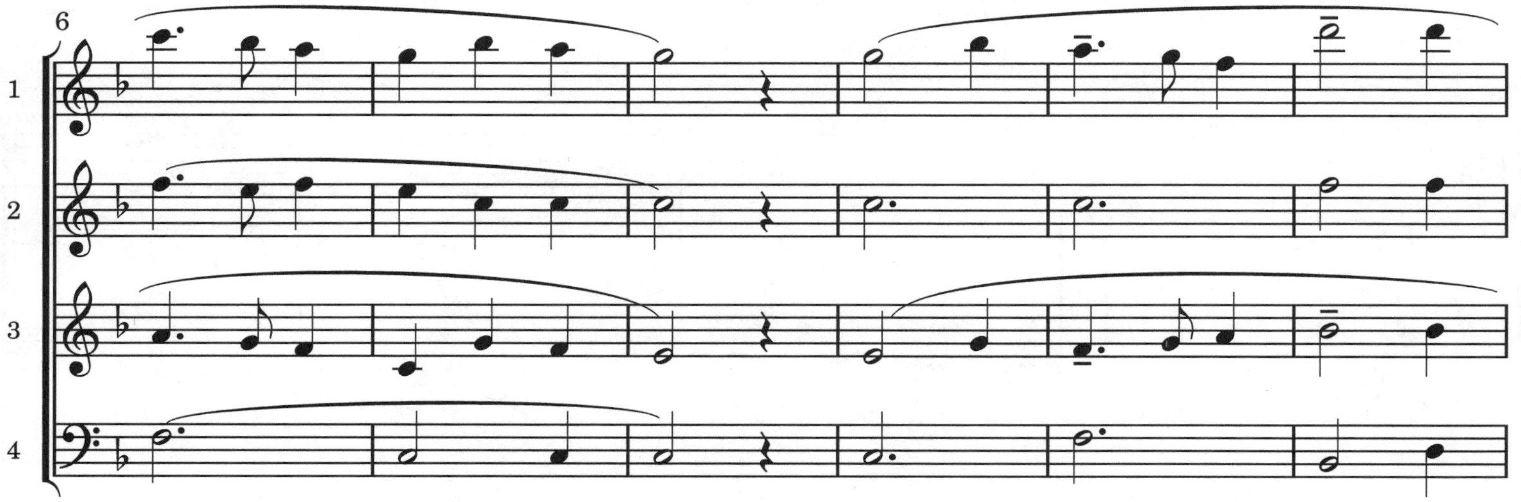

6

1

2

3

4

COMPOSITION

1. Compose a series of pieces in the style of the pentascale unisons on page 47–49. Trade with a classmate and sight-read each other's compositions.

SUBSEQUENT REPERTOIRE

1. *Echoing* employs imitation. Where in the piece does exact imitation cease?

Echoing

LOUIS KÖHLER, Op. 218
(1820–1886)

2. Look carefully at the "accompaniment" hand and the use of ties and slurs. Your fingering should be determined by looking at the *entire* phrase. A legato sound is appropriate. Notice the use of imitation, sequence, and repetition.

Etude

(Original in C)

CORNELIUS GURLITT, Op. 117, No. 3
(1820–1901)

Con moto

p

7

mf

cresc.

13

f

19

3. Improvise on all boxed pitches in *Inner View*.

Inner View

LYNN FREEMAN OLSON

3.

EXEMPLARY REPERTOIRE

TOPICS TO EXPLORE AND DISCUSS

RELATED SKILLS AND ACTIVITIES

SUBSEQUENT REPERTOIRE

Root Position Triads

EXEMPLARY REPERTOIRE **Scherzo, Op. 39, No. 12** Dmitri Kabalevsky

INQUIRY

1. Scan *Scherzo*. Observe:

    - repetitious shapes and their relationships
    - sequential patterns and direction
      — tones 1, 3, and 5 of a pentascale form a triad
      — the tones of a triad may be played singly or in various groupings
    - hand position shifts
    - contrasting articulations
    - unity and variety

2. Determine logical fingering.

PERFORMANCE

1. Play hands together as blocked triads with two pulses to each position.

2. Play as written.

Scherzo

from 24 *Pieces for Children*

DMITRI KABALEVSKY, Op. 39, No. 12
(1904–1987)

TOPICS TO EXPLORE AND DISCUSS

- Dmitri Kabalevsky: identify several musical contemporaries
- John La Montaine

RELATED SKILLS AND ACTIVITIES

TECHNIQUE

1. Play each example as written. Then play again using two hands, two octaves apart. Pay close attention to the indicated articulation.

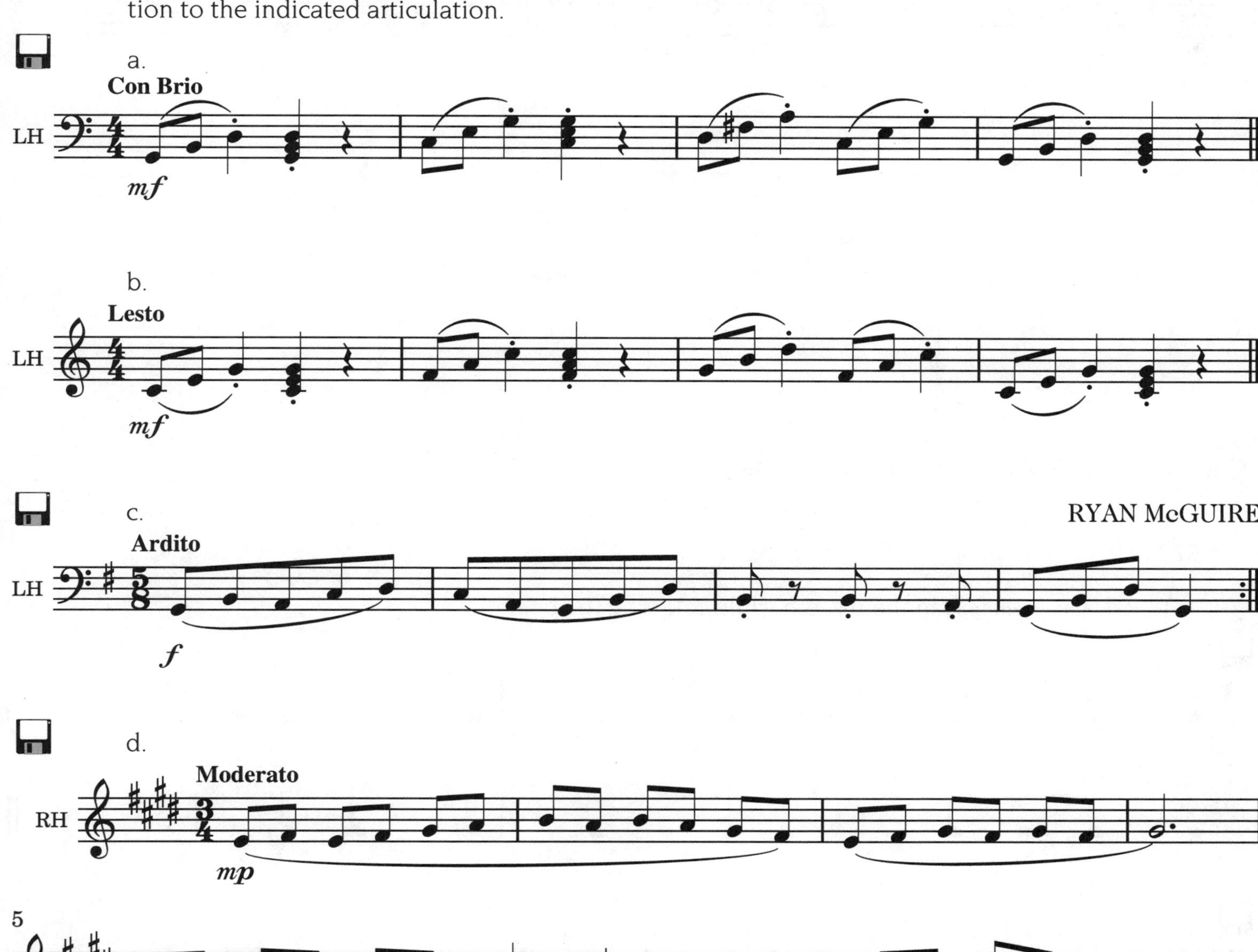

2. Play with the indicated hand; conduct with the other.

a.

b.

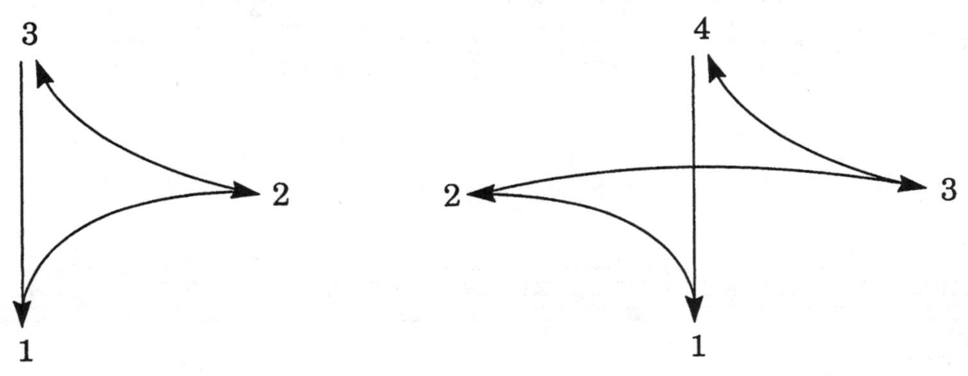

Go to the PDM Web site for more examples.

READING

1. *Rhythmic reading.* Tap the pattern while counting the beat.

2. Tap the following rhythms as two-part ensembles.

3. Tap the following rhythms while counting the beat. Perform as two-handed solos.

Go to the PDM Web site for more examples.

4. In the $\frac{4}{4}$ rhythm chart, use the following physical motions for given note values:

— CLAP

— TAP

— SNAP

— STOMP

Count aloud as you perform only the quarter notes.

Count aloud as you perform only the eighth notes.

Count aloud as you perform only the sixteenth notes.

Count aloud as you perform only the half notes.

Form a rhythm ensemble by assigning certain note values to certain students. When you perform together, you will hear all the rhythms given.

5. How many hand-position shifts are in A *Little Joke*?

A Little Joke

from 24 *Pieces for Children*

DMITRI KABALEVSKY, Op. 39, No. 6
(1904–1987)

6. Sight read the following examples using root position triads. Before playing, notice:
   - hand shifts
   - range of linear material
   - key signature
   - rhythmic "considerations"

a.

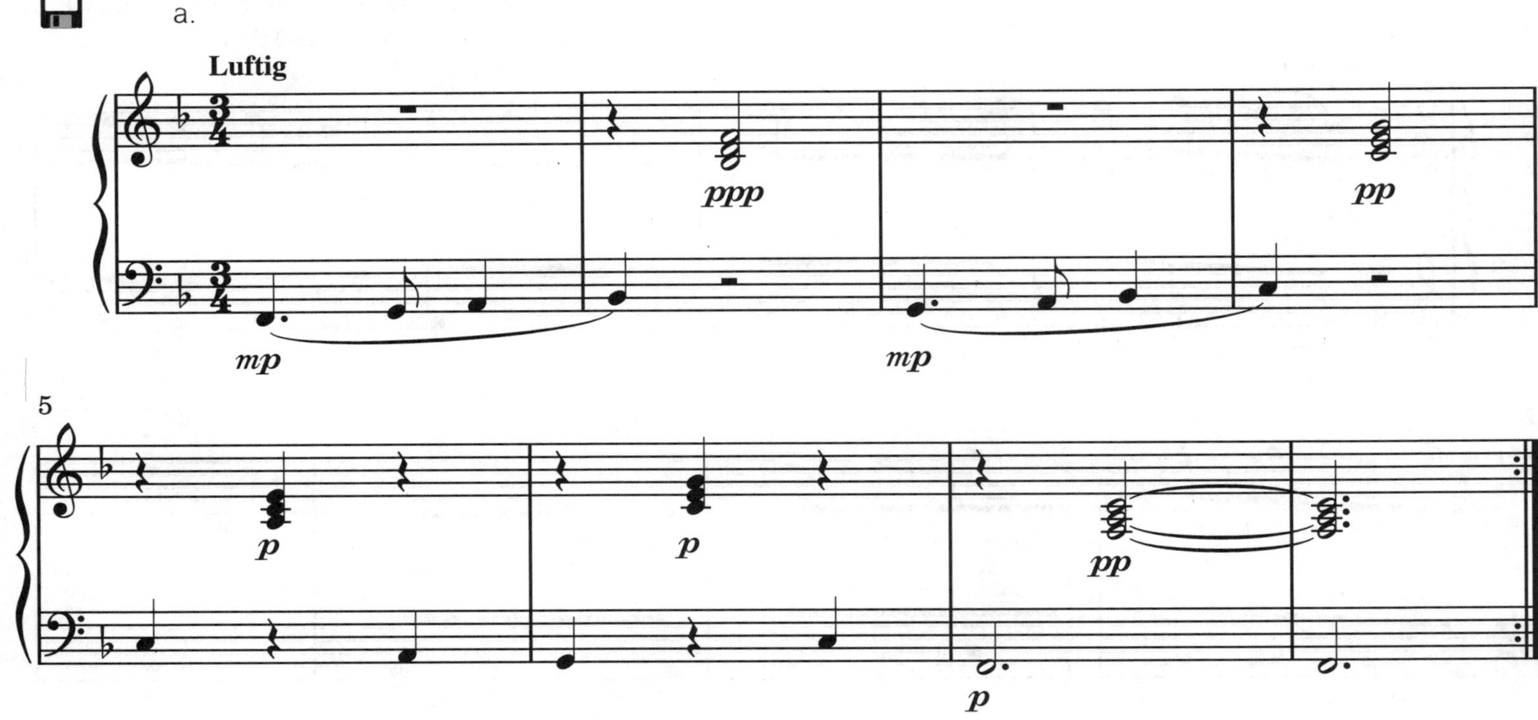

b.

c.

Go to the PDM Web site for more examples.

KEYBOARD THEORY

1. Play triads in the left hand built on each tone of the C major pentascale. Determine the quality of each triad (major or minor) and assign a Roman numeral to it.

2. Play triads in the left hand built on each triad of the following major pentascales:

D, E, F, G, and A.

Play triads in the right hand built on each triad of the following major pentascales:

D, E, F, G, and A.

3. Play triads hands together in the keys of C, D, E, F, G, and A major. There should be no pause between key changes.

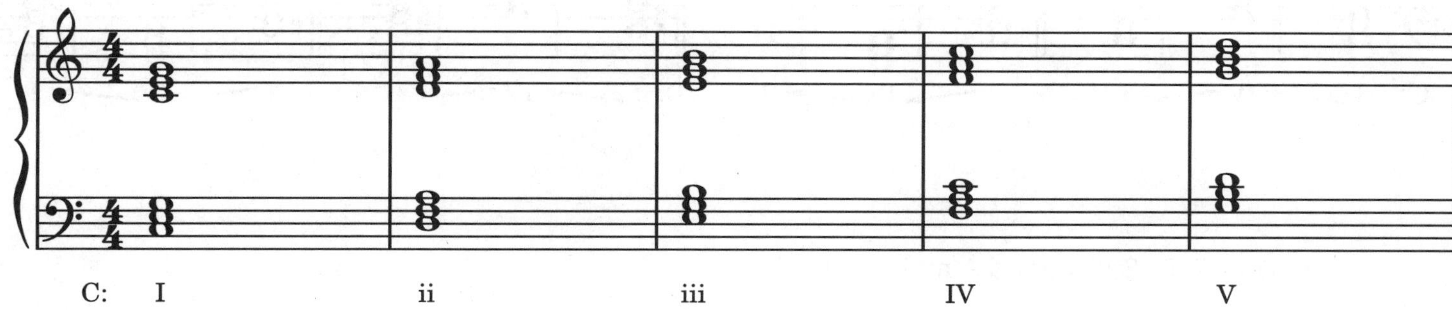

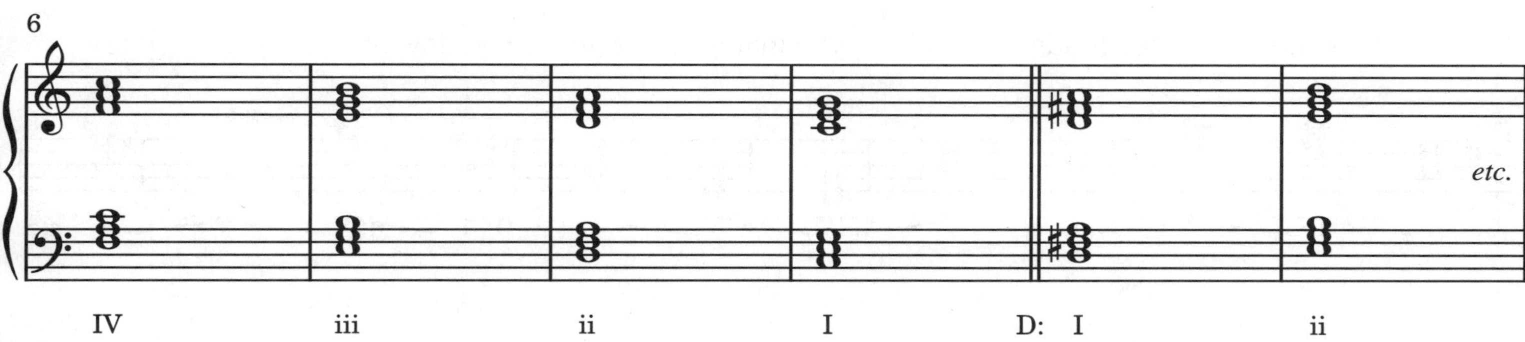

4. Play the same pentascale triads rhythmically in $\frac{6}{8}$, two measures to a triad— one measure broken, hand-to-hand, followed by one measure blocked, hand-to-hand.

5. Play the pentascale triads I and V in the major keys indicated. Follow the example.

Play in C, D, E, F, G, and A major.

6. Play the pentascale triads I and IV in the major keys indicated. Follow the example.

Play in C, D, E, F, G, and A major.

7. Play the pentascale triads I, IV, and V in the major keys indicated. Follow the example.

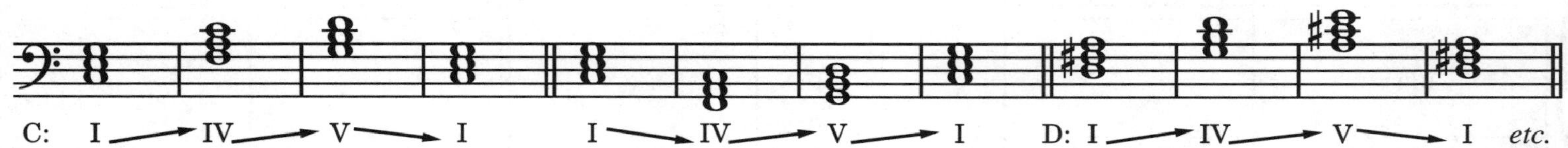

Play in C, D, E, F, G, and A major.

Go to the PDM Web site for more examples.

HARMONIZATION

1. Refer to the melodies on pages 51–52. Harmonize with triads instead of single tones.

2. When deciding harmonies to be used, consider the chord tones in the melody. Realize that for any single tones there are three triadic possibilities and that for two chord tones within one measure there are two possibilities.

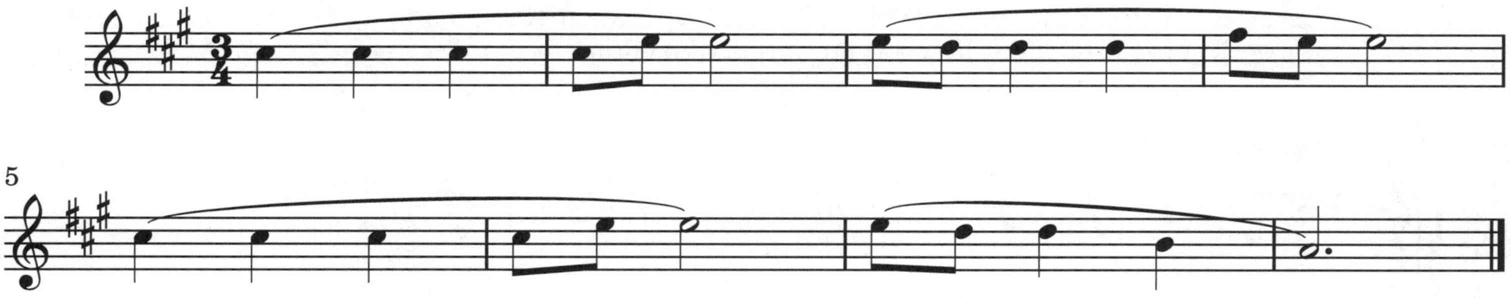

a. The following is one possible realization.

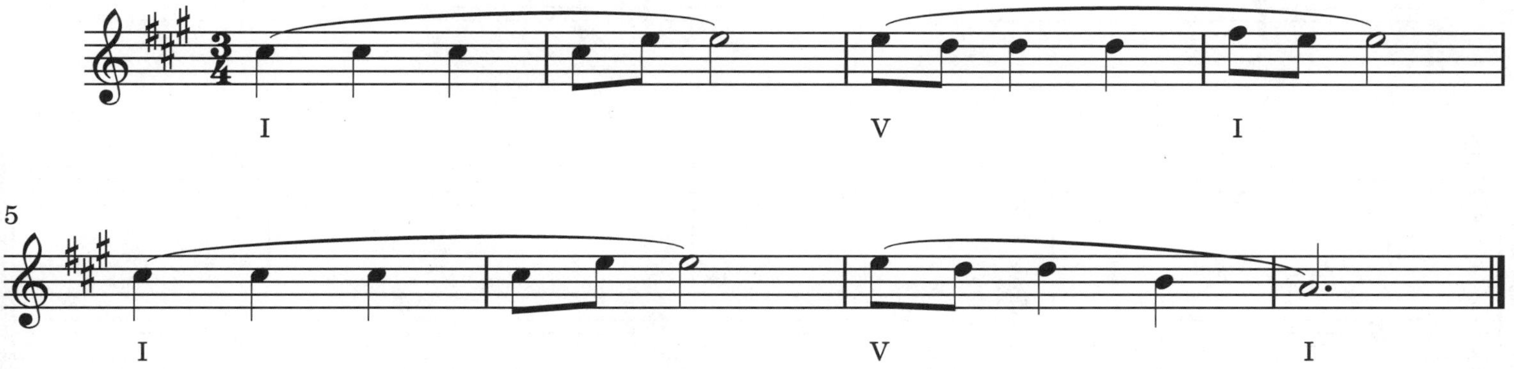

I V I

I V I

b. This is another possibility.

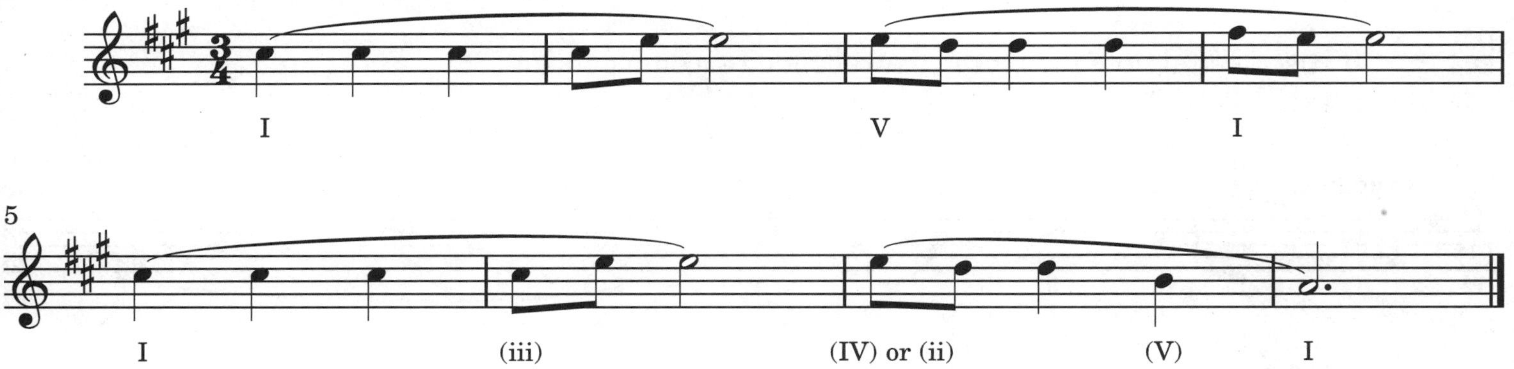

I V I

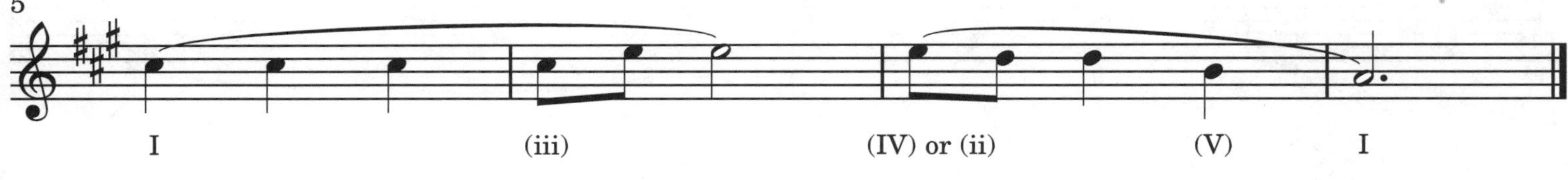

Try a two-handed accompaniment style for example b. Notice the "root-chord-chord" pattern.

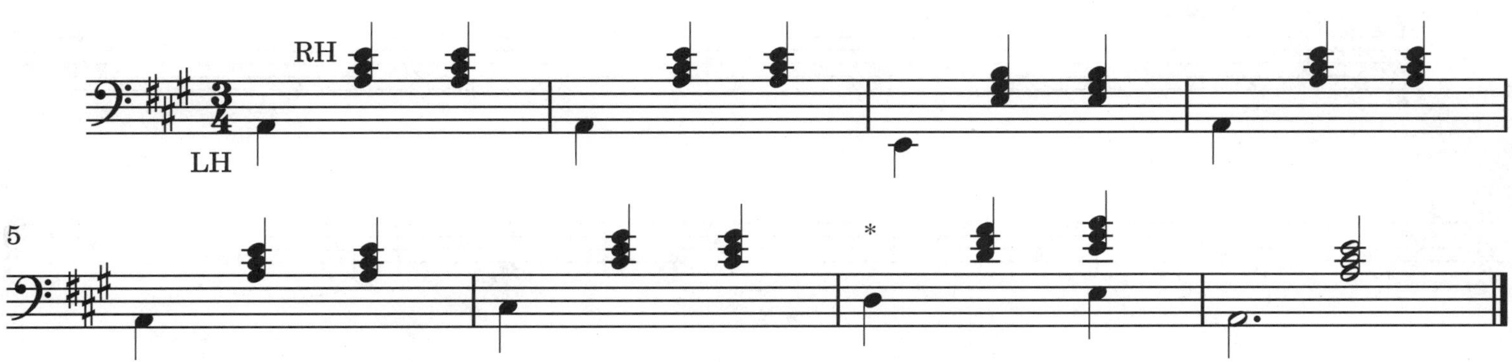

*Notice that the accompaniment pattern must change when the harmonic rhythm changes.

3. Choose from I, ii, iii, IV, and/or V to harmonize the following melodies. Chords have been furnished at first as an example.

   a. Listen for balance between melody and accompaniment. Your left hand must play softly. It is better to "double" the top note of the V chord with the melody than play the chord an octave lower. A general rule to follow—no root position chords below "B♭2."

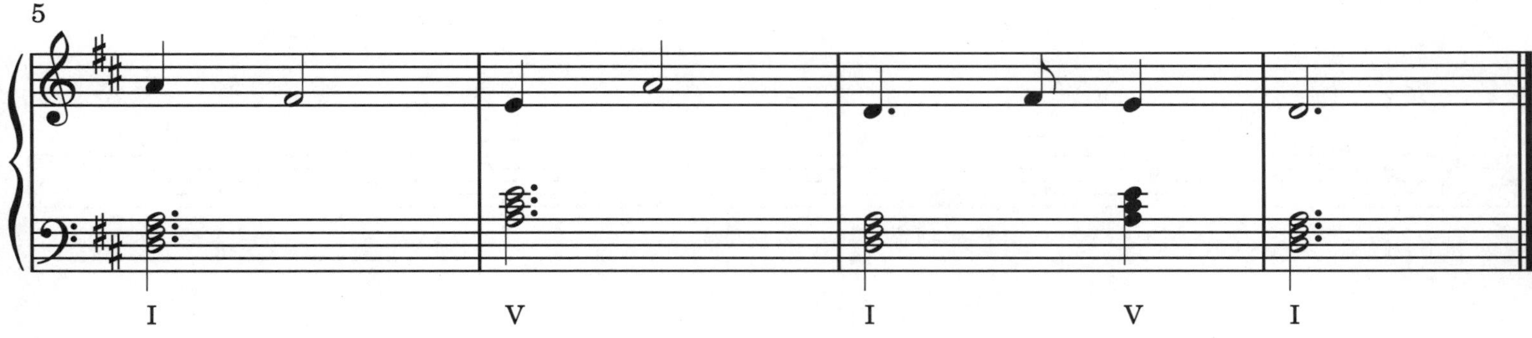

   b. Use quarter-note rhythms in a two-handed accompaniment.

   c. Write in Roman numeral designation and choose an appropriate accompaniment style.

4. The following are *challenge* melodies. Choose between two different accompaniment styles:

- RH melody and LH triads
- no melody; two-handed "root-chord"

Go to the PDM Web site for suggestions in choosing harmonies.

5. Return once more to the melodies on pages 51–52. Harmonize with a two-handed accompaniment while singing the melody.

TRANSPOSITION

1. Transpose item 3a of the Harmonization section (page 72) to F major and A major.

2. Transpose *Lullaby* to C, D, F, and A major.

Lullaby

LYNN FREEMAN OLSON

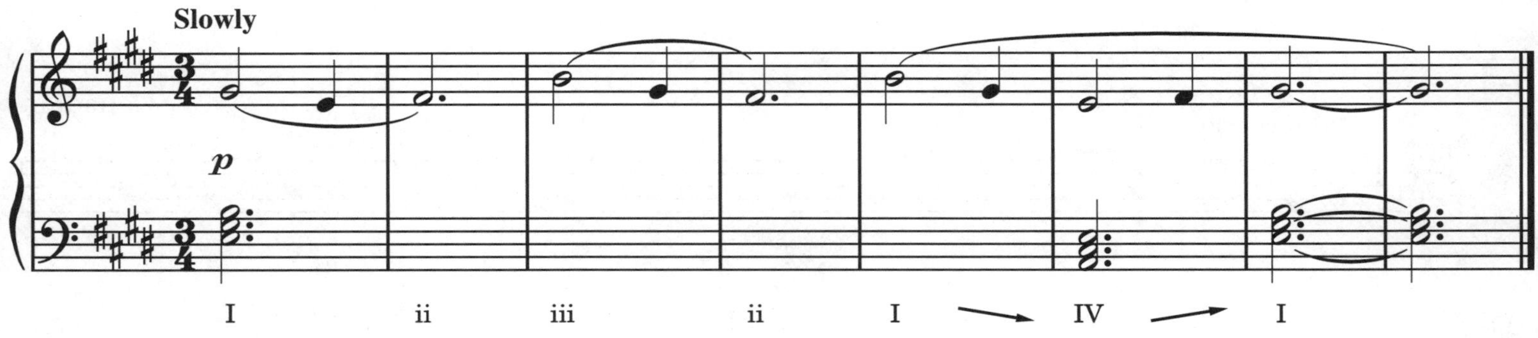

3. The following examples are to be transposed the interval of a tritone. To do so one note at a time is a difficult, if not impossible, task. Follow the steps listed to ensure success.
   - Do not play in written key
   - Determine melodic range
   - Observe melodic contour
   - Analyze harmonic content
   - Notice hand shifts
   - Determine beginning fingering

   a. Transpose to the key of C major.

b. Transpose to the key of A major..

c. Transpose to the key of G major.

Go to the PDM Web site for additional examples.

IMPROVISATION

Play through each example:

Weak:

Stronger:

Is the second example stronger because of pitch, or because of rhythm, or because of a combination of the two?

Working with a classmate on headsets, create four-bar phrases and assess the weakness and/or strength of your improvisation. As a team, determine a key and meter and play "Question and Answer" improvisations; each plays a four-bar phrase. Trade parts so each of you creates a question and each creates an answer.

Go to the PDM Web site for additional examples.

ENSEMBLE

1. Play *Country Dance* six times, moving to the next part down each time (Part 6 moves to Part 1).

- first time, ***p***
- second time, ***mp***
- third time, ***mf***
- fourth time, ***f***
- fifth time, ***p***
- sixth time, ***pp***

Country Dance

2. Play the Primo part (page 78) as your teacher or a classmate plays the Secondo.

Pop Goes the Weasel

Secondo

Folk Song
Arr. Marion Verhaalen

Pop Goes the Weasel

Primo

Folk Song
Arr. Marion Verhaalen

COMPOSITION

1. Compose a piece in the style of *Scherzo* (see page 62).

SUBSEQUENT REPERTOIRE

1. Look carefully for all ties before playing. While counting aloud, subdivide to ensure rhythmic accuracy through ties and dotted quarter notes. Notice the sign for pedal.

After the Rain

LYNN FREEMAN OLSON

Easily, but moving

p

pp

p

LH over

dim.

pp

Go to the PDM Web site for help with the rhythmic aspects of *After the Rain*.

2. *Questioning* uses primarily melodic thirds. Play each third as a sold harmonic interval using the indicated fingering. Then play the piece as written.

Questioning

JOHN LA MONTAINE

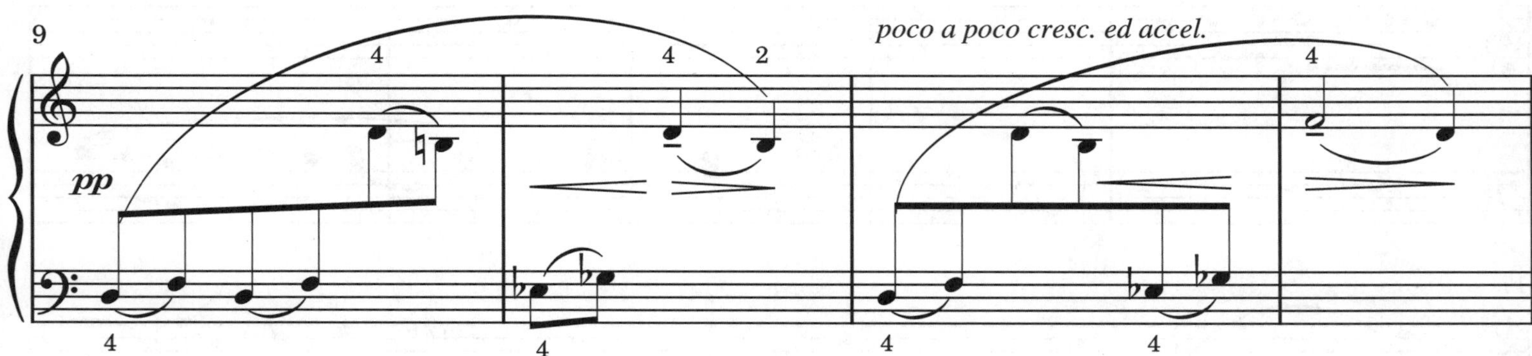

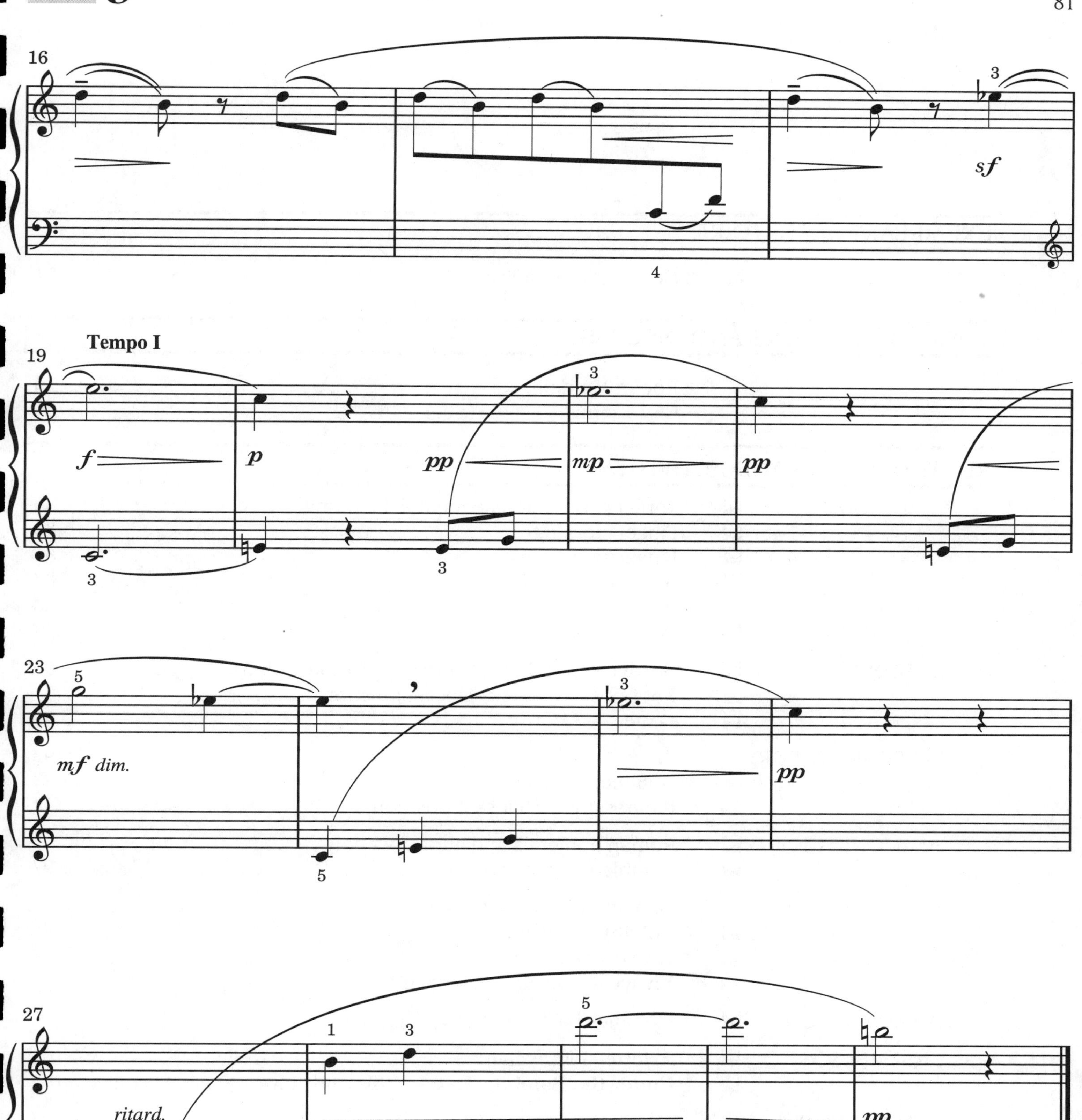
Tempo I
mf dim.
ritard.
over

4.

EXEMPLARY REPERTOIRE

TOPICS TO EXPLORE AND DISCUSS

RELATED SKILLS AND ACTIVITIES

SUBSEQUENT REPERTOIRE

Extended Use of Intervals, Pentascales, and Triads/ Dominant Seventh

EXEMPLARY REPERTOIRE — **Connections** Lynn Freeman Olson

INQUIRY

1. Scan *Connections*. Observe:

    - use of root position triads
    - use of broken chords
    - articulation
    - clef changes
    - form
    - Why the title *Connections*?

PERFORMANCE

1. As a class, discuss a sequence of practice steps that you feel will ensure success with this piece. List the steps in the space provided below.

    -
    -
    -
    -
    -

Connections

LYNN FREEMAN OLSON

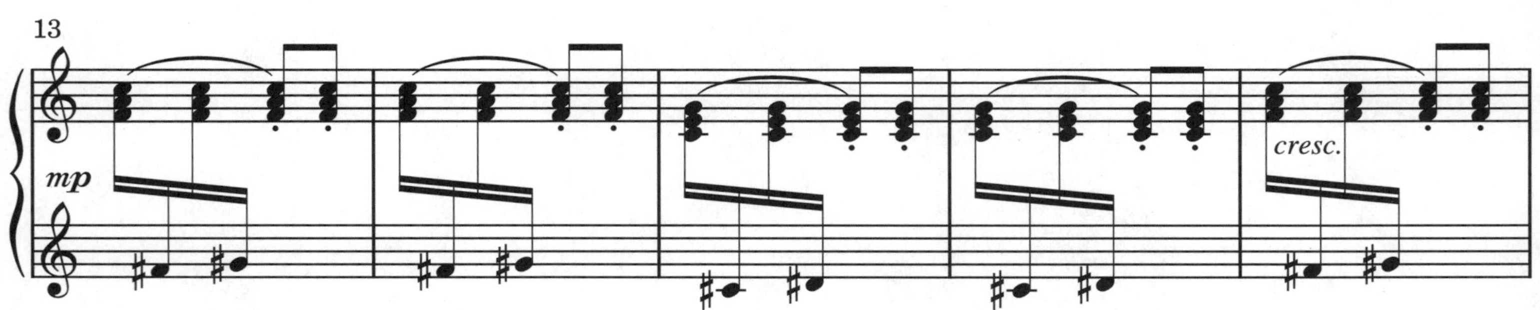

18
mf
mp
cresc.
23
mf
dim.
27
mp
cresc.
31
mf
dim.
molto cresc.
35
LH
ff

TOPICS TO EXPLORE AND DISCUSS

- Robert Vandall
- Carl Czerny

RELATED SKILLS AND ACTIVITIES

TECHNIQUE

1. Triplet subdivision of the basic pulse will aid in steady rhythm.

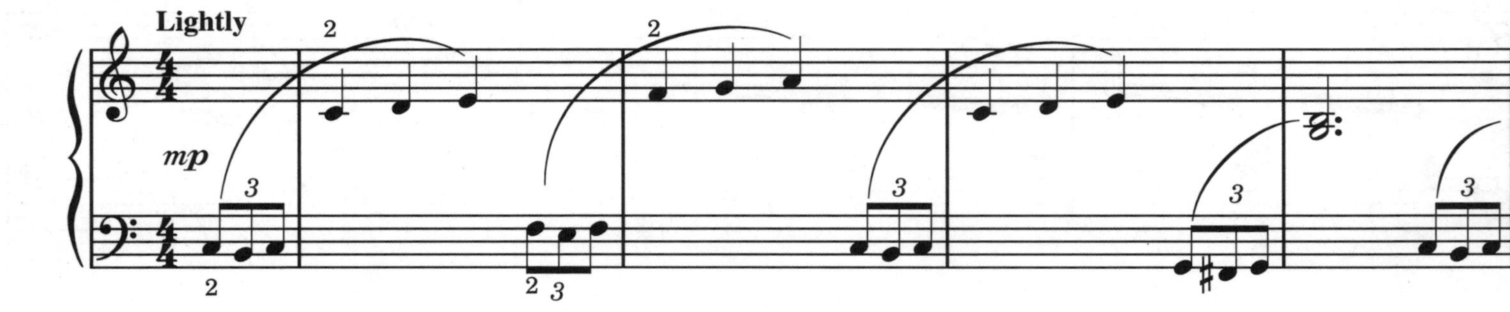

Go to the PDM Web site for further work with this example.

2. Play with careful attention to finger crossings.

a.

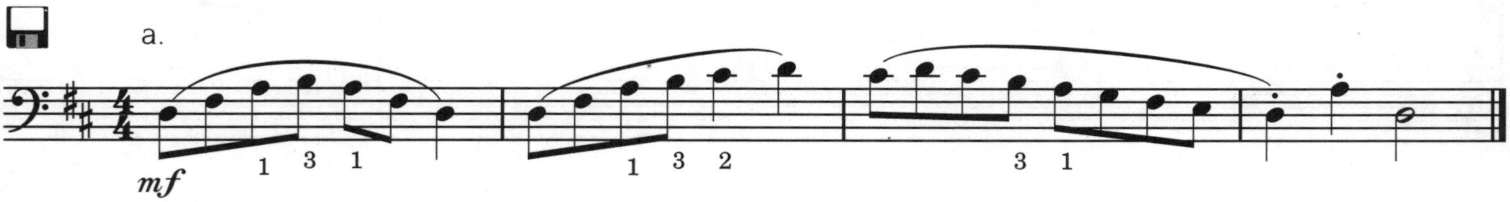

b.

3. Play with particular attention to extensions.

c.

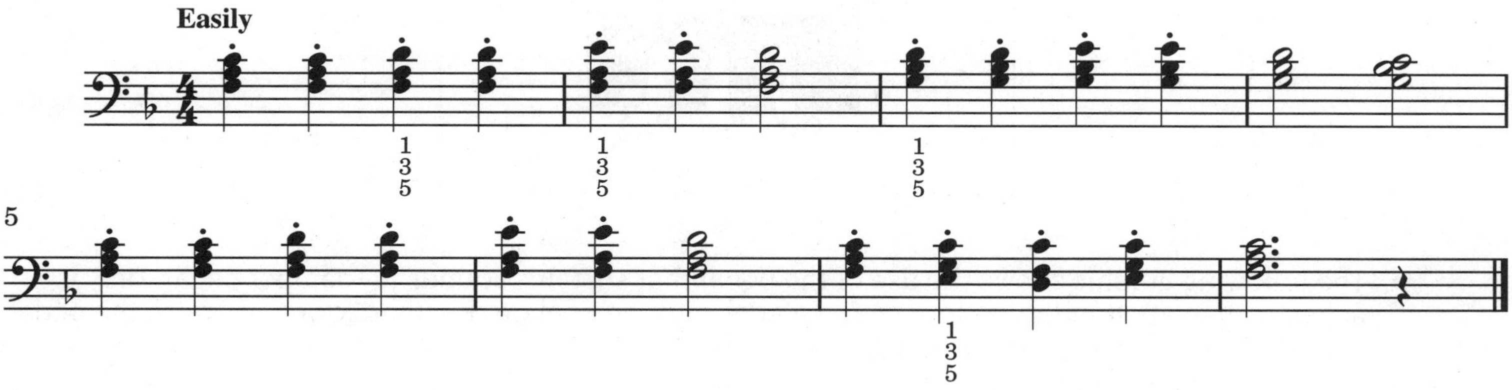

Easily

d.

mp

pp

4. The Bartók example uses a combination of staccato and legato articulation. What is the technical challenge in measures 6 and 7?

BÉLA BARTÓK
(1881–1945)

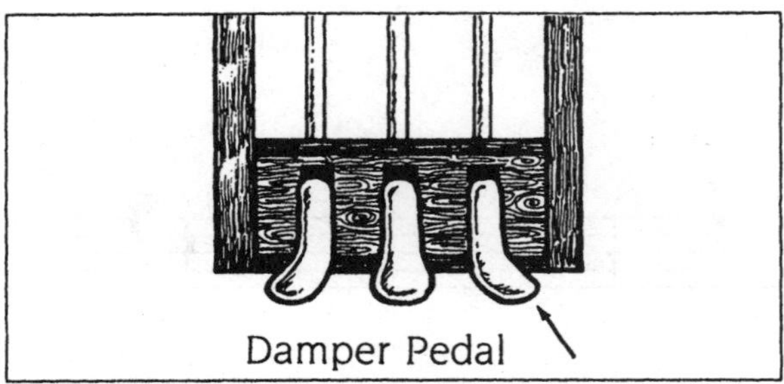

5. The following graphic shows the use of the pedal that sustains sounds (a "damper pedal" on acoustic pianos). It indicates foot action. Pedal with the heel on the floor; lower and raise the pedal with the ball of the foot. Use the right foot.

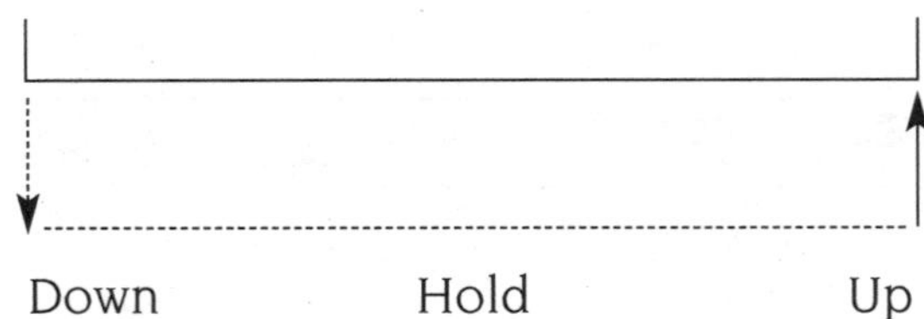

The graphic below shows connection of sounds. When the key or keys go down, the foot allows the pedal to raise to clear the previous sound and then lowers to catch the new sound. A seamless effect results.

6. With one finger, play the C major pentascale and connect one tone to the next with the pedal. The designation for pedal directs movement of the foot.

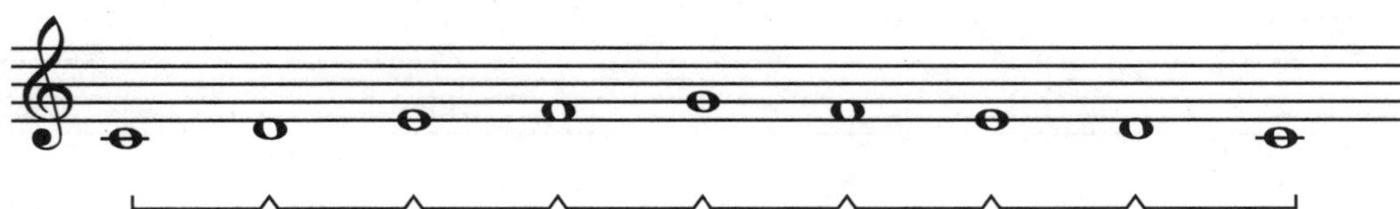

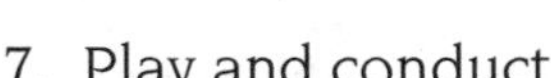

7. Play and conduct.

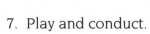

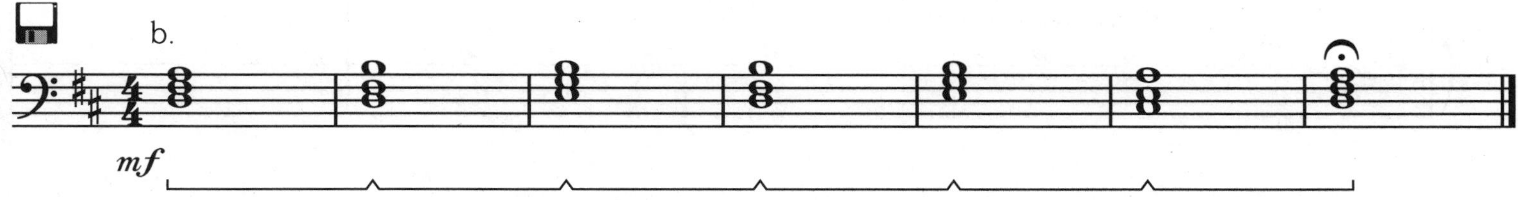

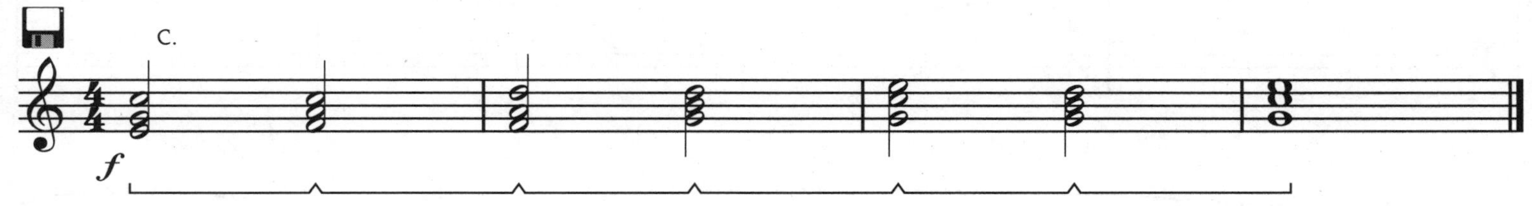

READING

1. Mark the places in the score where motion changes to contrary.

Study: Parallel and Contrary Motion

from *The First Term at the Piano*

BÉLA BARTÓK
(1881–1945)

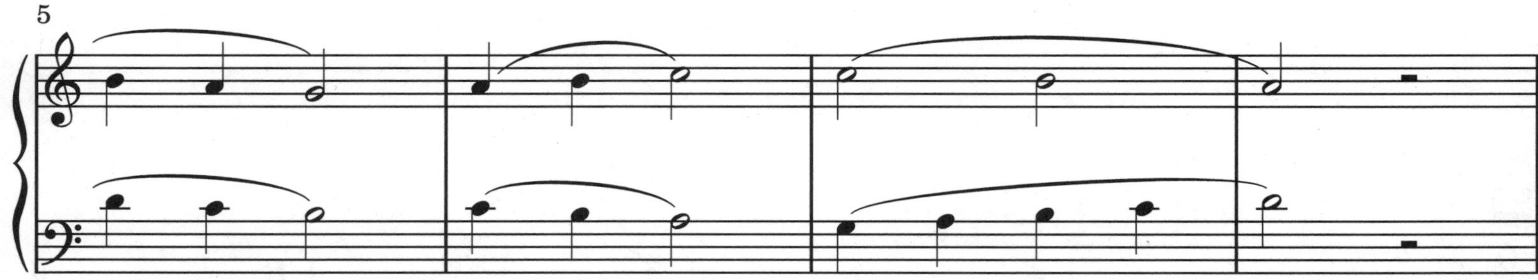

2. Each example has been written in two different ways. Which arrangement do you find easier to play?

a.

Andantamente

mp

*b.

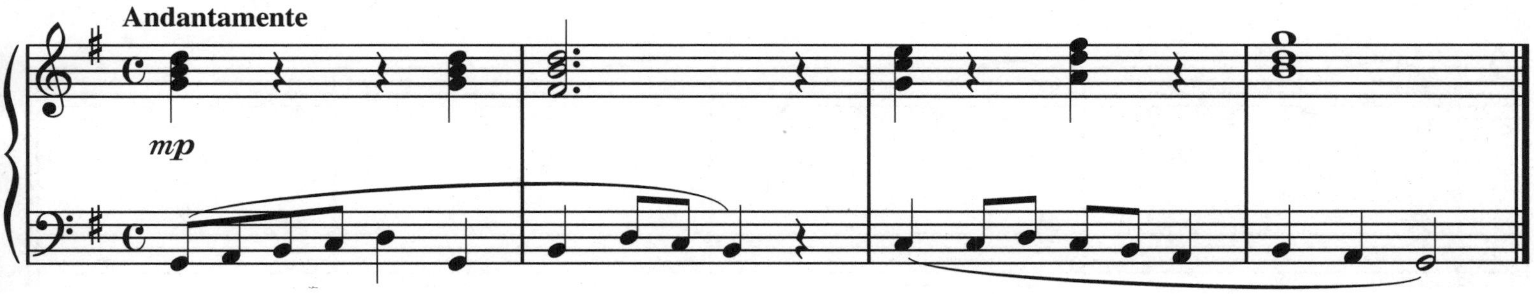

Andantamente

mp

c.

Schwungvoll

mf

*d.

Schwungvoll

mf

*(In these examples, the tones of the triads have been rearranged for convenience of playing.)

Go to the PDM Web site for additional examples.

3. Read through, blocking *both* hands; then play as written.

Dance

(Original in C)

CARL CZERNY, Op. 838, No. 11
(1791–1857)

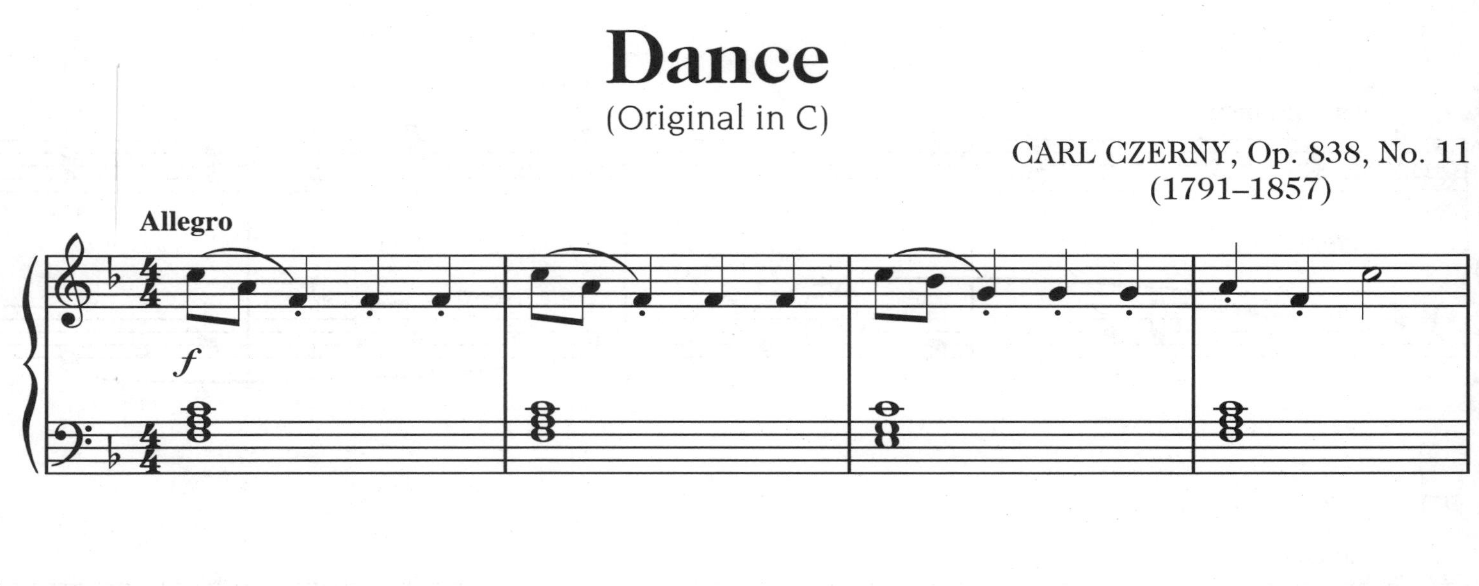

Go to the PDM Web site for further reading examples including random chord shapes.

KEYBOARD THEORY

1. The root position triads in this progression move by 4ths.

   In the left hand, double the roots of the triads and play the progression with hands together. Let the left hand also move in 4ths. Play in all white-key majors.

   You will have smoother motion using the *closest position* of the triads.

   To achieve the closest position, you will often move to an inversion (rearrangement) of the triad. In the preceding progression, the IV and V triads are inverted.

   Using this closest-position progression, add left-hand roots. Try both the "dominant above" and "dominant below" left-hand positions. Again, play in all white-key majors. Say the letter names of the roots as you play.

2. A dominant 7th chord (V7) is the dominant triad plus a minor 7th above the root.

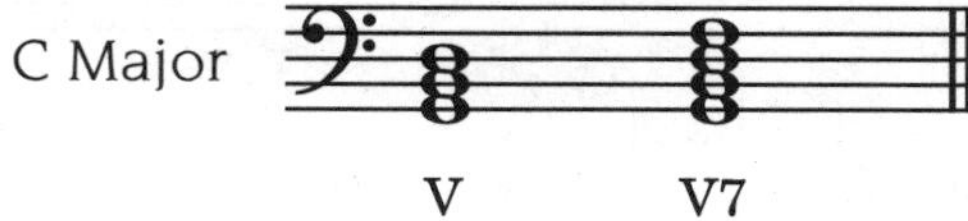

   In accompaniments, the 3rd is often not included in the left-hand V7 chord.

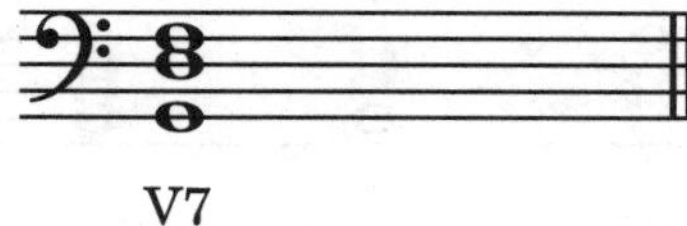

   For each major key shown, play a left-hand V7 chord omitting the 3rd. Supply the omitted 3rd an octave higher in the right hand.

3. A dominant 7th naturally leads to the tonic.

In this progression, economy of motion suggests omitting the 5th from the tonic. Play in the following keys:

D major:	A major:	F major:	E major:
V7–1	V7–1	V7–1	V7–1

4. Using the following harmonic progressions, verbally *spell* each chord in the root position but *play* the closest position.

a. C major

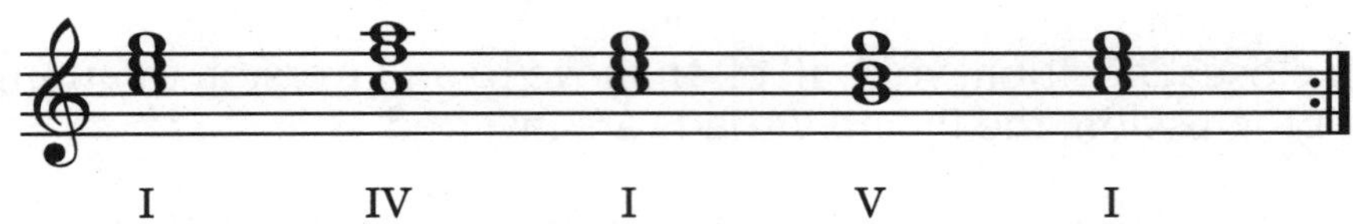

Also in
F major
A major

b. F major

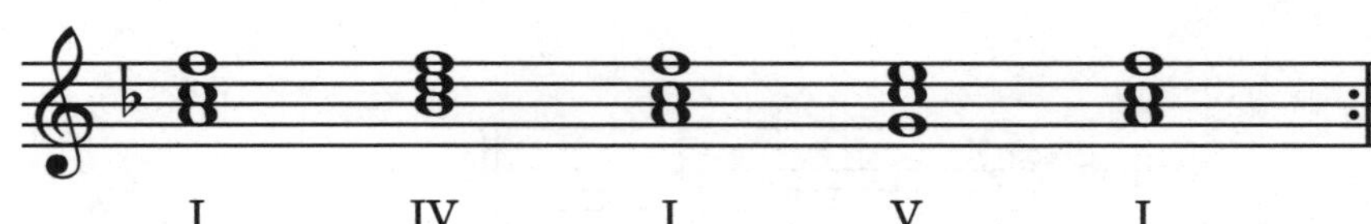

Also in
D major
B major

c. E major

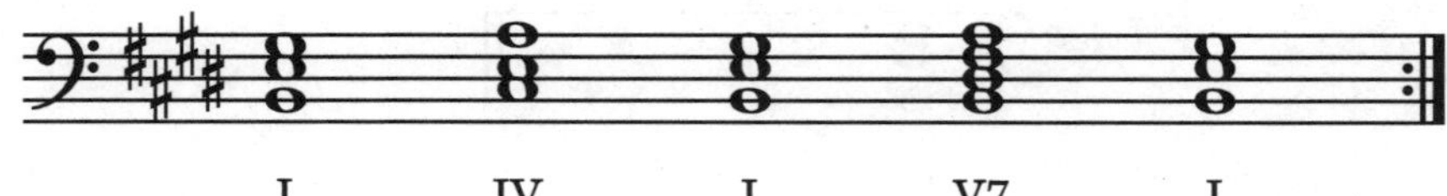

Also in
G major
C major

d. B major

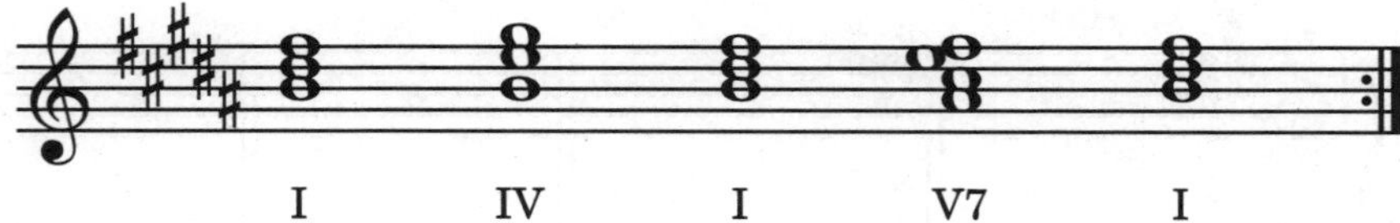

Also in
A major
G major

5.. Using the following progressions, verbally spell each chord in the root position but play the closest position.

a. D major

Also in
E major
A major

b. F major

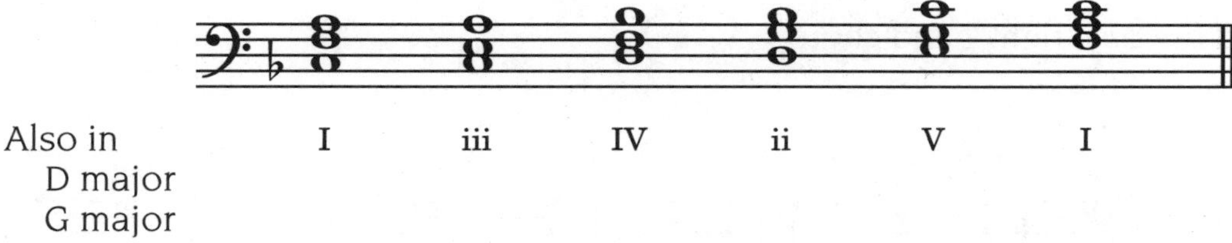

Also in
D major
G major

c. C major

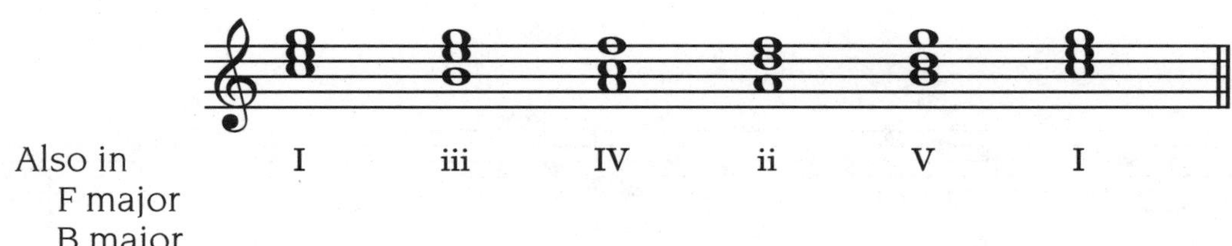

Also in
F major
B major

d. A major

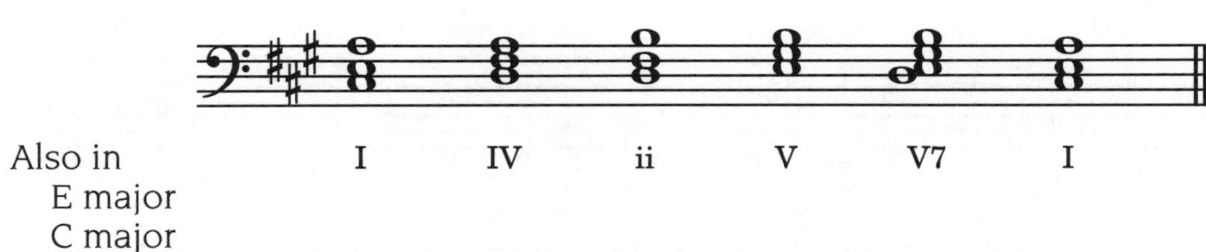

Also in
E major
C major

Go to the PDM Web site for further drill in closest-position progressions.

HARMONIZATION

1. Chords also may be designated by letter name instead of Roman numeral. Harmonize the following, moving to the closest chord possible each time..

a.

b.
Traditional
Slowly
D D G
expand
4
D
contract
A D A D
c. Left-hand melody, right-hand chords
English
Easily
F C7 F C7 F
d.
French
Sturdily
f
I V7 I V7 I V7 I V7 I
e. Accompany with a two-handed "root-chord" style. The RH chords should be in closest position.
American
With spirit
6
11
f.
British
Brightly
mf
5

2. Complete the following melodies in the style indicated.

a.

Go to the PDM Web site for suggestions in choosing harmonies and for additional melodies.

TRANSPOSITION

1. Return to the challenge harmonization examples on page 73 and transpose each to two different major keys.

2. Return to *Lullaby* on page 74. Play again in transposed keys, this time using a broken-chord accompaniment.

3. The following examples are to be transposed the interval of a tritone. As in Chapter 3, use the following steps:
   - Determine melodic range
   - Observe melodic contour
   - Analyze harmonic content
   - Notice common tones
   - Determine beginning fingering
   - Do not play in written key

   a. Play the last four bars in G major.

   b. Transpose *up* to A major.

c. Transpose *up* to B♭ major.

4. Efficient transposition includes an awareness of fragments, phrases, and sections that are repetitious. Scan *Vivace* for repetitions; then play in the keys of F major and G major. Do not play in the original key.

Vivace

CORNELIUS GURLITT, Op. 117, No. 8
(1829–1901)

Risoluto

f *mf*

1 3 2 5

5

f *mf*

9

mp *cresc.*

13

IMPROVISATION

1. Play the following triad progression hands together. Use the keys of D major, F major, and A major.

4/4	I	IV	ii	V	iii	ii	V	I :‖

2. Improvise a right-hand melody consisting of *chord tones only*. Select a ***maximum*** of three tones to use in your melody. For instance, in the key of B♭ major, you might choose D, E♭, and F. D is the third of the I chord and the root of the iii chord. E♭ is the root of the IV chord and the third of the ii chord. (It could also be used with the V chord as a natural extension to V7.) F is the fifth of the I chord, the root of the V chord, and the third of the iii chord.

   Your "improvisation" will consist of your choice of when to use each of the three tones and the rhythmic content. Both should be varied on the repeat.

Key of D major

Key of F major

Key of A major

(The balance of this page has been left blank to avoid a difficult page turn.)

ENSEMBLE

1.

Ariette

ALEXANDRE TANSMAN
(1897–1986)

Retenu

Primo

Secundo

p

p

5

9
4
1
4
13
3
3
3
1
4

17
21
Lunga
Lunga

2. Part 1 is to be improvised as a countermelody based on chord tones.

Under the Bamboo Tree

COLE AND JOHNSON
Arr. Lynn Freeman Olson

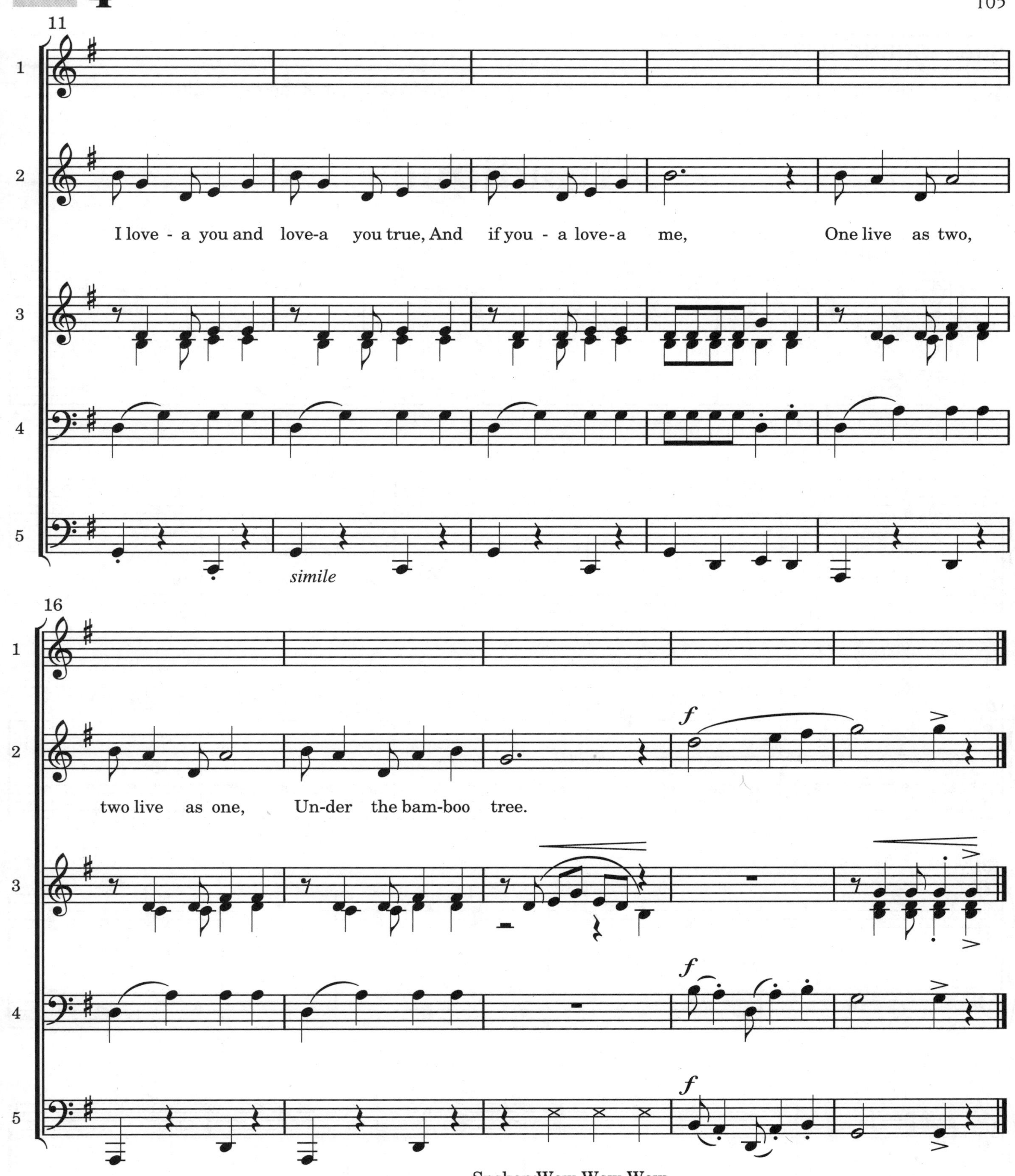
11
I love - a you and love-a you true, And if you - a love-a me, One live as two,
simile
16
two live as one, Un-der the bam-boo tree.
Spoken:Wow Wow Wow

COMPOSITION

Compose a piece using ABA form with the B section in the dominant. The composition should be a minimum of 24 measures in length.

- A section: Both hands are in the same pentascale position (any register), using parallel and/or contrary motion in a two-part texture.
- B section: Right hand plays melody against left-hand ostinato.

SUBSEQUENT REPERTOIRE

1. Use crisp staccato throughout. Discuss the form of *Triadique*. What is the major difference in the return of the A section?

Triadique

LYNN FREEMAN OLSON

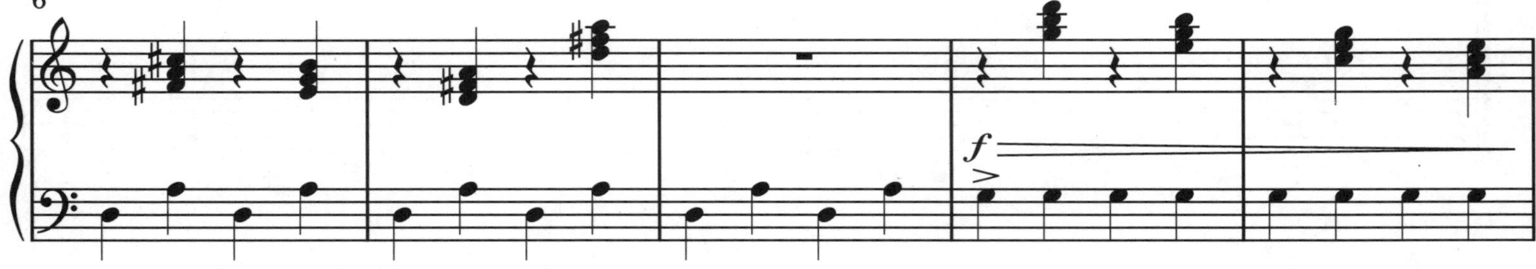

2. Pay close attention to pedal markings, but don't forget to listen to the effect of your foot!

3

Adagio

ROBERT D. VANDALL

3 1 3 1 3 1

p f p

5

f p

9

p f p

13

p f rit. p

3. What is "different in measures 9–12?

Summer Mood

from *Pop! Goes the Piano, Book I*

LYNN FREEMAN OLSON

21
dim.
p
p
26
31
36
41
pp
p
pp

5.

EXEMPLARY REPERTOIRE

TOPICS TO EXPLORE AND DISCUSS

RELATED SKILLS AND ACTIVITIES

SUBSEQUENT REPERTOIRE

Chord Shapes/Pentascales with Black-Key Groups

EXEMPLARY REPERTOIRE **Flickering Candle** Lynn Freeman Olson

INQUIRY

1. Scan *Flickering Candle*. Observe:

   - bass clef motion
   - broken-chords shapes
   - use of augmentation
   - use of diminution

PERFORMANCE

1. A consistent fingering is essential to the performance of *Flickering Candle*.

2. Practice the right hand as blocked chords.

3. Isolate measures 31–39. These should determine the overall tempo.

Flickering Candle

LYNN FREEMAN OLSON

TOPICS TO EXPLORE AND DISCUSS

- Philip Keveren
- Glenda Austin
- Chorale style/Keyboard style

RELATED SKILLS AND ACTIVITIES

TECHNIQUE

1. Play the following shapes.

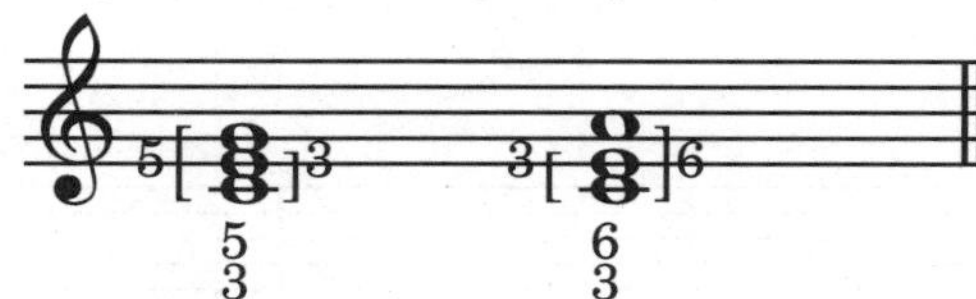

On white keys only, play a sequence of ${}^{5}_{3}$ to ${}^{6}_{3}$ shapes.

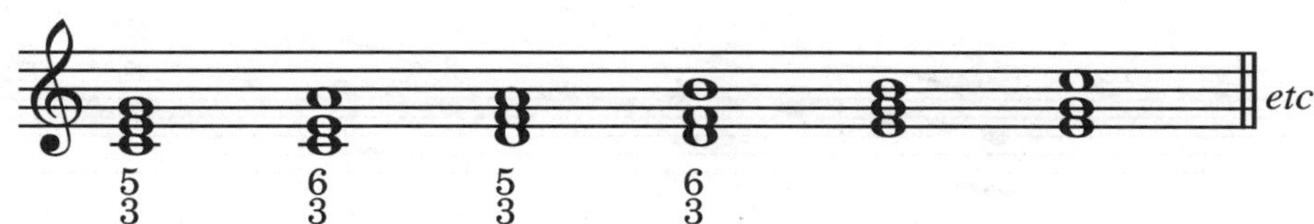

Play the same sequence with the left hand one octave lower.

Repeat the ${}^{5}_{3}$ to ${}^{6}_{3}$ sequence with each hand, this time sharping each F. Repeat, sharping each F and C. Repeat the sequence using major keys up through and including three sharps and three flats.

Key of G

Key of F

Key of D

Key of B♭

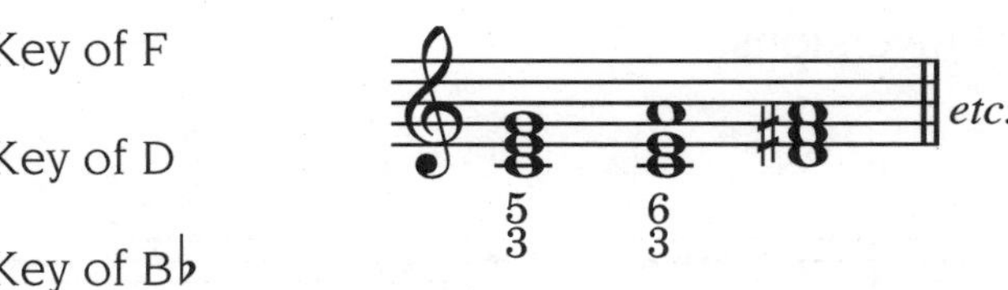

2. Using a pointer finger, play and name a major pentascale on each of the following black keys.

D♭/C♯ G♭/F♯

Play the two and three black-key groups, hands together, blocked.

RH	2	3	2	3	4
LH	3	2	4	3	2

Play again, and this time use thumbs as pivots to move from one black-key group to the other (thumbs on F).

Using the same principle, block the pentascale. Play the pentascale again as single tones, hands together.

Follow the same steps with G♭/F♯ and C♭/B (in B pentascale, left hand begins on finger 4, right hand on finger 1).

3. Play the following black-key-group pentascale drills, hands separately.

a.

RH

LH *(8va lower)*

b.

(8va higher)

RH

LH

4. Play the following exercises, which use chord inversions.

a.

5. Repeat the preceding two exercises, adding connecting pedal. Let your ear be your guide.

READING

1. Play these closest-position examples. Follow these steps with each item:

- Notice key signature
- Determine melodic range
- Observe melodic contour
- Quickly analyze LH closest-position chords
- Notice common tones
- Determine beginning fingering

2. Play these black-key-group pieces.

3. Play through with right-hand blocked chords before playing as written.

Prelude in G

(Original in C)

FRITZ SPINDLER
(1817–1905)

KEYBOARD THEORY

1. In a major key, the triad built on the 6th scale degree is minor.

C major 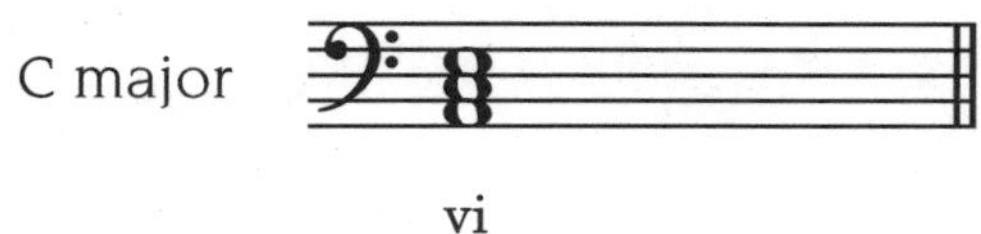

Using the following progression, verbally spell each chord in the *root* position but play the closest position.

C major 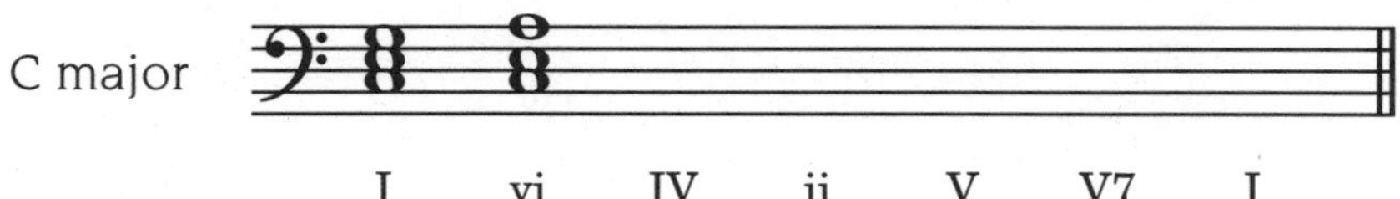

Also spell and play this progression in

D major

G major

A major

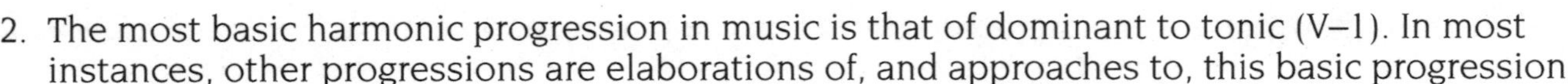

2. The most basic harmonic progression in music is that of dominant to tonic (V–1). In most instances, other progressions are elaborations of, and approaches to, this basic progression.

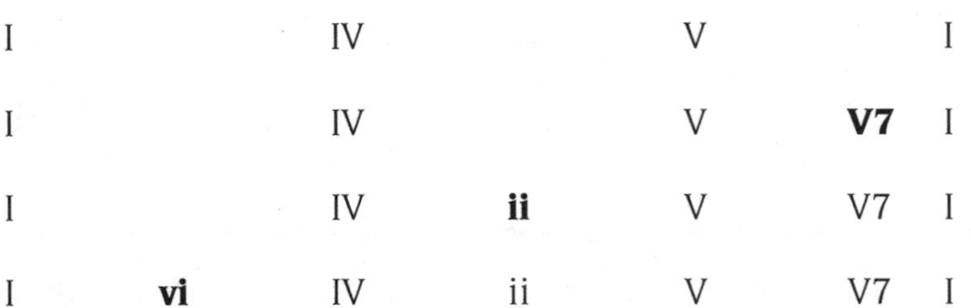

I IV V I
I IV V **V7** I
I IV **ii** V V7 I
I **vi** IV ii V V7 I

Go to the PDM Web site for more drill on this progression.

There is a secret life among chords. The vi has an affinity for IV; the ii is the stranger that comes in and ultimately strengthens the V–I relationship.

In V versus V7, there is more tension owing to the *tritone* provided by the 7th.

3. In playing four-part harmony, one may use *chorale style* or *keyboard style*.

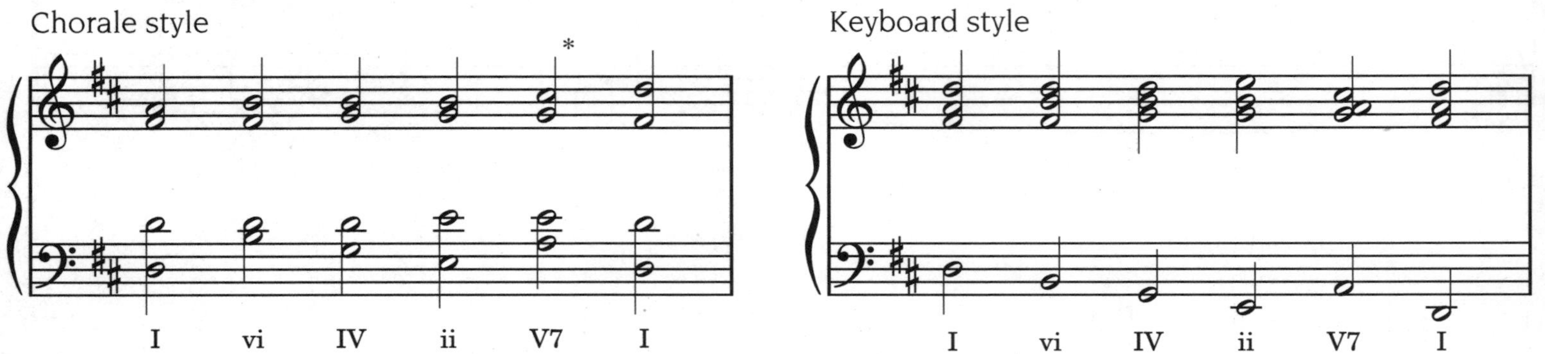

*The tritone (E–B♭) must resolve to F–A, omitting the 5th in 1.

As a general rule to follow, if the dominant 7th contains all four tones, the tonic will not contain a 5th. The reverse is generally true: If the 5th is omitted from the dominant 7th, the tonic resolution will contain all tones of the triad. Both instances allow for proper resolution of the augmented 4th/diminished 5th of the V7.

4. For each of the following examples, play in keyboard style. After playing, notate in the space provided.

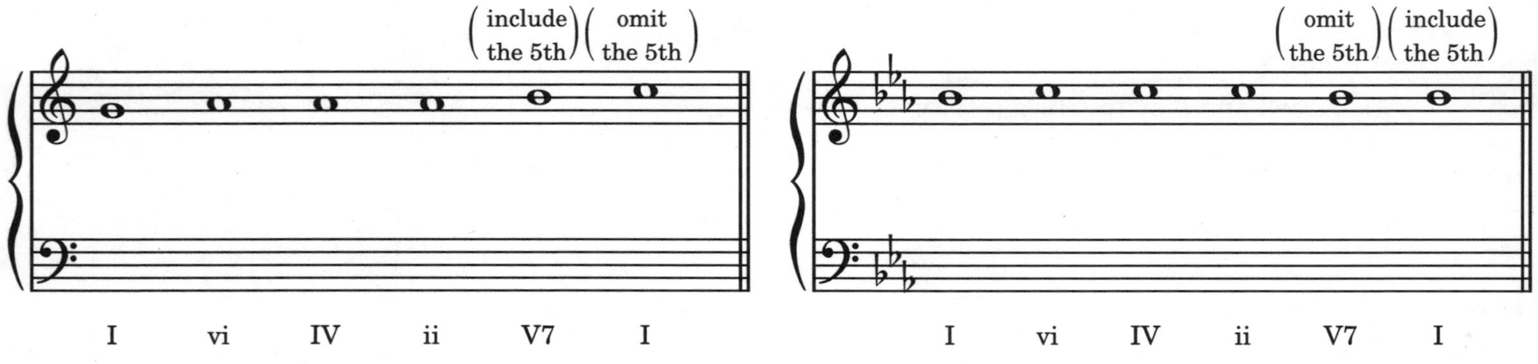

5. Inverted chords are nothing more than root position rearranged. Their shapes are most clearly seen through figured-bass designations.

They are usually abbreviated as follows:

I   I6 I^6_4 V7 V^6_5 V^4_3 V^4_2 (V2)

6. All figured-bass designations are built on the *lowest sounding tone* regardless of the octave placement of the other tones.

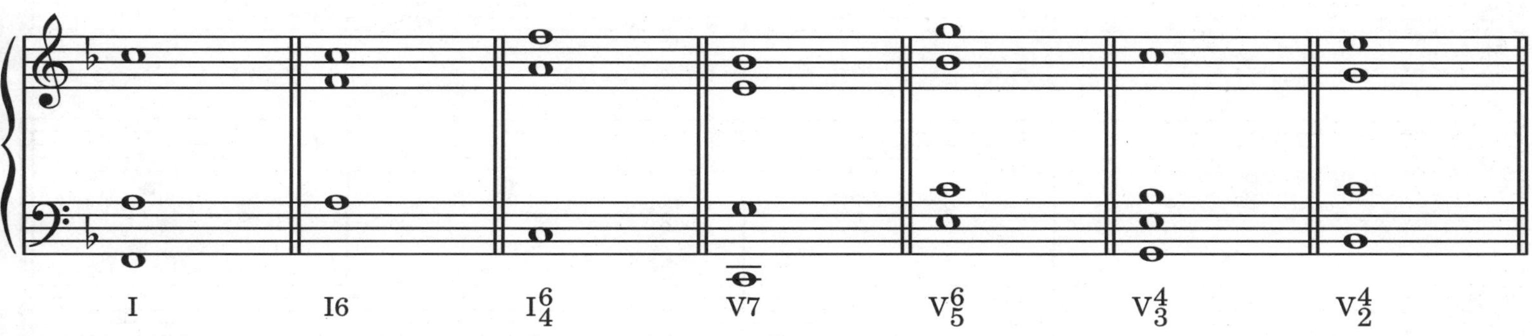

7. Chord inversions also may be designated by letter names (guitar symbols).

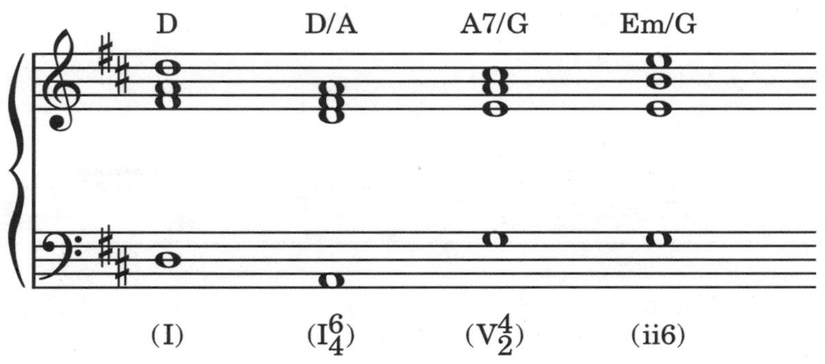

HARMONIZATION

1. Choose from I, V, V7, IV, ii, vi, and iii when harmonizing the following. Accompanying styles have been suggested for most examples.

a. Swiss

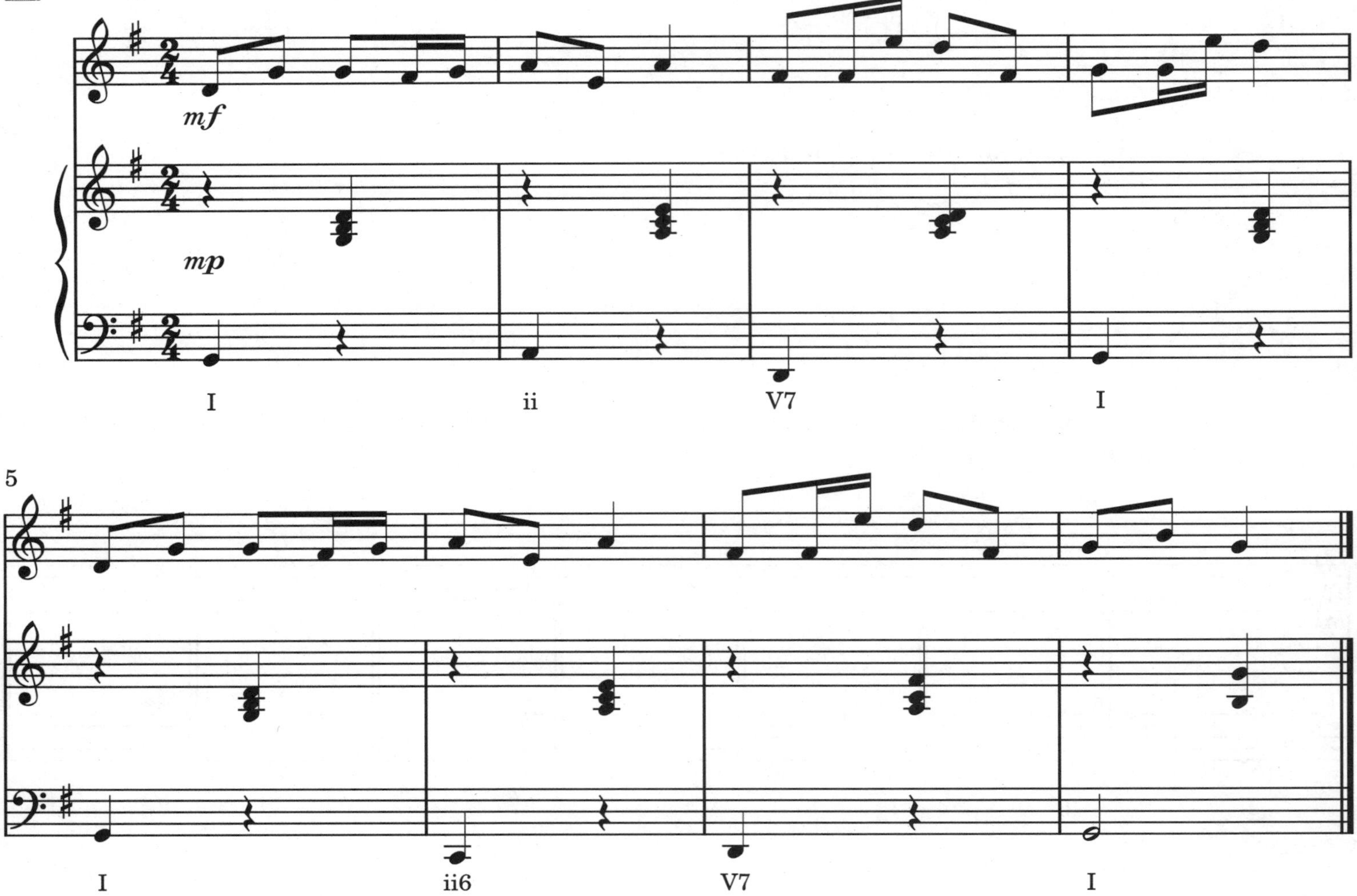

mf
mp
I
ii
V7
I
5
I
ii6
V7
I

b. Closest-position chords; notice the octave placement for the accompaniment.

STEPHEN C. FOSTER
(1826–1864)

Lively
I V I etc.
5
iii vi ii V7

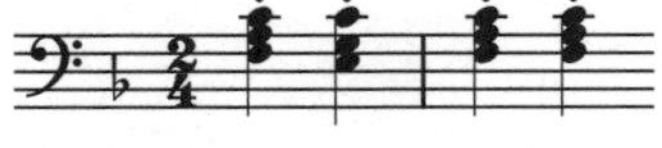

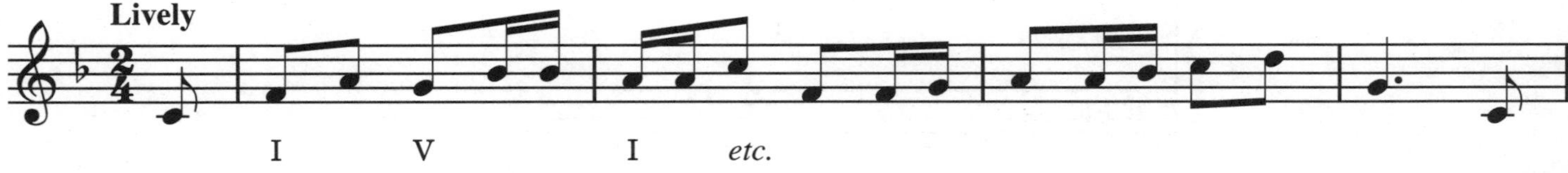

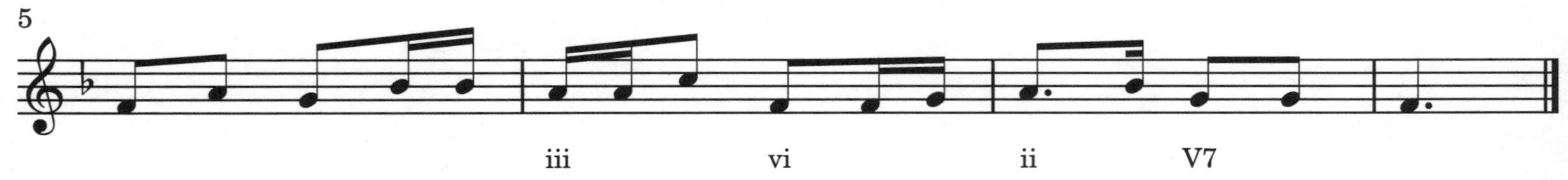

c. Broken chord

d. Two-handed accompaniment

Traditional

With a bounce

Go to the PDM Web site for further drill on this accompaniment.

e. Closest-position chords
Traditional
A
E7
Bm
E7
A
5
A
C♯m
D
Bm
E7
A
f. Two-handed accompaniment
American Folk
8
g. Modified keyboard style (challenge)
Two-handed broken chord
p
pp
JAMES R. MURRAY
5
11

h. Left-hand broken chord

American

6

11

i. Two-handed accompaniment

j. Closest-position left-hand broken chords. (challenge)

Go to the PDM Web site for further drill on this accompaniment.

TRANSPOSITION

1. The following examples are to be transposed the interval of a tritone. As before, use the following steps:
   - Determine melodic range
   - Observe melodic contour
   - Analyze the harmonic content
   - Notice common tones
   - Determine beginning fingering
   - Do not play in original key!

a. Transpose *up* to B♭ major.

b. Transpose *down* to D major.

Go to the PDM Web site for more examples.

c. Transpose *up* to G major.

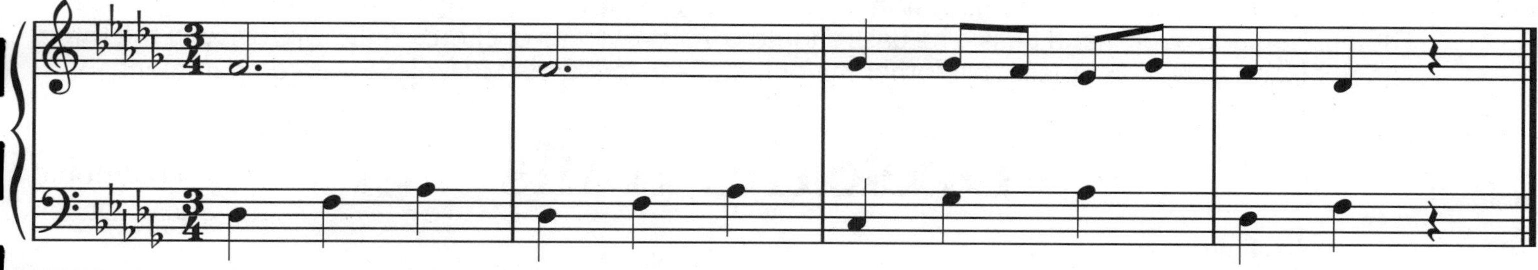

2. Transpose H*opak* by Goedicke to the keys of A major and B major.

Hopak

ALEXANDER GOEDICKE
(1877–1957)

Allegro

f

5

9

mp

13

f

3. Transpose Harmonization items g and i (pages 122–123) to at least two other major keys.

IMPROVISATION

1. Return to the improvisation progression on page 100. This time, play a right-hand melodic improvisation as you add a left-hand bass. The bass should consist of roots of chords only. Improvise in the three original keys as well as at least two other major keys. Transpose the MIDI disk for accompaniment.

ENSEMBLE

1.

9
1
2
3
4
5
6
14

2. Think about chord names and quality before playing.

Etude in A

Secondo

MARTHA HILLEY

Secondo

Etude in A

Primo

MARTHA HILLEY

Primo
9
11
13
RH
LH
15

COMPOSITION

Select a holiday melody and create a theme with at least two variations. The following is given as an example.

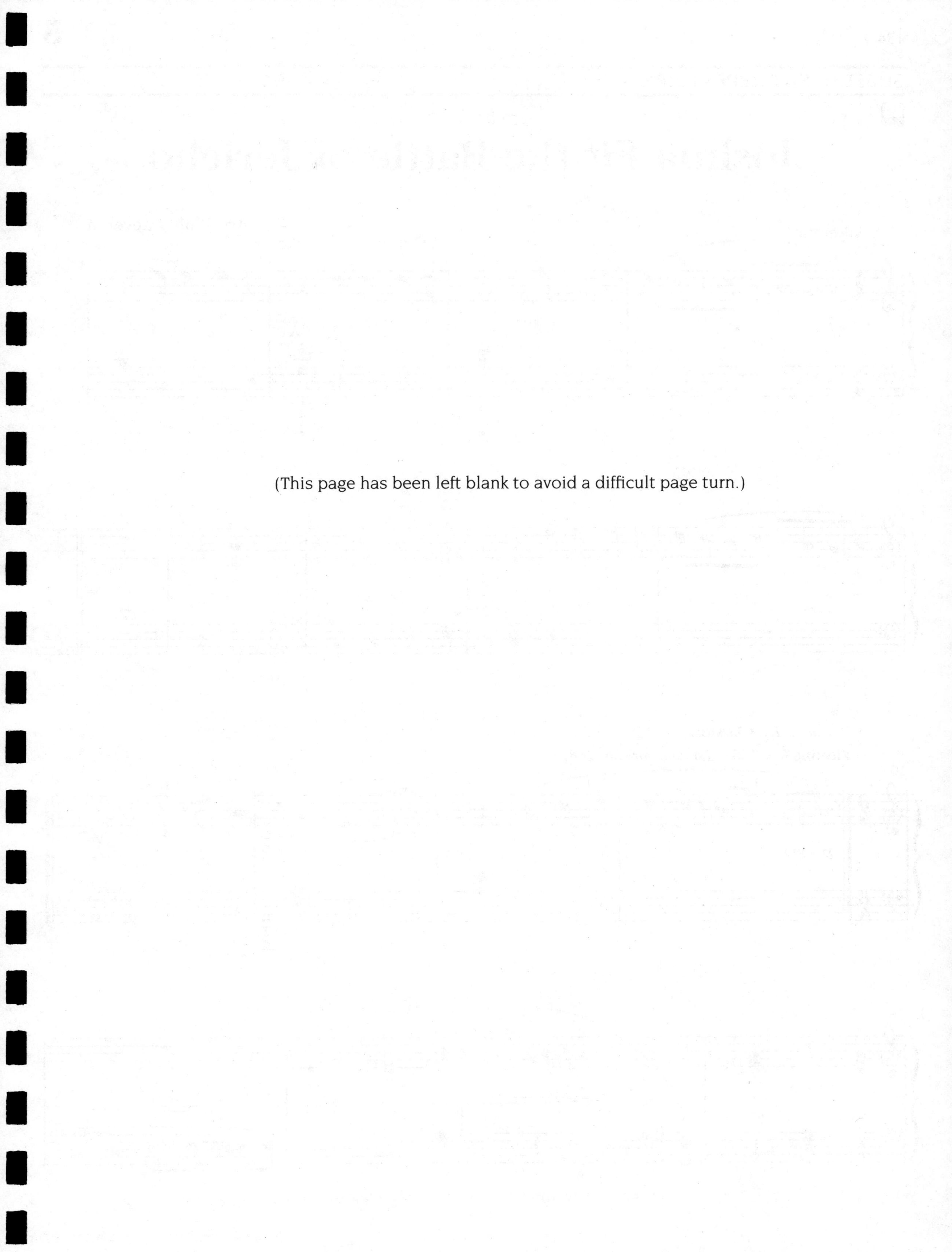

(This page has been left blank to avoid a difficult page turn.)

1.

Joshua Fit the Battle of Jericho

Jamie 5/3/05

Arr. Phillip Keveren

Allegretto

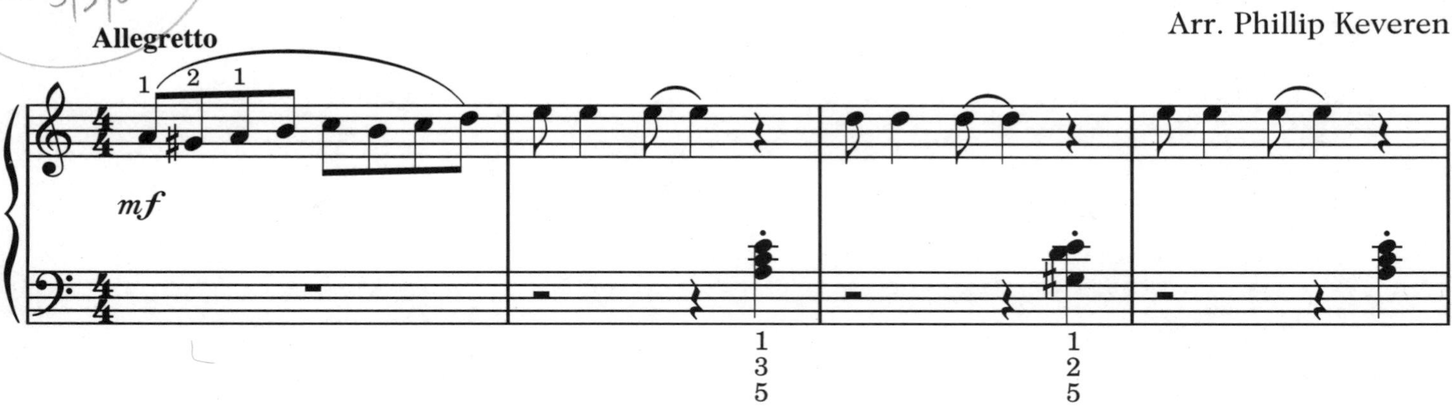

Variation I: **Classical**

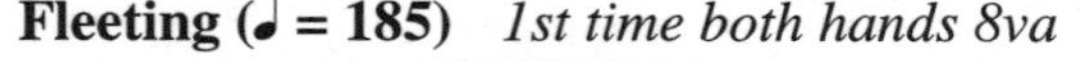
Fleeting (♩ = 185) *1st time both hands 8va*

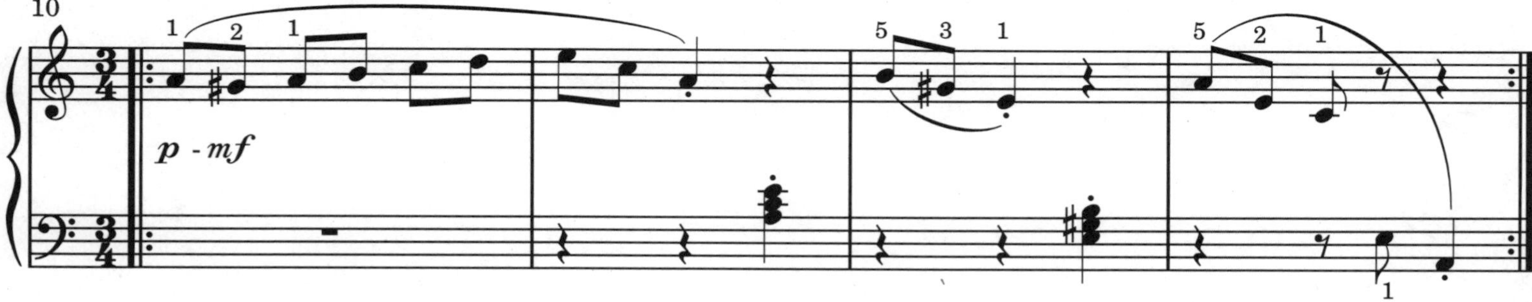

18
p
Variation II: Swing
Laid-back Jazz (♩ = 150)
23
mf
27
31
f
35
p
f

2.

O Hanukah

21
25
29
33
37
molto rit.

3.

The First Noël

The first Noël the angel did say,
Was to certain poor shepherds in fields as they lay;
In fields where they lay keeping their sheep
On a cold winter's night that was so deep.
Noël, Noël, Noël, Noël
Born is the King of Israel.

18th-Century French Melody
Arr. Glenda Austin

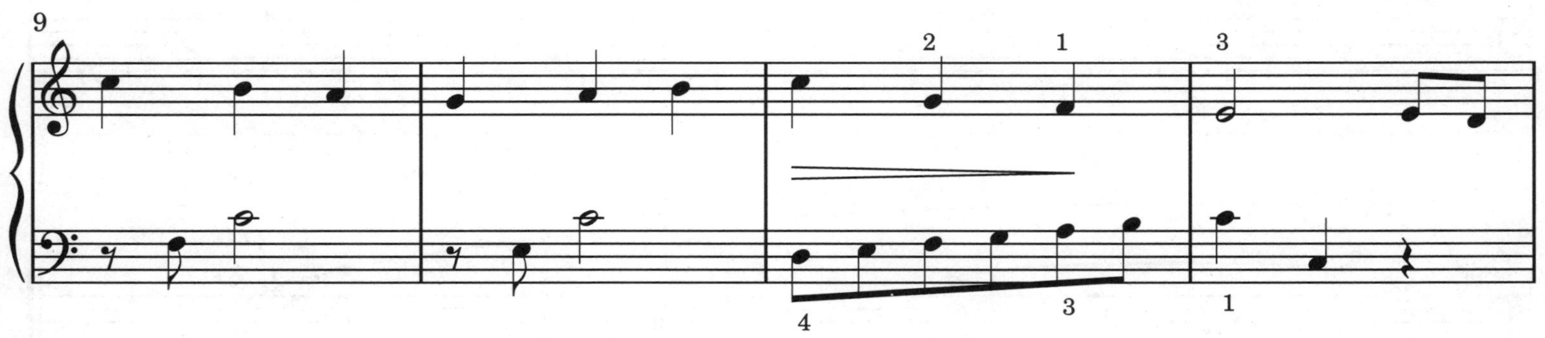

13
1
17
3
21
5
2
3
2
1
3
5
4
2
cresc.
deliberate
f
Lunga
2
3
2
4
2
1
3
5
1
2
4
25
a tempo
rit.
mf
a tempo
30
morendo
pp

6.

EXEMPLARY REPERTOIRE

TOPICS TO EXPLORE AND DISCUSS

RELATED SKILLS AND ACTIVITIES

SUBSEQUENT REPERTOIRE

Scalar Sequences/Modal Patterns/Black-Key-Group Major Scales

EXEMPLARY REPERTOIRE — **Prelude, Op. 37, No. 5** Giuseppe Concone

INQUIRY

1. Scan *Prelude*. Observe:

   - scalar sequences
   - clef changes
   - open chord structure: root position and inversion (analysis)
   - chromatic scale

PERFORMANCE

1. Play the following sequence on a flat surface.

   ♭3 2 ♭3 5 4 ♭3 2 1

2. Play the following sequence on a flat surface.

   ♭3 2 ♭3 5 4 ♭3 2 1 ↘ 4 ♮3 4 5 4 ♭3 2 1 ↘ ♭3

Repeat several times until position shift is secure.

3. Play the first four measures from the score, repeating the right-hand scalar pattern.

4. A common fingering for the chromatic scale is:

   - white to black—1 to 3
   - white to white—1 to 2

   Play the three-octave chromatic scale from the score.

5. Play all bass tones and chords in rhythm. (Teacher fills in scalar passages.)

6. Look away from the score and "talk it through."

7. Take a deep breath and play as written.

Prelude

GIUSEPPE CONCONE, Op. 37, No. 5
(1801–1861)

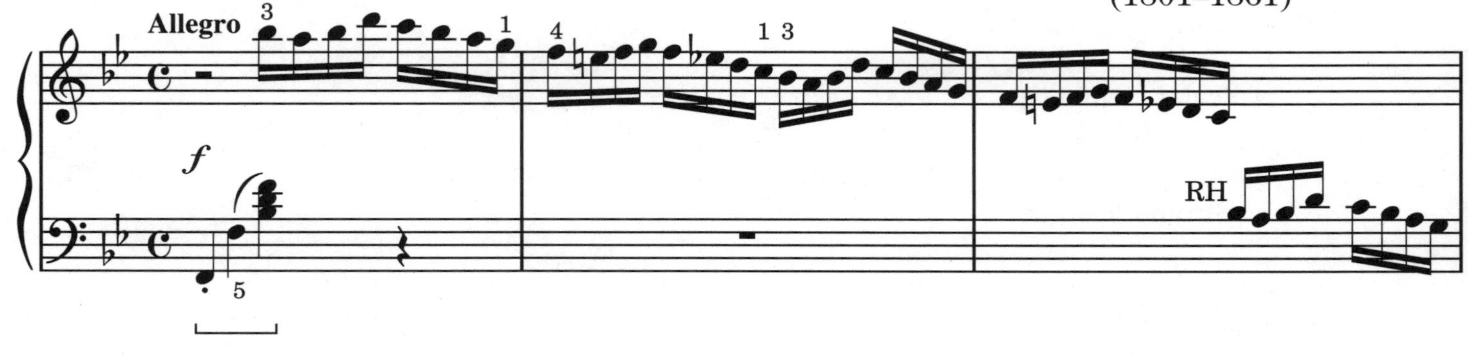

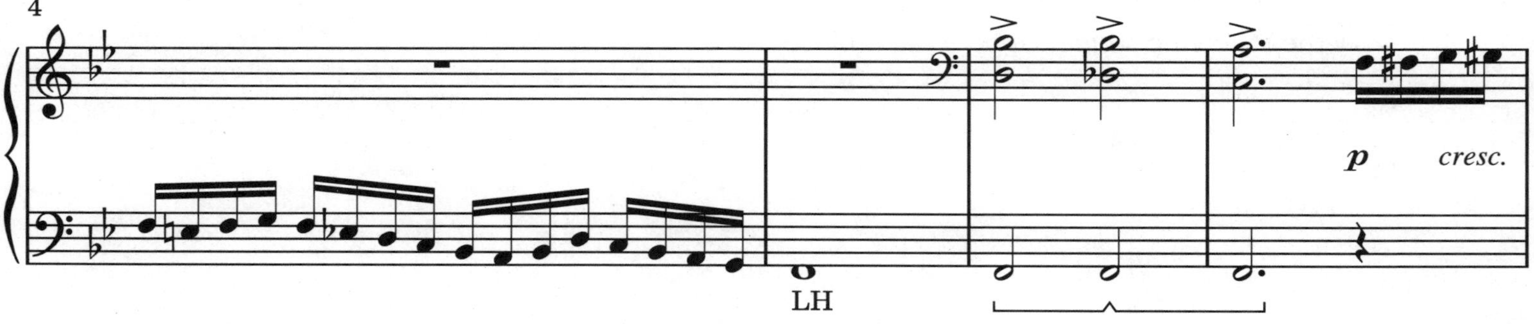

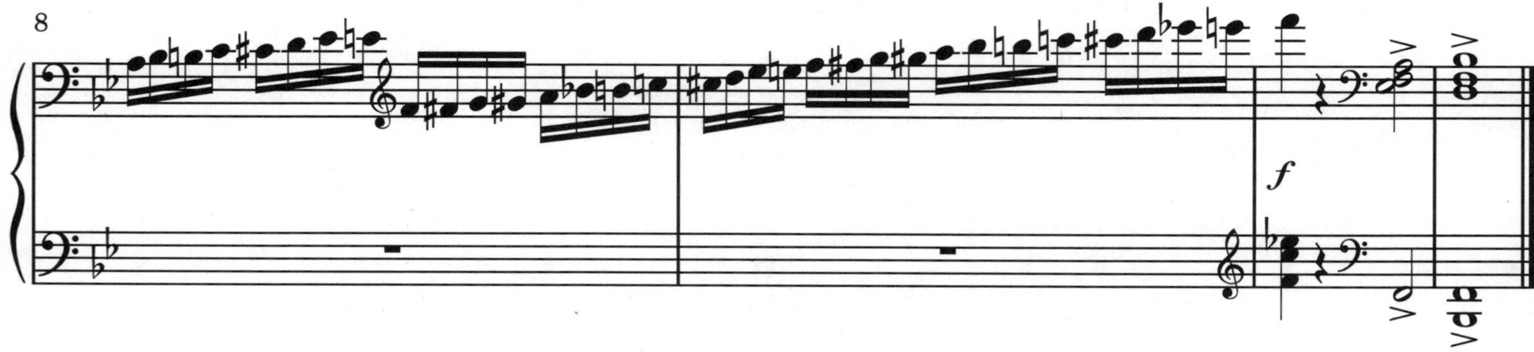

TOPICS TO EXPLORE AND DISCUSS

- Giuseppe Concone
- Robert Starer

RELATED SKILLS AND ACTIVITIES

TECHNIQUE

1. Chromatic exercises

- Using the principles of chromatic scale fingering stated on page 142, determine a right-hand fingering for the following example.

- Play with right hand.
- Determine a left-hand fingering for the same example and play the left hand one octave lower.
- Play with hands together, paying particular attention to fingerings for natural half steps.

2. Play the following as written with the nondominant hand.

3. Play again. This time fill in the rests by playing C's (when you end a pattern on C) or G's (when you end on G) with the other hand.

4. Swing the exercise by playing the eighth notes in a long-short pattern ♩♪ (triplet, 3) and syncopating the fill-in tones.

5. In Chapter 5, you used the black-key-group fingering principle. This principle forms the basis of fingering for the following major scales.

D♭/C♯ G♭/F♯ C♭/B

- Block the D♭ major scale with hands together, two octaves up and down.
  2 blacks–thumbs–3 blacks–thumbs, etc.
- Play the D♭ major scale as individual tones. Keep fingers close to the keys, covering positions as shifts occur.
- Transfer the same principle to the other black-key-group scales and play.

READING

1. Plan a fingering before playing.

2. Place fingerings in the score where shifts occur.

3. Think about melodic "turn-arounds" before you play.

Go to the PDM Web site for additional black-key-group reading.

4. Play the following combinations: Sopr 1/Sopr 2; Sopr 1/Alto; All voices.

Benediction

JOSEPH M. MARTIN

5. On what tonality is *Medieval Garden* based?

Medieval Garden

SALLY ETTER

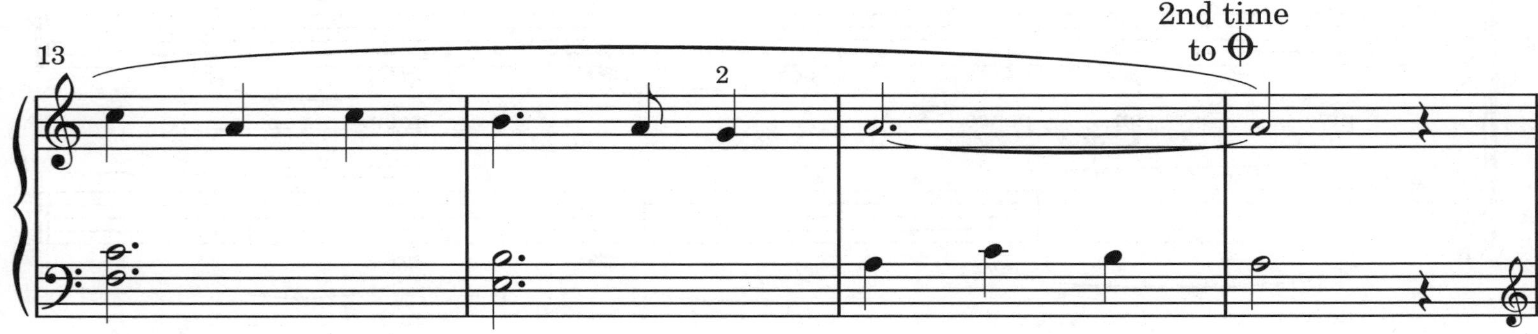

17
mf
21
25
mp
29
2
3
D. C. al Coda
Coda
pp
2
rit.
8va

6. Would this be considered use of alternating meter or variable meter? Perform at an "up" tempo.

Evens and Odds

ROBERT STARER
(1924–2001)

KEYBOARD THEORY

1. Think the key of D♭ major and play a scale beginning on the 2nd degree and ending on the 2nd degree an octave higher. This is the E♭ *Dorian* mode. We can build seven different modes starting on the seven tones of a major scale:

    - Ionian—1st degree (major scale)
    - Dorian—2nd degree
    - Phrygian—3rd degree
    - Lydian—4th degree
    - Mixolydian—5th degree
    - Aeolian—6th degree (natural minor)
    - Locrian—7th degree

    Think the B major key signature and play a scale beginning on the 2nd scale degree and ending on C♯ an octave above. This is the C♯ Dorian mode.

    Experiment with other modal scales. Always think of the major key signature.

2. Determine major key signatures and fingering before playing:

    - C♯ Ionian
    - C Locrian
    - A♭ Dorian
    - E Lydian

Go to the PDM Web site for additional drill on modes.

HARMONIZATION

1.

a. Closest-position chords

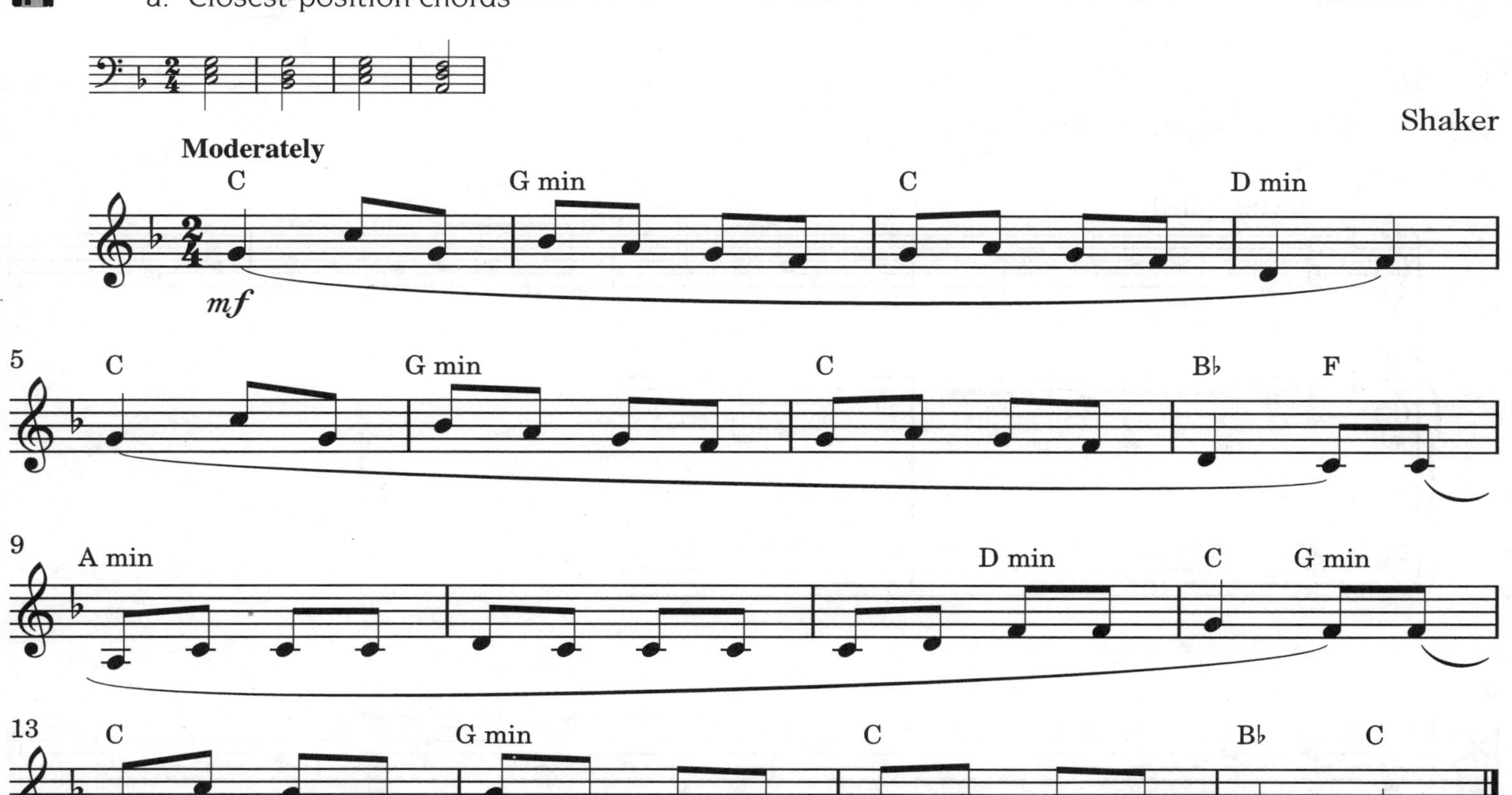

b. Closest-position chords

c. Modified keyboard style (challenge)

d. Complete in the style indicated.

e. Two-handed style.

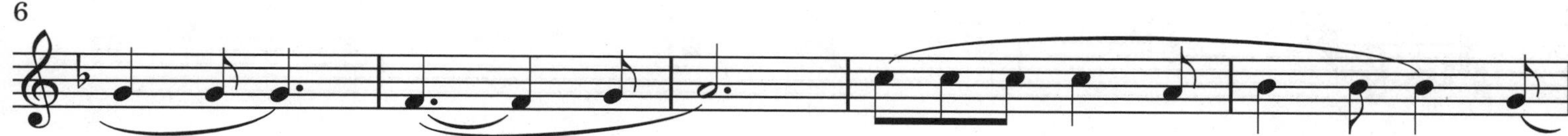

Go to the PDM Web site for "original" modal harmonization examples.

TRANSPOSITION

1. The following examples are to be transposed the interval of a tritone. As before, use the following steps:
   - Determine melodic range
   - Observe melodic contour
   - Analyze the harmonic content
   - Notice common tones
   - Determine beginning fingering
   - Do not play in original key!

a. Transpose *down* to the key of E major.

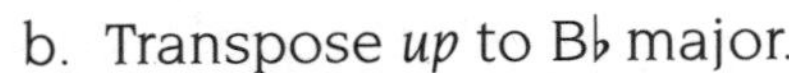

b. Transpose *up* to B♭ major.

c. Transpose *down* to C major.

2. Transpose *The Chase* to E major and A major.

The Chase

from *First Lessons for the Piano*

CORNELIUS GURLITT, Op. 117, No. 15
(1820–1901)

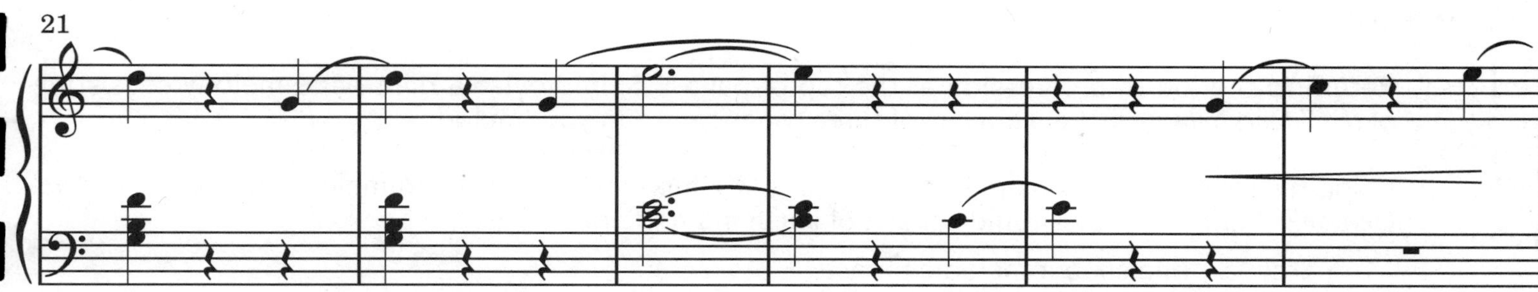

3. Transpose *Plaint* so that
   - tonic is G
   - tonic is D

   Do not change mode. What is the signature for each?

Transpose *Plaint* so that
   - mode is Dorian
   - mode is Lydian

Do not change the tonal center of E. What is the signature for each?

Plaint

LYNN FREEMAN OLSON

Adagietto

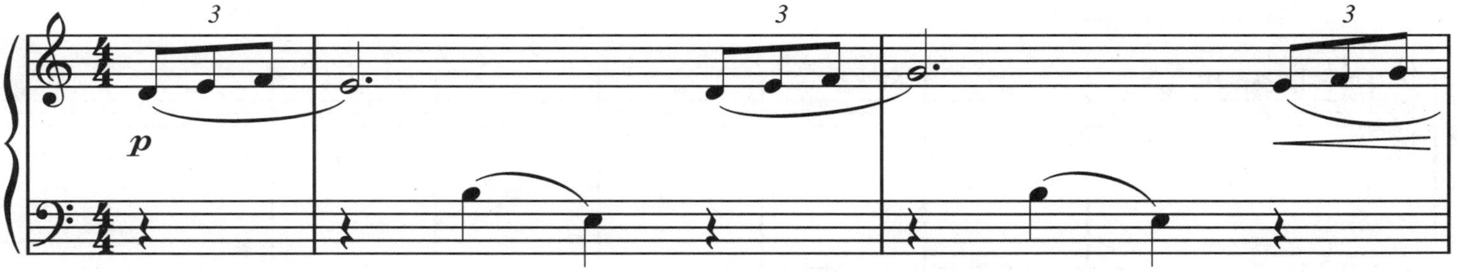

p

3

6

p

IMPROVISATION

1. Return to the fourth progression at the top of page 118. Improvise a right-hand melody consisting of *chord tones only*. Select a *maximum* of three tones to use in your melody.

2. Using the four progressions in item 5 on page 95, improvise a right-hand melody consisting of *chord tones only*. Your bass line should consist of left-hand roots of chords.
   - Item a—one six-bar melodic phrase
   - Item b—two three-bar melodic phrases
   - Item c—two three-bar melodic phrases
   - Item d—one six-bar melodic phrase

   Choose from the major keys listed on page 95.

3. Determine the modal scale for each example and improvise melodically. Item "a" has been started as an example. Your improvised melody should consist of two "easily heard" four-bar phrases. You might want to partner with a classmate who plays the ostinato as you improvise your first melody. Above all, keep going!

a. F♯ Dorian

b. ____________

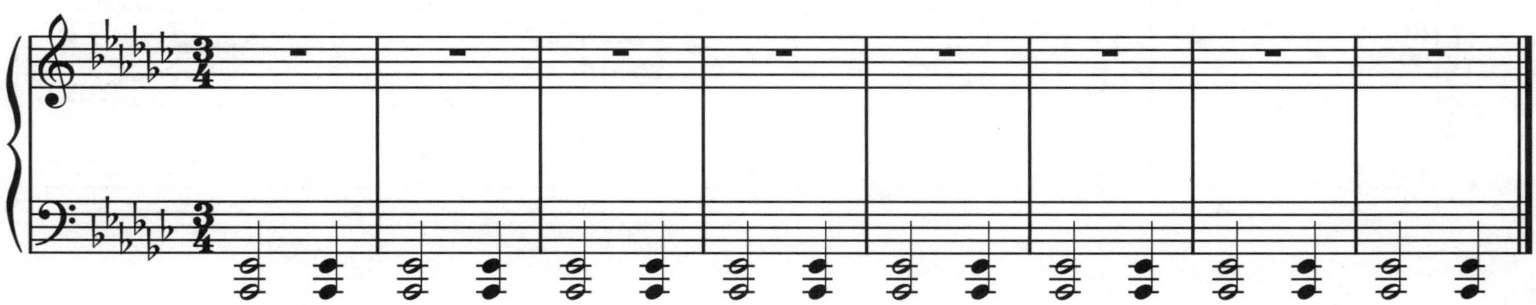

c. ____________

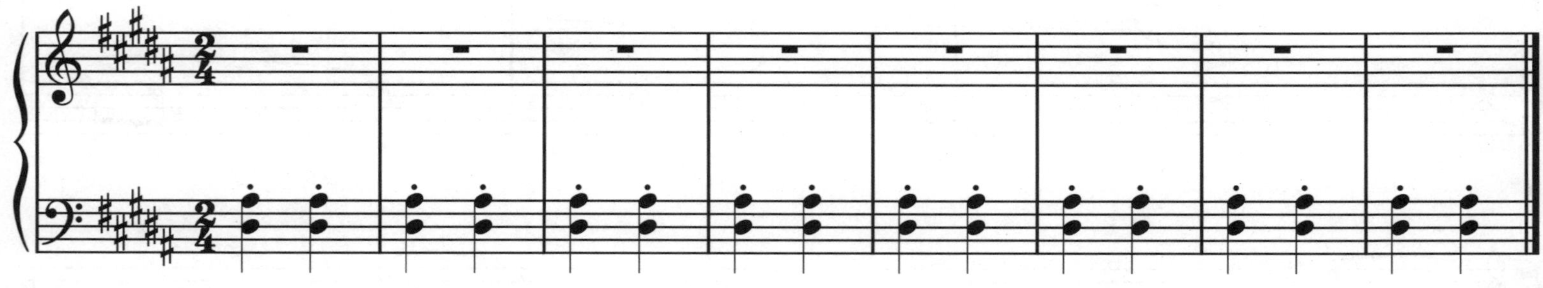

ENSEMBLE

1. Play with disk accompaniment.

Shuffle

11
1
2
3
4
5
6
cresc.
cresc.
cresc.
cresc.
cresc.
cresc.
16
f
f
f
f
f
f
simile

21
8va
mf
f
26
cresc.
subito p
sfz

2. Play Parts 5 and 6 together as one part.

Jingle, Jangle, Jingle
(I Got Spurs)

JOSEPH J. LILLEY
Arr. Lynn Freeman Olson

12
1
2
3
4
5
6
17
1
2
3
4
5
6

23
1
2
3
4
5
6
29
1
2
3
4
5
6

35
1
2
3
4
5
6
41
1
2
3
4
5
6

COMPOSITION

Create modal pieces to match the words of these two poems by Ogden Nash.

1. For "The Panther," use C Dorian.

The Panther
The panther is like a leopard,
Except it hasn't been peppered.
Should you behold a panther crouch
Prepare to say Ouch.
Better yet, if called by panther,
Don't anther.

2. For "The Pizza," use a combination of G Lydian and G Locrian.

The Pizza
Look at itsy-bitsy Mitzi!
See her figure slim and ritzy!
She eatsa
Pizza!
Greedy Mitzi!
She no longer itsy-bitsy!

Go to the PDM Web site to see examples of student compositions.

SUBSEQUENT REPERTOIRE

1. Eighth notes remain equal throughout. Is this an example of alternating or variable meter?

ZOLTÁN KODÁLY
(1882–1967)

6

8
11
pp
simile
14
accelerando
cresc.
17
f
20
più f
sf
allargando
dim.
Tempo I
p
p
p
ppp
23
ritard.
pp
ppp

2. Careful attention to indicated articulation will make this piece less difficult.

German Dance

LUDWIG van BEETHOVEN
(1779–1827)

3. Notice the quality of all triads. What is the meaning of "svegliato"?

Furtive Gestures

LYNN FREEMAN OLSON

7.

EXEMPLARY REPERTOIRE

TOPICS TO EXPLORE AND DISCUSS

RELATED SKILLS AND ACTIVITIES

SUBSEQUENT REPERTOIRE

White-Key Major Scale Fingerings/Blues Pentascale and the 12-Bar Blues

EXEMPLARY REPERTOIRE **Menuet Pastoral** Johann Philipp Kirnberger

INQUIRY

1. Scan *Menuet Pastoral*. Observe:
   - phrase markings
   - sequence
   - articulation—wedge-shaped mark and staccato notes under a slur
2. Considering the period and the dance form, discuss an appropriate tempo and dynamic markings.
3. Determine logical fingering with particular attention to cadences.

PERFORMANCE

1. Work with the right-hand material. Pay particular attention to indicated phrasing and articulation.
2. When you feel confident with the nuances of the treble, add the left hand.

Menuet Pastoral

JOHANN PHILIPP KIRNBERGER
(1721–1783)

TOPICS TO EXPLORE AND DISCUSS

- Johann Philipp Kirnberger and his contemporaries
- Origin of the blues
- Scat syllables
- 12-tone row

RELATED SKILLS AND ACTIVITIES

TECHNIQUE

1. The following is traditional C major scale fingering (two octaves).

RH	1	2	3	1	2	3	4	1	2	3	1	2	3	4	5
LH	5	4	3	2	1	3	2	1	4	3	2	1	3	2	1

Away from the keyboard on a flat surface, play the scale upward and downward. Say "3"s and "1"s when those fingers play together. Now play on the keyboard, slowly and steadily. This fingering also is used for D major, E major, G major, and A major.

2. Play the C major scale upward and stop on A. Now *flat* the A and continue with the same finger combinations to play the scale of A♭ major.

3. Review the black-key-group scales.

Go to the PDM Web site for additional drill of white-key major scales.

READING

1. Use traditional scale fingerings.

Moderato

CORNELIUS GURLITT, Op. 117, No. 12
(1829–1901)

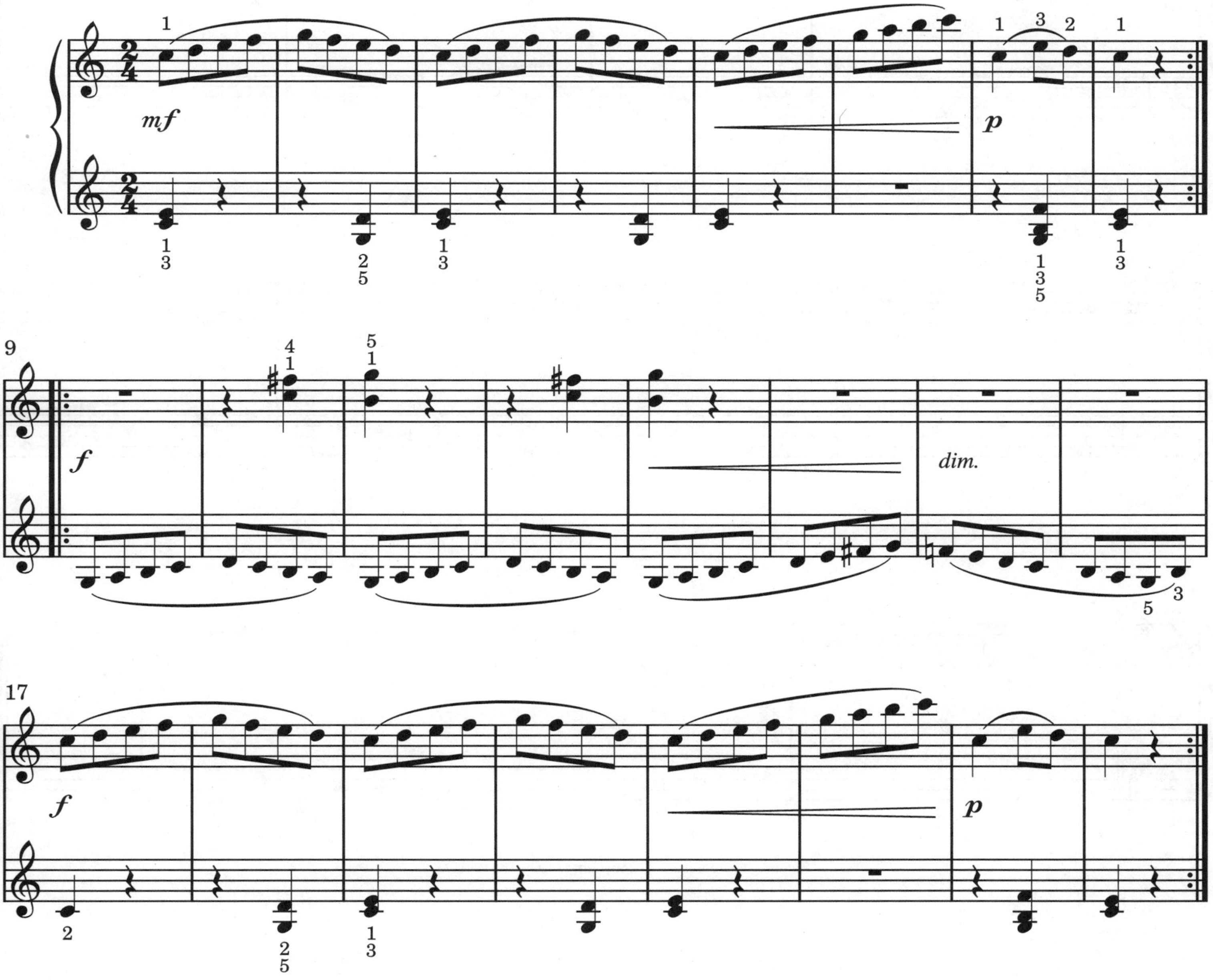

9

dim.

17

2. First practice the scale of A major. Then play *The Chase*.

The Chase

KATHERINE K. BEARD

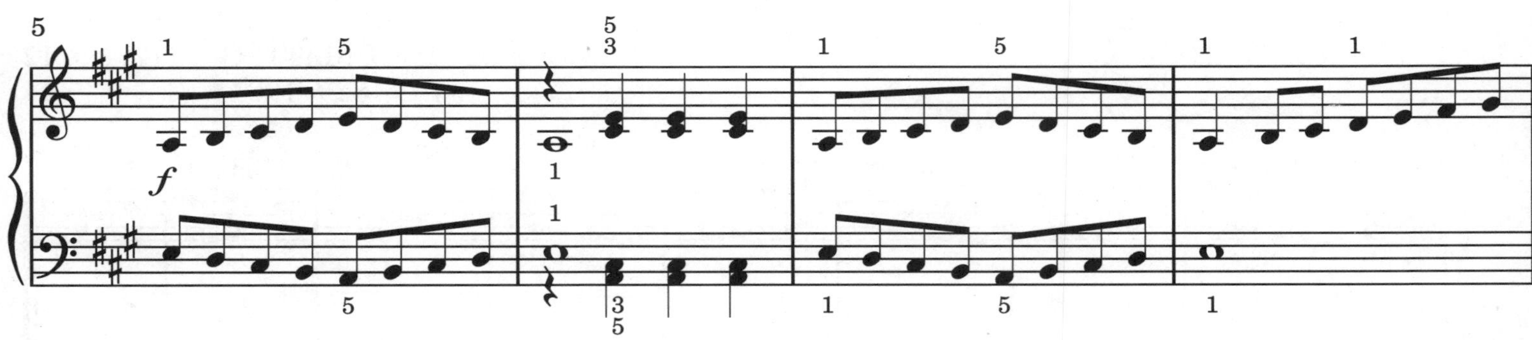

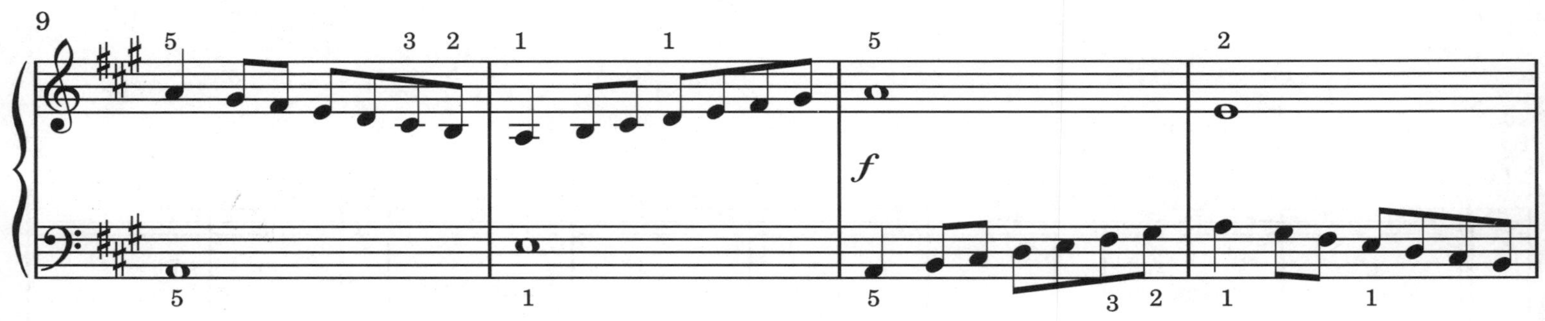

3. What is unusual about the phrase structure? (Challenge)

Petit Menuet

JEAN-NICOLAS GEOFFROY (1633–1694)

4. Study the scalar sequences carefully before you play.

5. Think about the fingering in measure 3.

Go to the PDM Web site for additional scalar pattern pieces.

KEYBOARD THEORY

1. The note given is the leading tone in a major key. Play a *keyboard style* cadence pattern, V7–I, with the leading tone and its neighbor tonic in the soprano voice.

   Example:

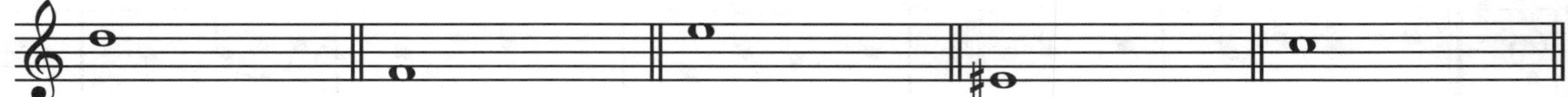

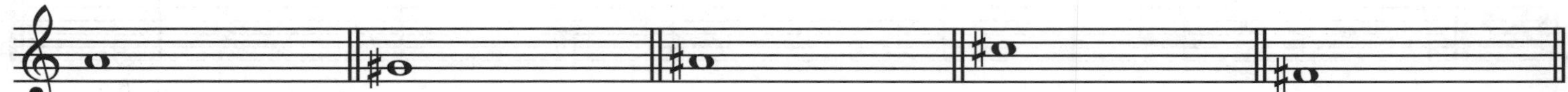

Go to the PDM Web site for additional drill on item 1.

2. In which major scales can the following melodic intervals function as written?

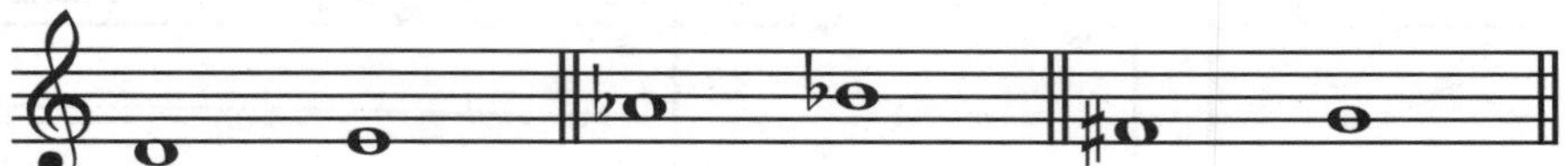

   Play each scale and sing only the given interval in numerals.

3. The numerals here refer to scale degrees. Complete a major scale upward on the keyboard while singing the degree numbers. Finish with a tonic root-position triad.

   Example:

4. Play the following in three major keys using right hand only.

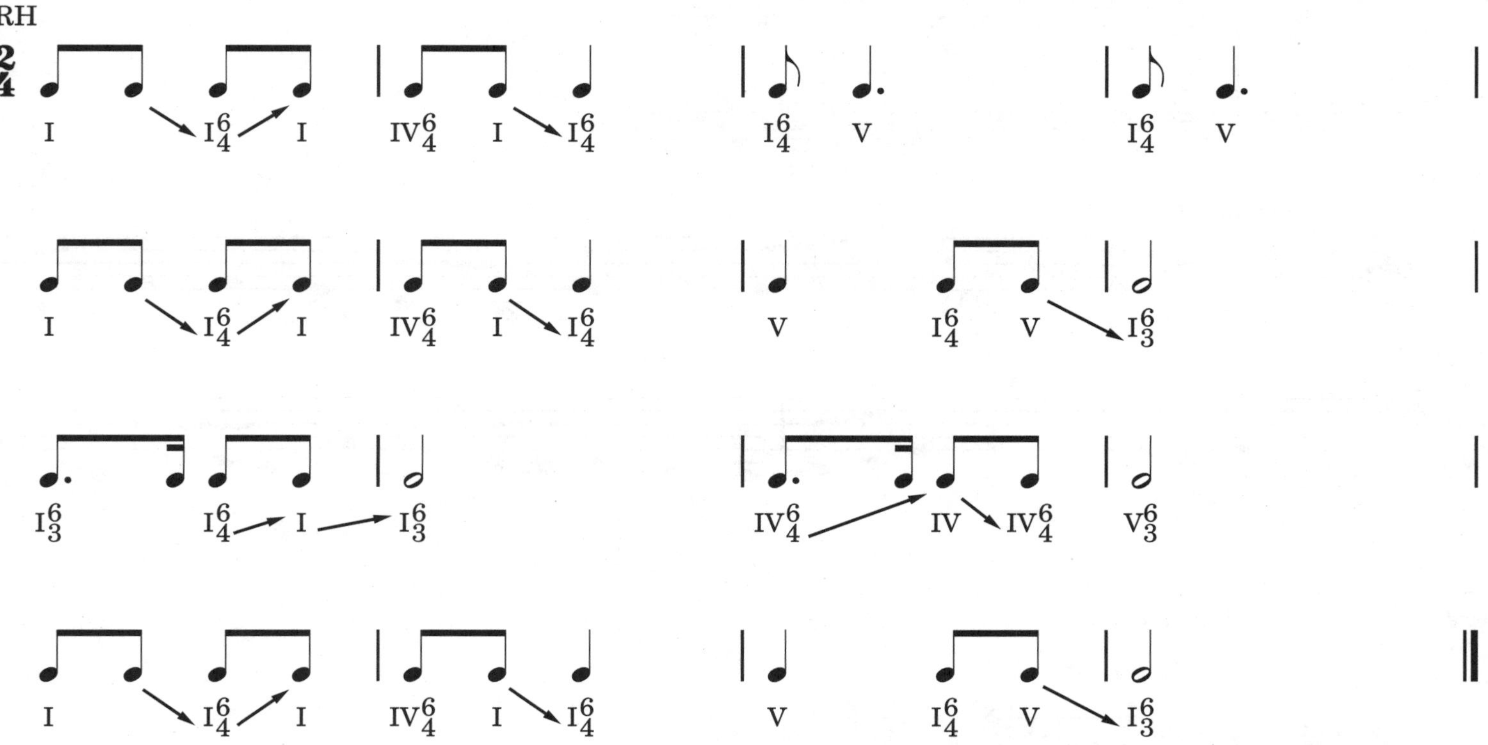

5. For each example, give the key signature and then play the modal scale (decide fingering).

- Phrygian on F
- Locrian on G
- Lydian on D♭
- Dorian on B
- Mixolydian on F♯
- Aeolian on E

HARMONIZATION

1. Complete in the indicated style.

a. Two-handed accompaniment

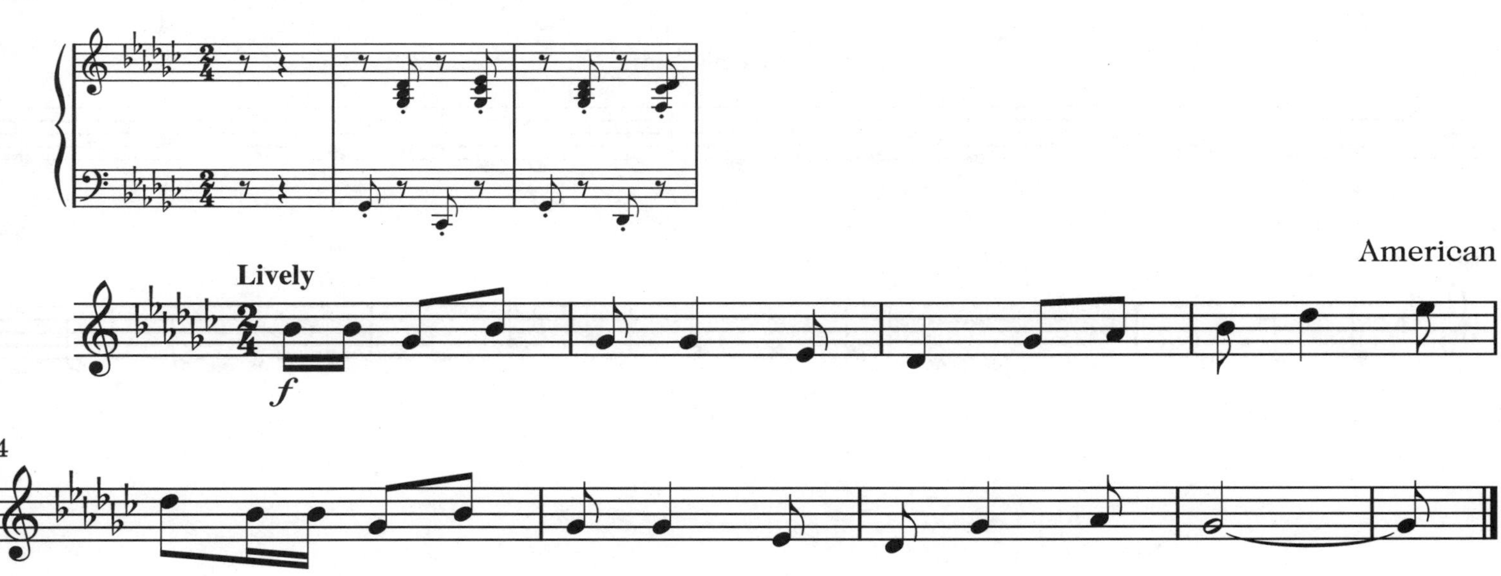

b. Two-handed broken chord

American

c. Two-handed style

American

d. Play through first with melody and indicated bass.

American

Easily

F F/C F F/C F D min

mf

mf

4 C7 F F/C F F/C

etc.

7 F C7 F F/E F/D F/C F F/C

10 D min D min/A F/C F C7/E C7

13 F F/C D min D min/A F/C C7 F

e. Left-hand broken chord

American

G Bm/F♯ C/G D7/F♯ G

5 *etc.*

TRANSPOSITION

1. Transpose the Concone *Prelude* in B♭ (page 142) to C major. Plan a fingering that will facilitate transposing the same prelude to B major.

2. The following exercises are to be transposed the interval of a tritone.

   a. Transpose *down* to D♭ major.

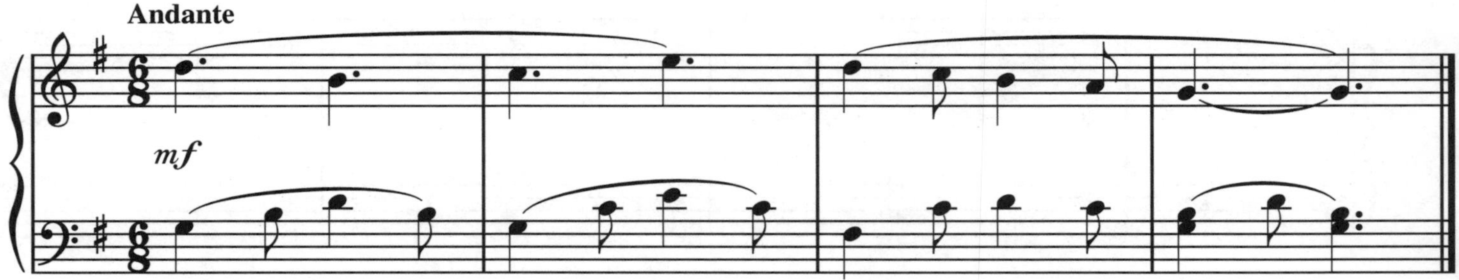

   b. Transpose *up* to A major.

   c. Transpose *down* to C major.

IMPROVISATION

1. The blues pentascale is 1, 4, and 5 of a major pentascale with a flat 3 and an added flat 5.

   Key of C: C, E♭, F, G♭, G♮

   In beginning blues improvisation, this pentascale provides a foolproof vehicle because the melodic tones fit the basic harmonies used.

   Play:

Traditional blues eighths are played with a swing, with the emphasis on the second note in each pair. Play the preceding example with "swinging eighths."

(The balance of this page has been left blank to avoid a difficult page turn.)

2. *Scat syllables* offer a natural model for rhythmic ideas in blues improvisation. It makes no difference how inexperienced or technically advanced you are at the keyboard—you should start memorizing these nine rhythms immediately. By practicing scat every day, you will program these rhythms into your subconscious "bank" of rhythmic ideas. With subconscious control, you will find that you can create an infinite number of new rhythms that automatically suit your own musical moment. Next practice scatting and playing these ideas using the F blues pentascale.

3. The following is a possibility for the first four bars of a chorus of 12-bar blues. Write in your choice for the other eight bars and play a blues melody using the G blues pentascale.

Repeat the pentascale scats, this time adding left-hand roots of triads. Follow this blues progression:

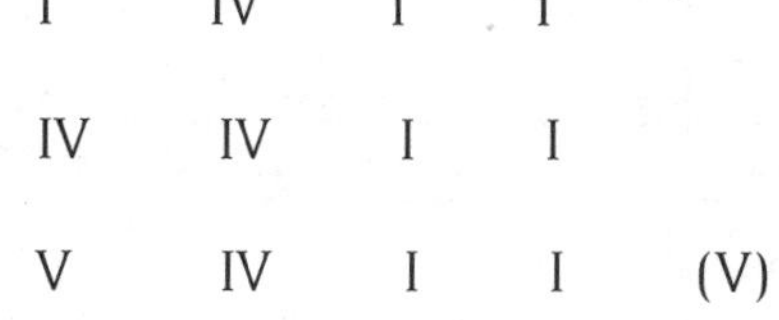

Used as a turn-around chord in place of the first chorus final "I" when playing two choruses.

ENSEMBLE

1. Eighth notes are *not* in a swing style.

Solitude

CHRISTOPHER NORTON

4
7
10
mf
mf

13
f
dim.
dim.
16
poco rit.
mp
mp

2. As a challenge, play Parts 4 and 5 as one part.

Hello! Ma Baby

JOSEPH E. HOWARD
Arr. Olson/Ogilvy

9
1
2
3
4
5
6
f
f
13
mf
f
mf
f

17
1
2
3
4
5
6
21
p
mp
p
mp
p
mp

25
1
2
3
4
5
6
mf
cresc.
cresc.
cresc.
mf
29
1
2
3
4
5
6
mf
mf
mf
mf

(The balance of this page has been left blank to avoid a difficult page turn.)

Play through *Dripping Faucet* by Alan Shulman. Compose a light "descriptive miniature."

Dripping Faucet

ALAN SHULMAN

Allegro giocoso, ♩ = 176

p

6

11

16

mf

21

dim.

ppp

Go to the PDM Web site to see examples of student compositions.

SUBSEQUENT REPERTOIRE

1. Where does a mode first occur? What is the form?

In Row and Mode

from *Shorties*

DAVID FEINBERG

Moderately slow

p *legato sempre, semplice ed espressivo*

No pedal at the beginning

rit. poco

a tempo

p

mp

espressivo

rit.

a tempo, dolce

Più lento

rit.

Go to the PDM Web site to see further details about a 12-tone row.

2. The surprise sforzandi help to lend definition to the title of the piece.

CORNELIUS GURLITT
(1820–1901)

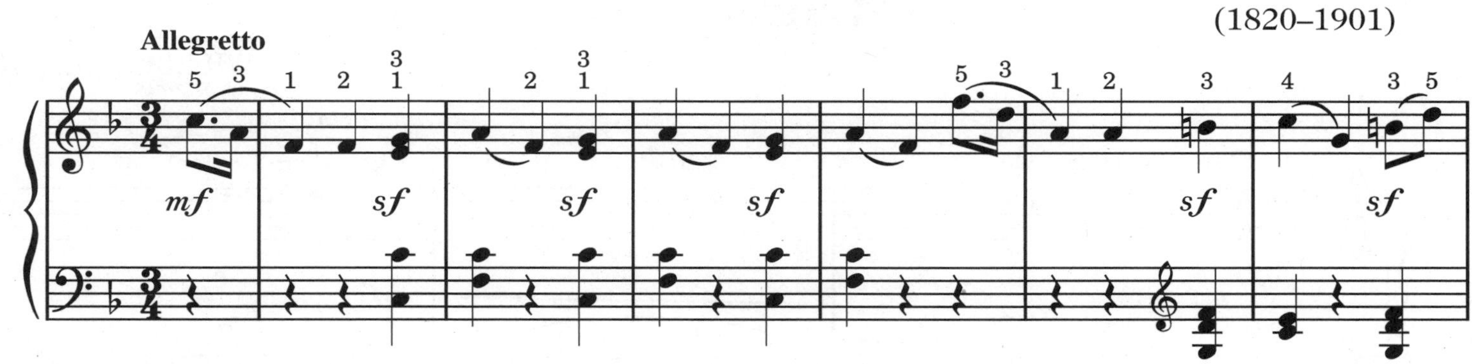

3. Although the composer prefers that all eighth notes be played literally as written, the player may take the liberty of treating any or all as ♩♪ (triplet) patterns.

Blues Motif

WILLIAM GILLOCK

13
p
16
19
mf
22
f
mp
25
p
retarding
RH
LH
RH

8.

EXEMPLARY REPERTOIRE

TOPICS TO EXPLORE AND DISCUSS

RELATED SKILLS AND ACTIVITIES

SUBSEQUENT REPERTOIRE

White-Key Minor Scale Fingerings/Diatonic Harmonies in Minor

EXEMPLARY REPERTOIRE — Invention No. 9 in C Minor — Katherine K. Beard

INQUIRY

1. Scan *Invention No. 9 in C Minor*. Observe:

   - theme entrances; indicate all entrances in your score
   - use of fragments

   - key at measure 11; relationship?
   - key at measure 15; relationship?
   - harmonies used in measures 27–28
   - use of *stretto*
   - *false entrance*
   - mordents

The *mordent* is an ornament that decorates the melody and makes one note sound more prominent. The mordent sign (⁓) always stands for three notes: the written note, the lower neighbor, and the written note again. The first note of a mordent must be played *on the beat*. An accidental under the mordent sign applies to the lower neighbor.

PERFORMANCE

1. Play as a duet, eliminating the mordents for the first reading. Listen carefully for all entrances.

2. Add ornamentation, trade parts, and play again as a duet.

3 Practice hands together, slowly, in the following sections:
   - measures 1–6, 7–11, 9–15, 13–17, 17–19, 19–23, 23–27, 26–30

Invention No. 9 in C Minor

With solemn dignity

KATHERINE K. BEARD

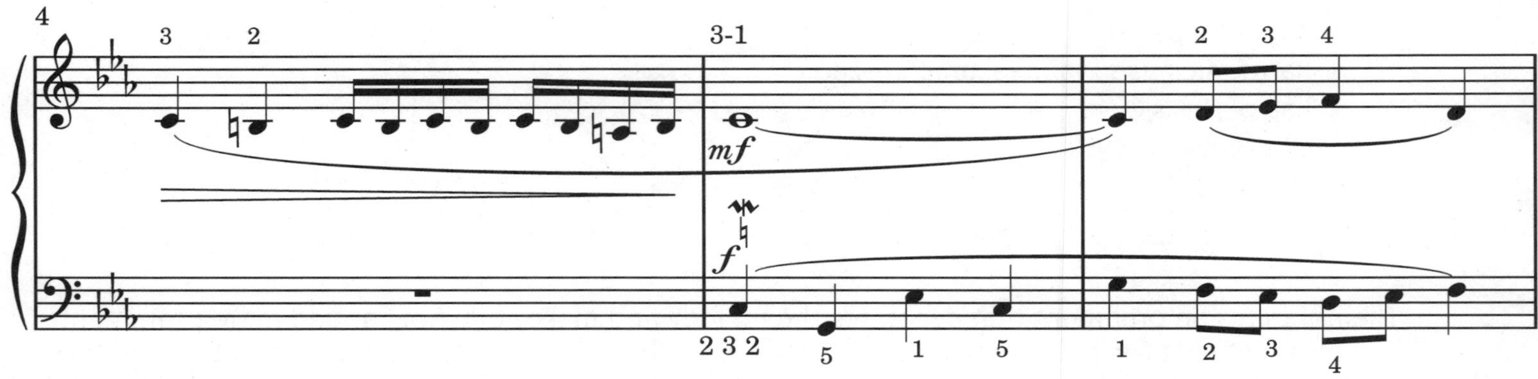

Broader
Freely
ritard.

TOPICS TO EXPLORE AND DISCUSS

- Parallel minor versus relative minor
- Pentatonic scale
- Samuil Maykapar

RELATED SKILLS AND ACTIVITIES

TECHNIQUE

1. Indicated mordents begin on the beat.

2. Determine the quality of scalar passages and the use of sequence before playing.

Etude in A Minor

CORNELIUS GURLITT
(1820–1901)

READING

1. Articulation, fingering, and a "sense of key" are critical for success.

2. Play the following combinations. Soprano–Baritone; Soprano–Alto–Baritone.

Morning Song

Text*

GIOVANNI PIERLUIGI DA PALESTRINA
(ca. 1525–1594)

Con moto

mf

Soprano: Now with cre - a - tion's morn - ing song, Let us, as chil - dren of the

Alto: Now with cre - a - tion's morn - ing song, Let us, as chil - dren of the

Baritone: Now with cre - a - tion's morn - ing song, Let us, as chil - dren of the

5

Soprano: day, With wak - ened heart and pur - pose strong, The

Alto: day, With wak - ened heart and pur - pose strong, The works of dark - ness

Baritone: day, With wak - ened heart and pur - pose strong, The works of dark - ness

10

Soprano: works of dark - ness cast a - way, The works of dark - ness cast a - way.

Alto: cast a - way, The works of dark - ness cast a - way.

Baritone: cast a - way, The works of dark - ness cast, cast a - way.

* Aurelius Clemens Prudentius, fifth century, adapted by Samuel Longfellow, 1864.

Go to the PDM Web site for additional three-part reading.

3. Discuss harmonies before playing.

Etude

LUDVIG SCHYTTE
(1848–1909)

4. What scale degrees are missing?

American Tune

Traditional
Arr. Lynn Freeman Olson

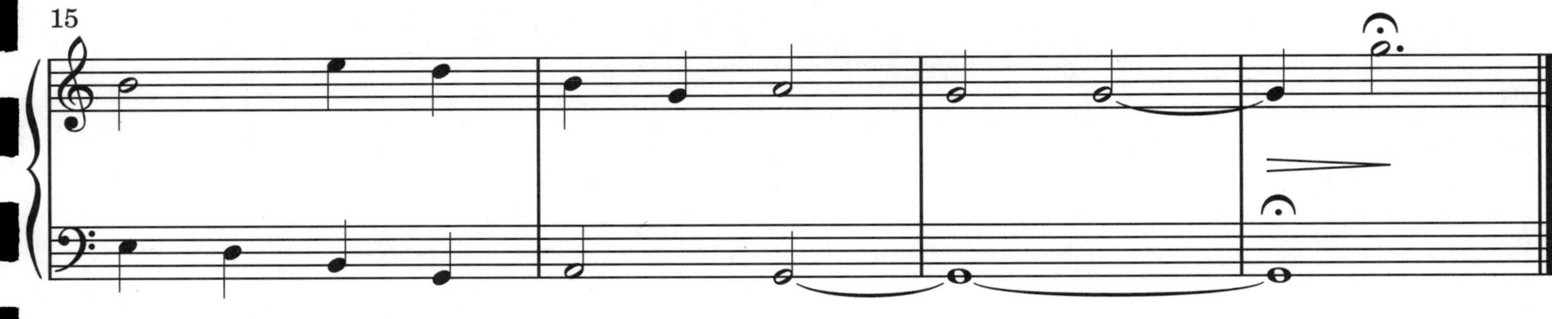

KEYBOARD THEORY

1. Play triads on each tone of the major scale as indicated.

Root on top:

Root on middle:

2. Play this triad sequence with the root on top. Play in all major keys except B♭ and E♭.

Play again, doubling the root in the bass.

Play the same triad sequence with the root in the middle. Repeat with a left-hand doubled root.

3. All minor scales are derived from their relative majors and use the same key signatures. The natural minor scale can be observed within the major scale pattern, beginning on the 6th scale degree.

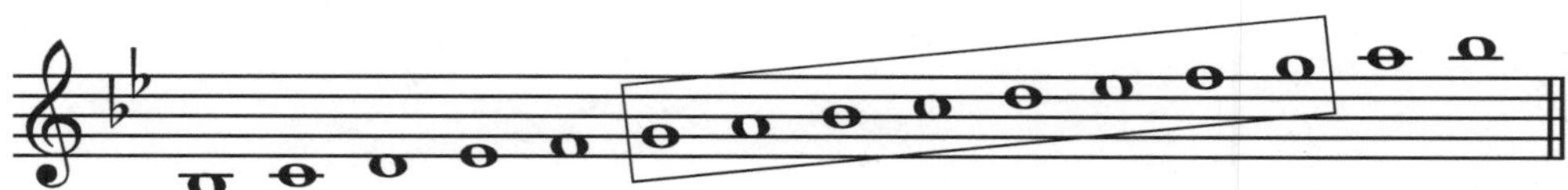

There are two commonly used altered forms of the natural minor scale. The *harmonic* form is the result of the major quality of the dominant 7th chord and therefore uses an accidental to produce a leading tone that is a half step below tonic.

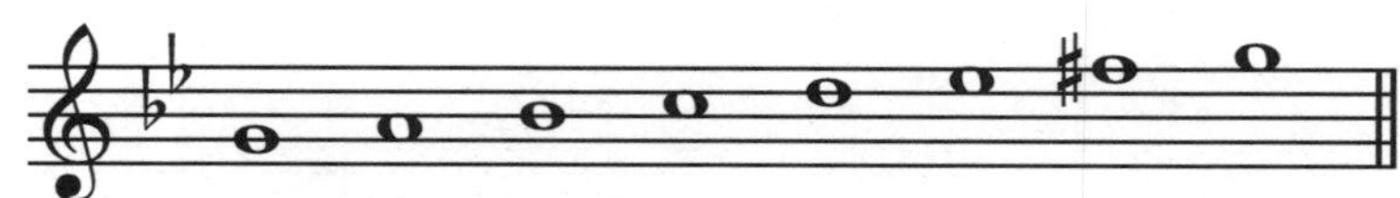

The *melodic* form uses an additional accidental in the ascending pattern to avoid the awkward augmented 2nd.

When descending, melodic returns to the natural form of the minor.

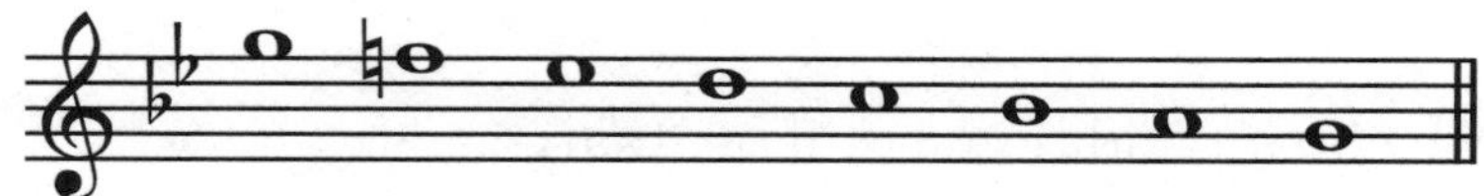

4. The following white-key minor scales use the same fingering as their parallel major scales. Refer to the fingerings used on page 168.

   - C natural, harmonic, and melodic minor
   - D natural, harmonic, and melodic minor
   - E natural, harmonic, and melodic minor
   - G natural, harmonic, and melodic minor
   - A natural, harmonic, and melodic minor

   Play these minor scales two octaves, up and down (natural, harmonic, melodic) with no break between keys.

5. *Diatonic triads in minor*. Play the following triads in D minor.

Using the following harmonic progression, verbally *spell* each chord in root position but *play* the closest position possible.

a. G minor

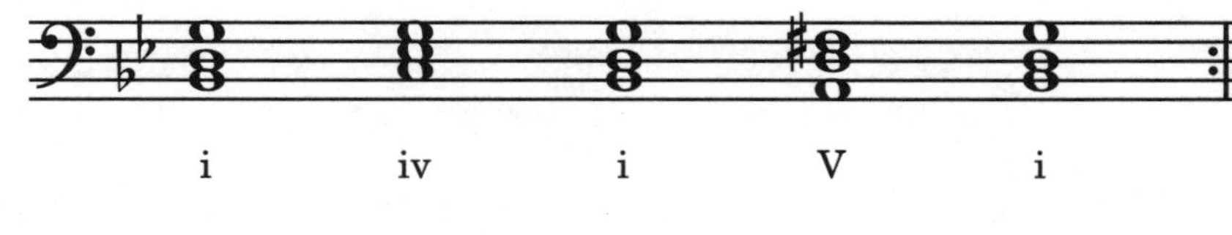

Also in
D minor
A minor

b. E minor

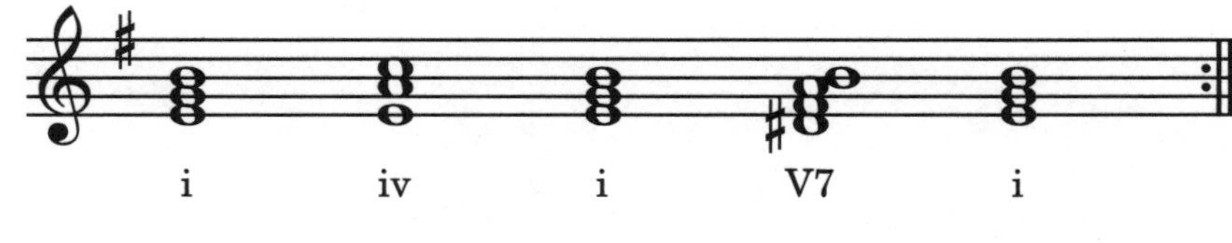

Also in
C minor
F minor

c. F♯ minor (Challenge)

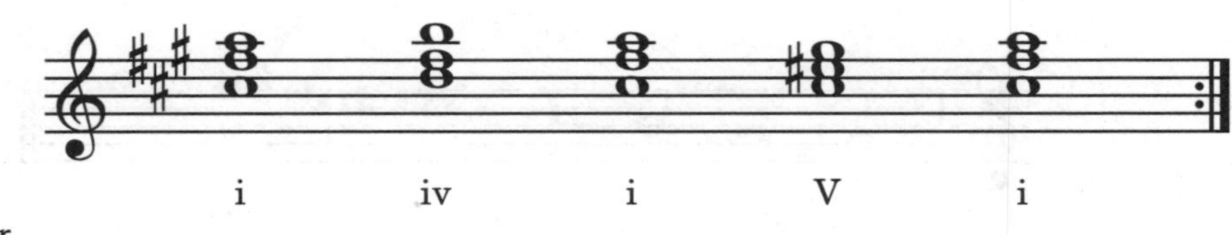

Also in B minor, C♯ minor: i iv i V i

Go to the PDM Web site for additional drill on items 5a, 5b, and 5c.

6. Using the following progression, verbally spell each chord in root position but play the closest position.

a. D minor

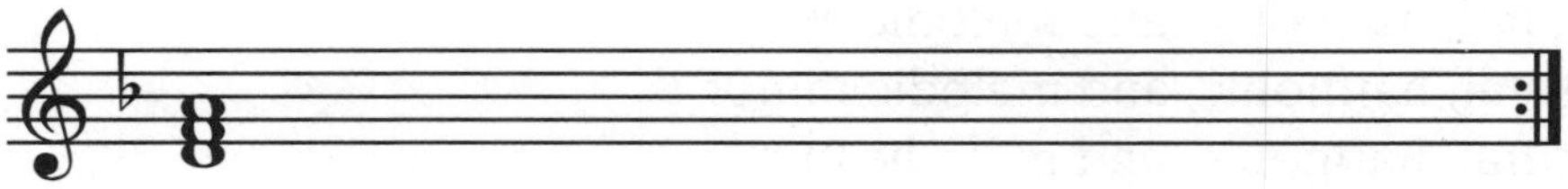

Also in G minor, E minor: i VI iv ii° V i

b. C minor

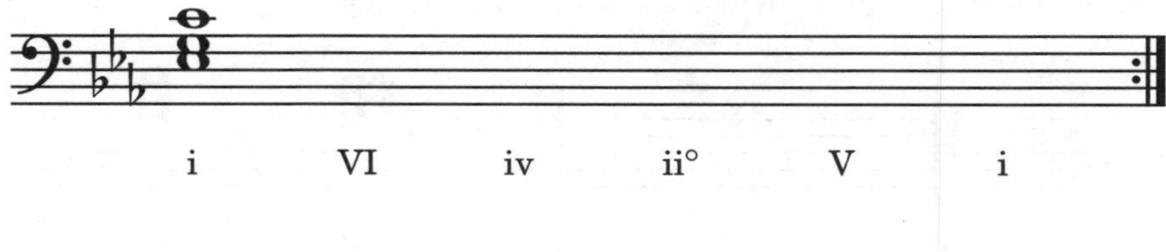

Also in D minor, F minor: i VI iv ii° V i

c. C♯ minor (Challenge)

Also in E♭ minor, A minor: i iv ii° V i

8

HARMONIZATION

1. Harmonize the following with chords given. Suggested styles of accompanying are furnished.

   a. Broken chord

French

Go to the PDM Web site for further drill on item a.

   b. Two-handed

British

Go to the PDM Web site for further drill on item b.

   c. Choose an appropriate accompaniment style.

2. Complete the following:

a. Spanish

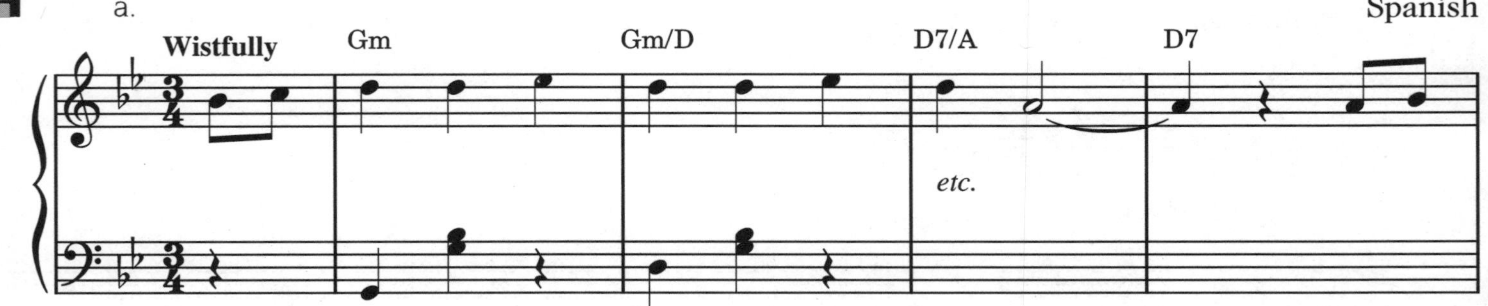

b.

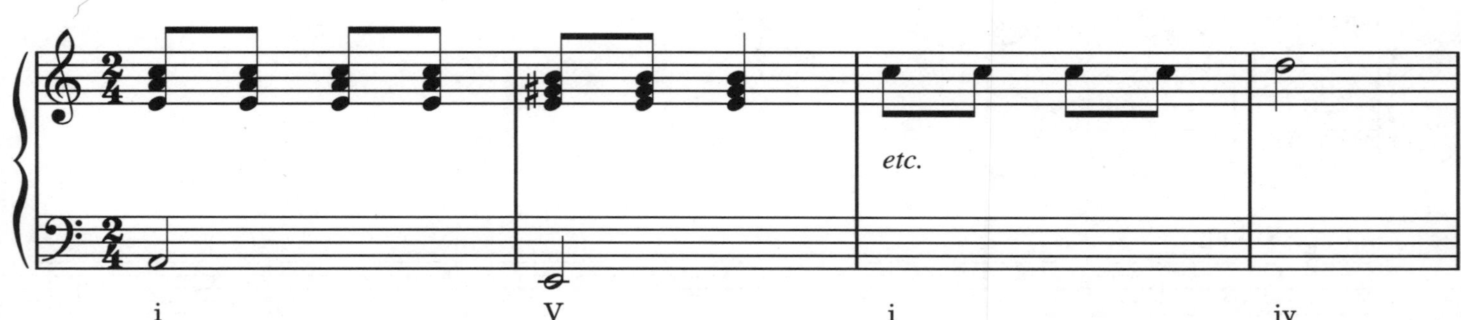

3. Play the following melodies by ear and determine appropriate harmonies for each.

- *Johnny Has Gone for a Soldier*
- *Joshua Fit Da Battle of Jericho*
- *Sometimes I Feel Like a Motherless Child*
- *Scarborough Fair*

Go to the PDM Web site for help in getting started with these melodies.

TRANSPOSITION

1. The following are to transposed an interval of a tritone.

Adapted from Lancaster/Renfrow

a. Transpose *down* to C minor.

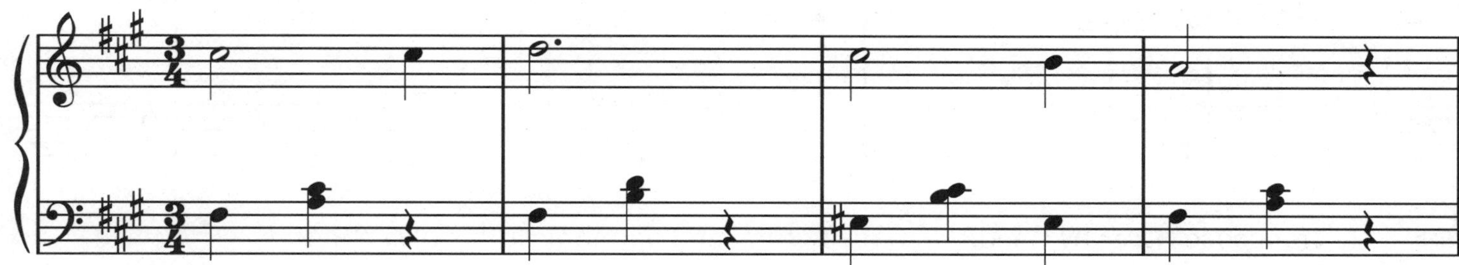

b. Transpose *up* to B minor.

K. RICHMOND

c. Transpose *down* to E minor.

S. RAMAWY

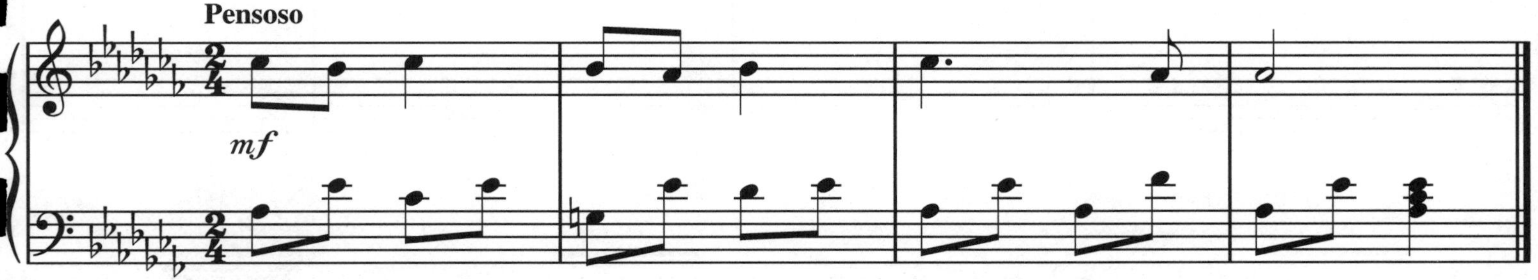

2. Transpose *Etude* by Schytte (page 200) to B minor.

3. Transpose the following extension exercise to the keys of A♭ and C♯ major.

4. Transpose *Hopak* by Goedicke to the natural and harmonic forms of G minor.

Hopak

ALEXANDER GOEDICKE
(1877–1957)

Allegro

f

f

5

9

mp

13

f

IMPROVISATION

1. Play the following expansion of the blues pentascale in F.

2. The beginning 12-bar blues progression is based on three chords: I, IV, and V. To expand this harmonic basis, each triad may be given a dominant 7th quality.

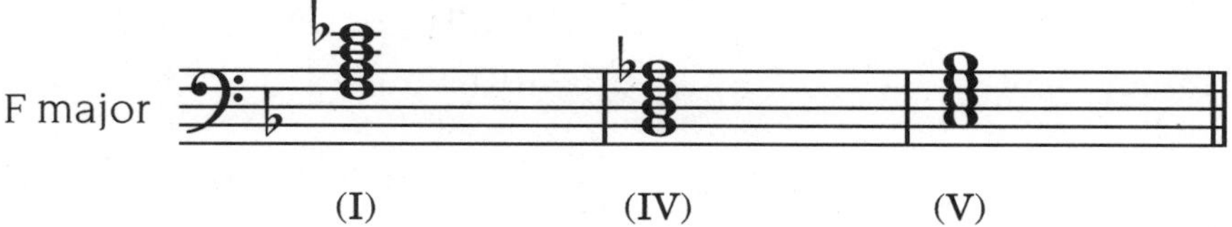

Play open 7ths that follow this blues progression in F

I	IV	I	I
IV	IV	I	I
V	IV	I	I

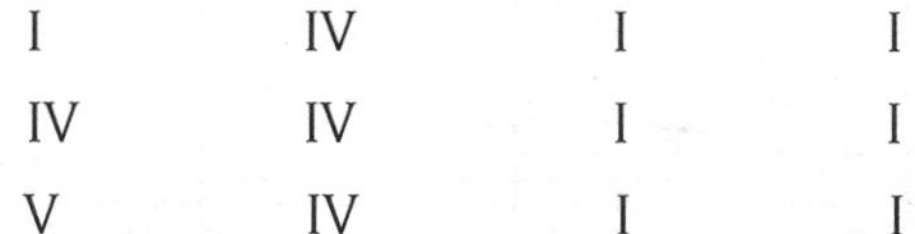

3. Choose a partner. One person will scat and play melody as the other plays 7ths. Use the key of F major.

4. For ease of movement around the keyboard, tritones substitute quite effectively for mid-range seventh chords. Compare these tritones to the full seventh chords used above.

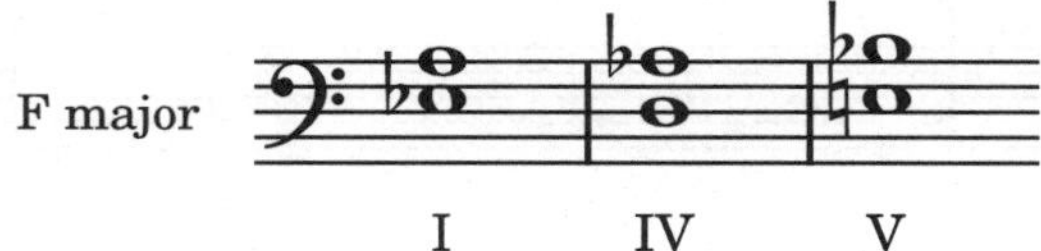

5. Choose a partner. Play an "up-tempo" blues improvisation ensemble in F major.

   Part 1—one chorus of blues scale melody followed by one chorus of tritones

   Part 2—one chorus of tritones followed by one chorus of blues scale melody

   Note the Octave Placement of the Tritones!

Two choruses will have a V chord turn-around at the end of the first chorus.

6. Return to *Etude* on page 200. As your teacher or a classmate plays the score as written, improvise a melody at least one octave above. Your improvisation should consist of chord tones, passing tones, neighbor tones, etc.

ENSEMBLE

1. Trade parts for the second 16 bars.

Minuet

(*Don Juan*)
Secondo

W. A. MOZART
(1756–1791)

Minuet

(Don Juan)
Primo

W. A. MOZART
(1756–1791)

2. The *Galop* as a part of a French suite is a lively round dance in duple meter. Minimum tempo for this should be approximately 192 to the quarter note. Enjoy!

Secondo

WELLS

Vivace

mf leggiero

7

marcato

12

cresc.

17

f leggiero

23

marcato

28

ff

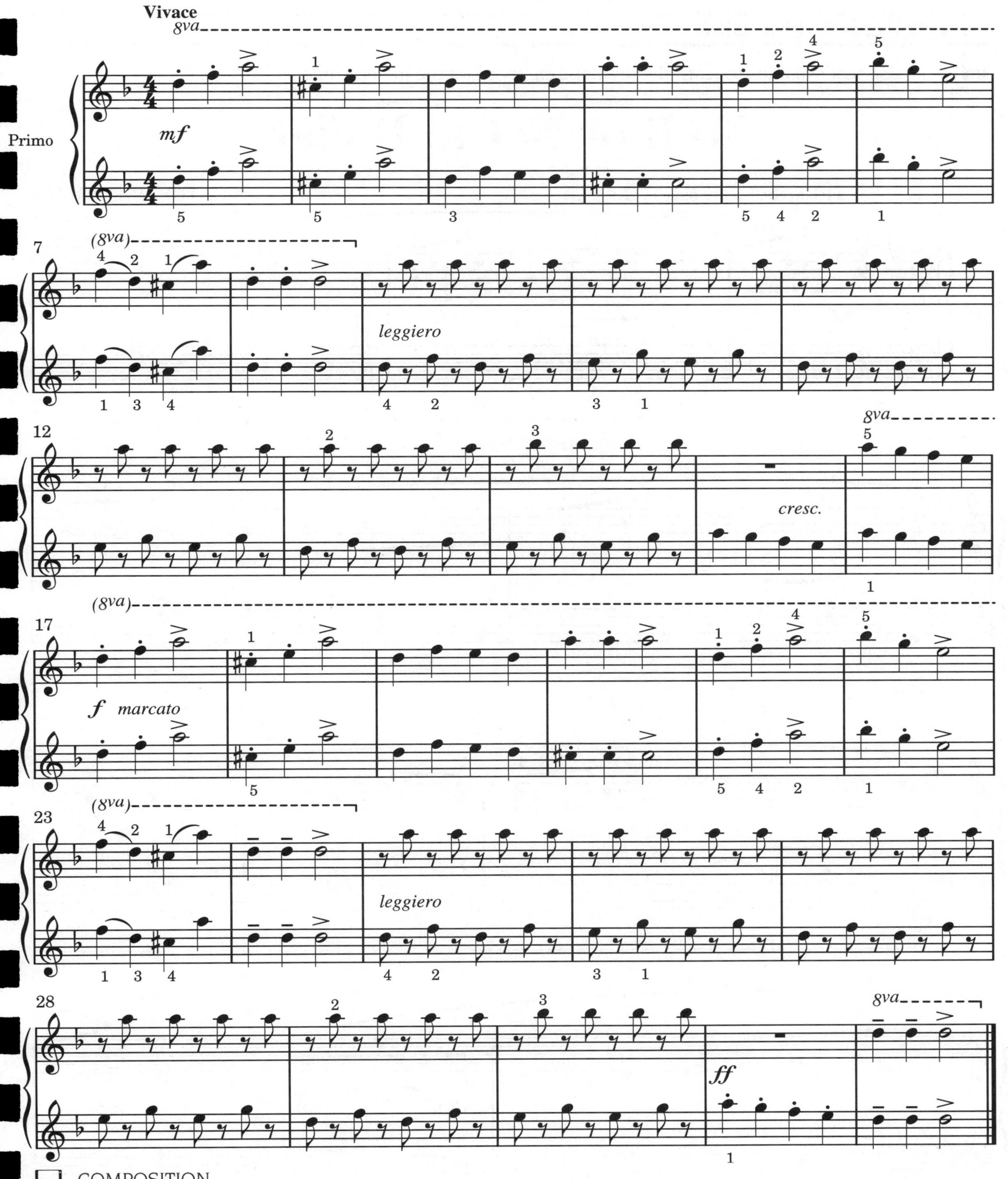

COMPOSITION

1. Compose a two-chorus blues solo in the key of F or G. The melody should come from the blues scale of the key and the accompaniment will consist of tritones in whatever rhythm you feel is appropriate. The MIDI disk will furnish a bass line and drums to complete the "Blues Trio." You may transpose the key of the disk and adjust the tempo as needed. Use the progression from page 209 with a dominant turn-around at the end of the first chorus.

SUBSEQUENT REPERTOIRE

1. Use scat syllables to learn the rhythmic emphasis of the melodic line.

To B or Not to B Flat

At a leisurely, bluesy pace

CATHERINE ROLLIN

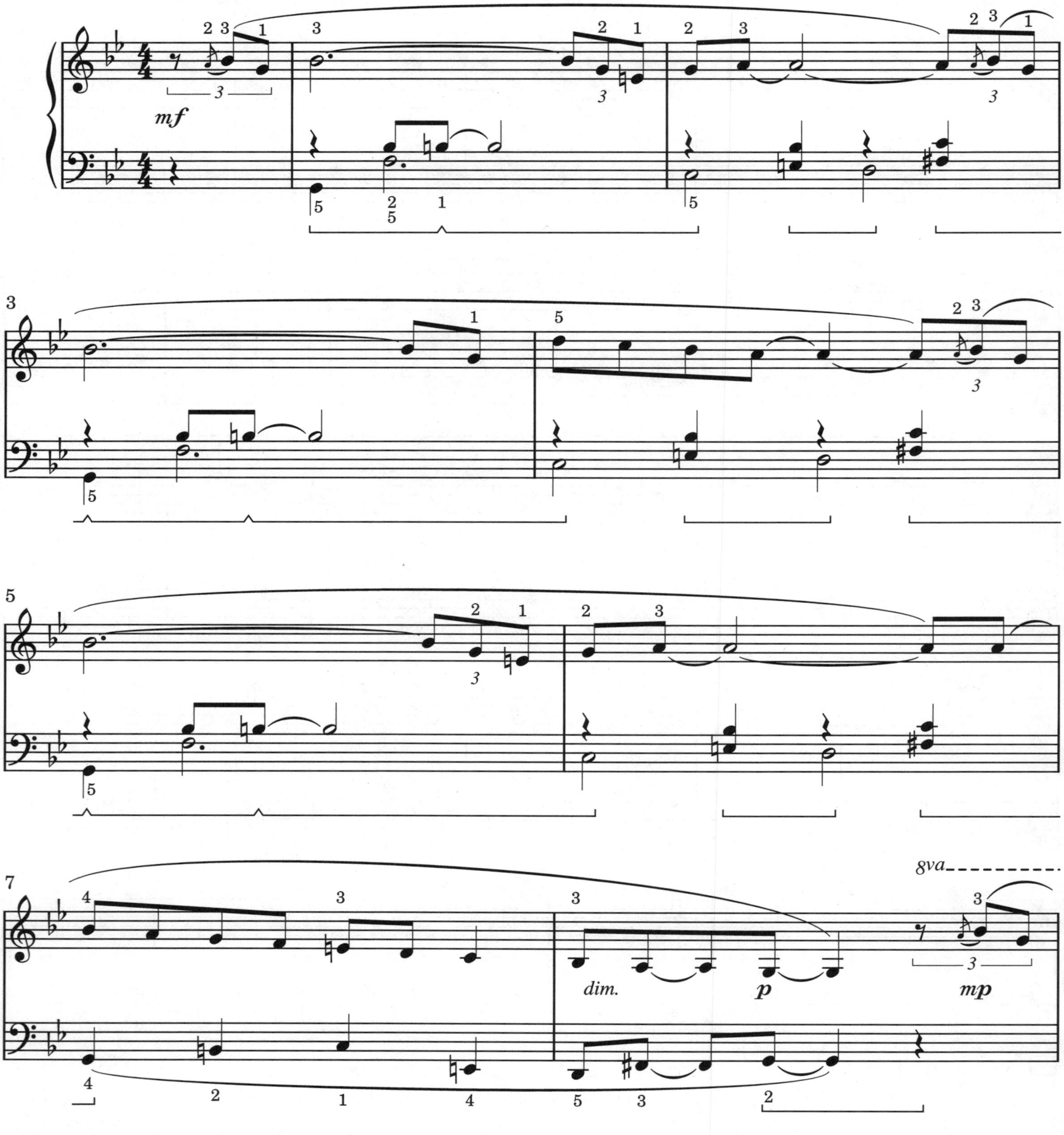

9 (8va)

11 (8va)

mf

13 (8va)

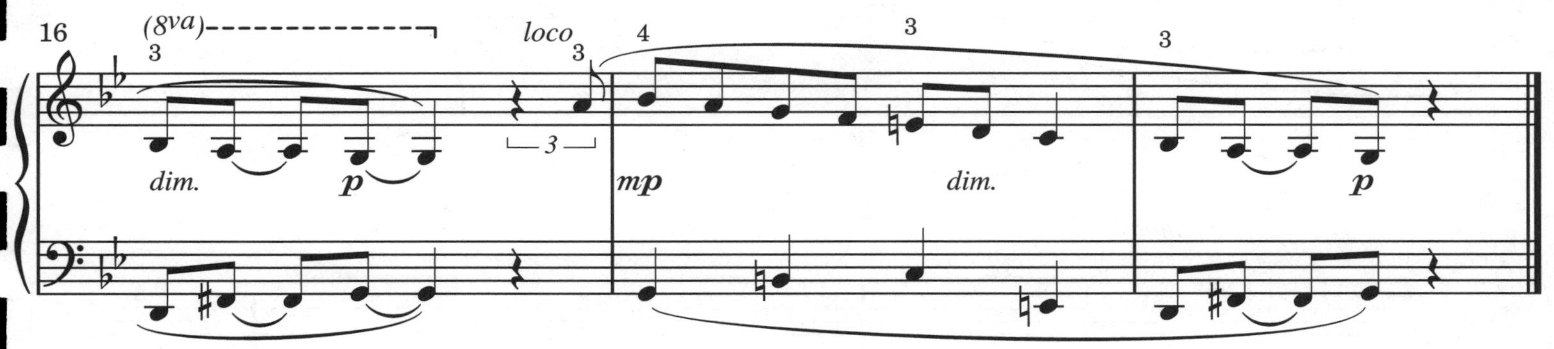

2. Note the tempo marking.

Left Behind

Wistfully (♩ = 132)

JEANINE YEAGER

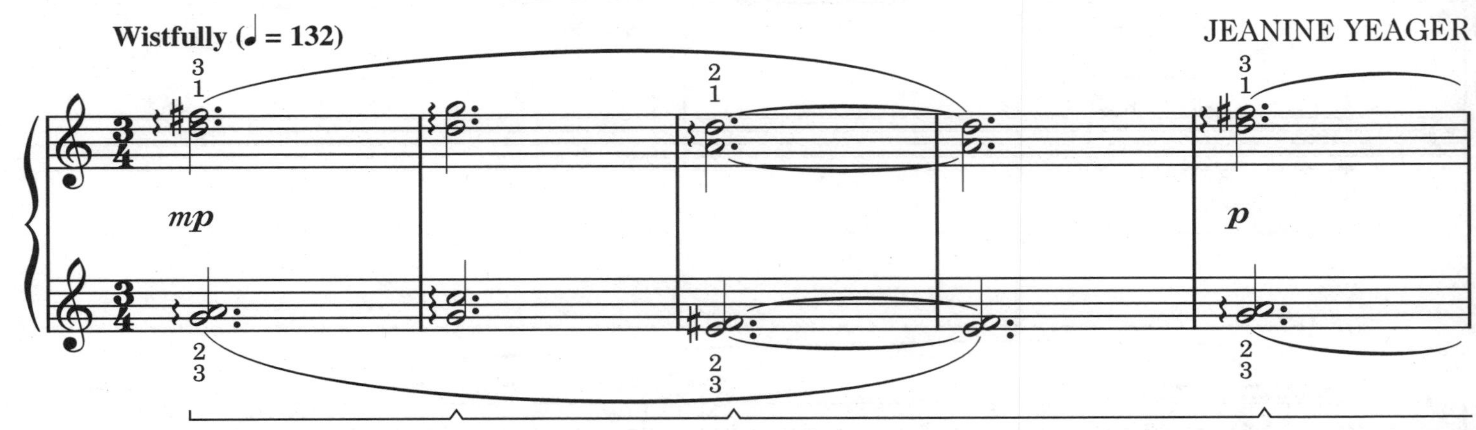

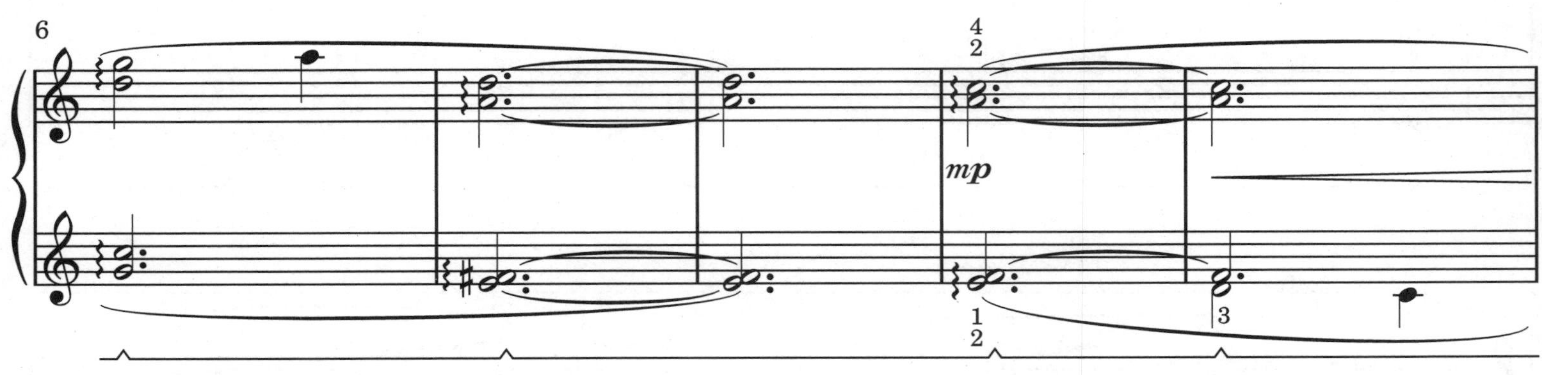

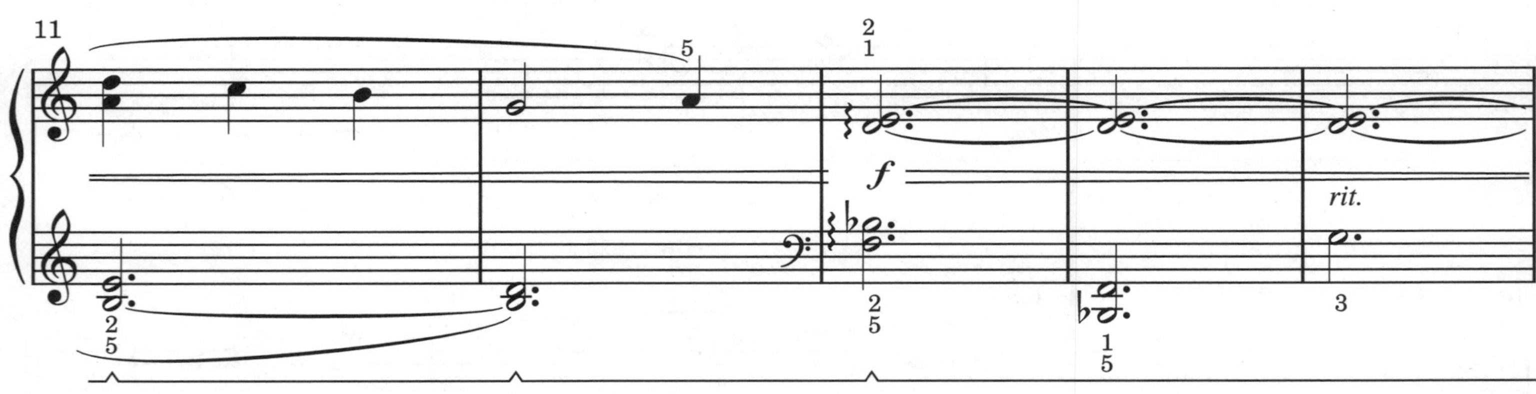

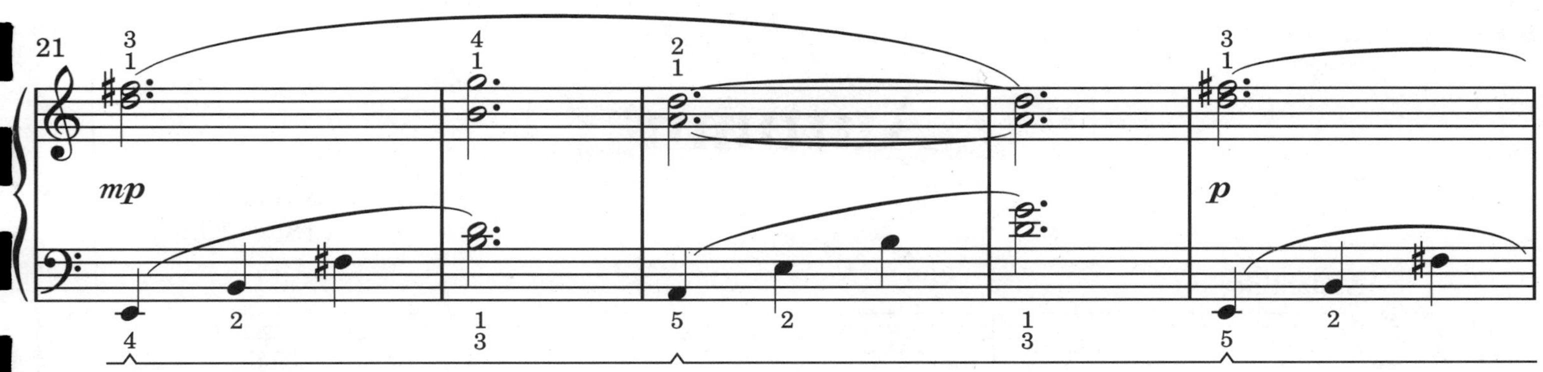
21
mp
p

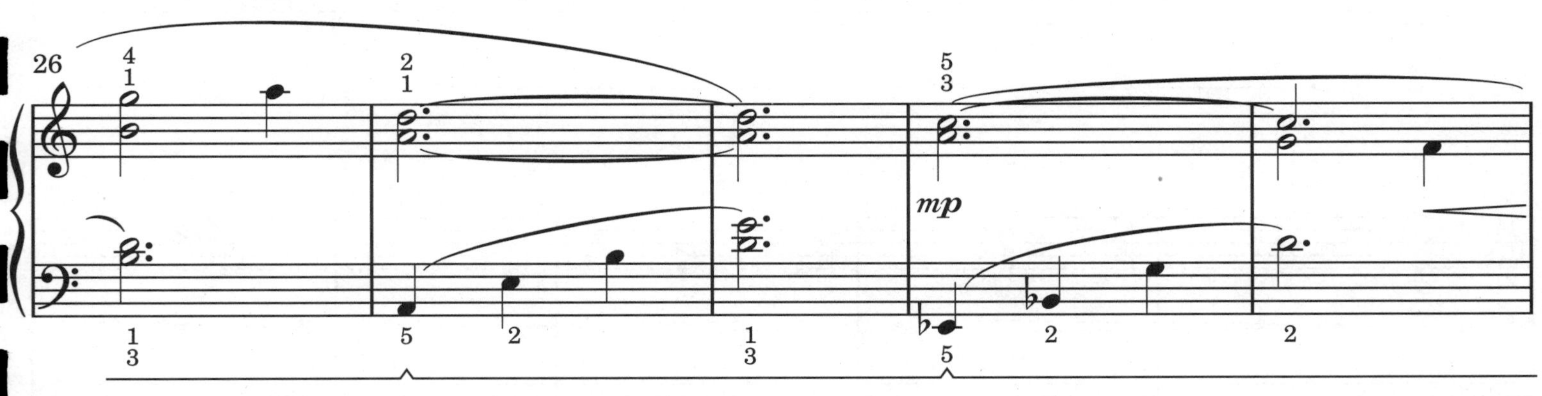
26
mp

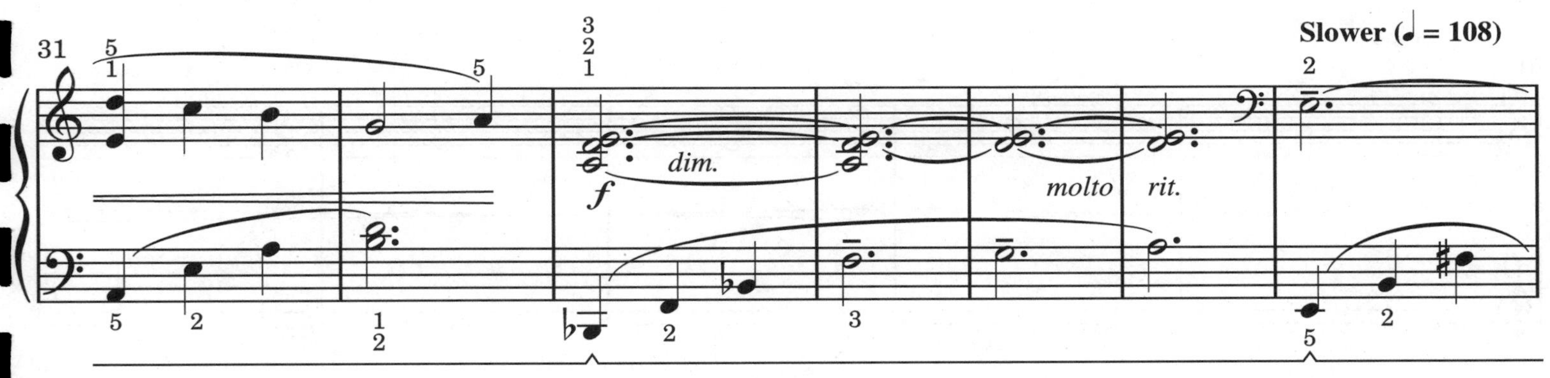
31
Slower (♩ = 108)
f
dim.
molto
rit.

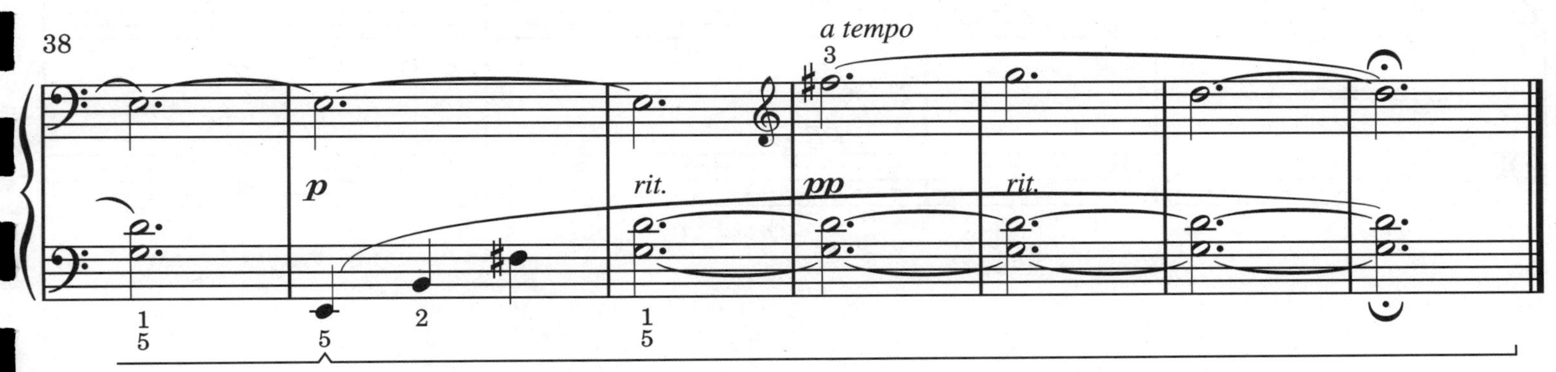
38
a tempo
p
rit.
pp
rit.

3. Plan for the articulation changes in *Autumn*.

Autumn

SAMUIL MAYKAPAR, Op. 28
(1867–1938)

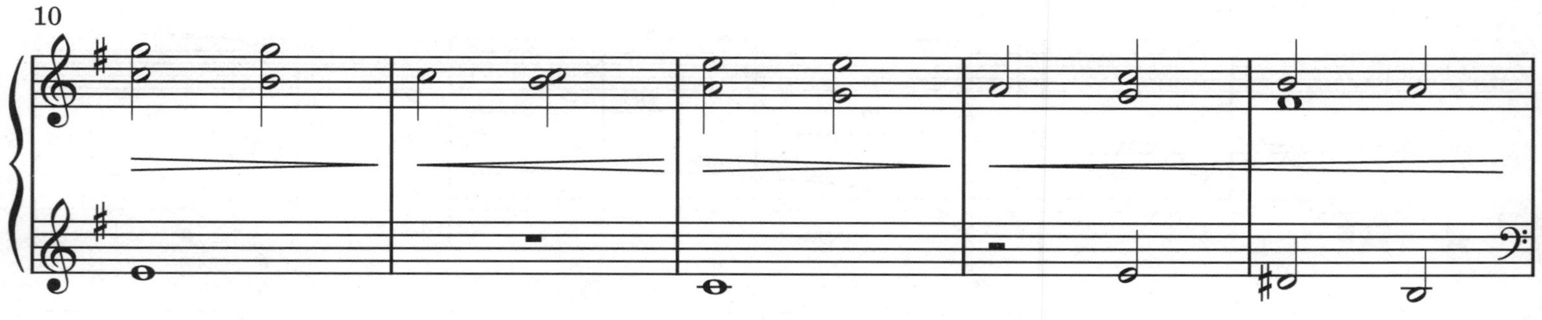

19
23
mf
p cantabile
pp legato
27
31
pp
rall.

9.

EXEMPLARY REPERTOIRE

TOPICS TO EXPLORE AND DISCUSS

RELATED SKILLS AND ACTIVITIES

SUBSEQUENT REPERTOIRE

The ii–V7–I Progression

EXEMPLARY REPERTOIRE **Lemonade** Lynn Freeman Olson

INQUIRY

1. Scan *Lemonade*. Observe:
   - chord shapes
   - form
   - harmonic progression
2. Determine fingering.

PERFORMANCE

1. Block right-hand chord shapes.
2. Play as written. Count aloud.

Lemonade

LYNN FREEMAN OLSON

14
17
f
20
p
23
mf
26

TOPICS TO EXPLORE AND DISCUSS

- Jean-Louis Gobbaerts
- Anton Diabelli
- Gigue
- Domenico Zipoli

RELATED SKILLS AND ACTIVITIES

TECHNIQUE

1. Review all white-key major scales (C, D, E, G, A).

RH:	1	2	3	1	2	3	4	1	2	3	1	2	3	4	5
LH:	5	4	3	2	1	3	2	1	4	3	2	1	3	2	1

2. Play *Pleasant Morning.*

Pleasant Morning

STREABBOG (JEAN-LOUIS GOBBAERTS)
(1835–1886)

10
14
17
p
20
23
f
f
26

READING

1. The alto clef positions middle C on the third line of the staff.

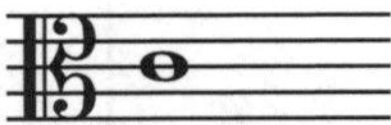

Play the following viola excerpt using alto clef.

String Quartet in E-Flat Major

(Viola excerpt)

WOLFGANG AMADEUS MOZART
(1756–1791)

2. Before playing, look for chord outlines and scalar passages.

String Quartet in G Major

(Viola excerpt)

WOLFGANG AMADEUS MOZART
(1756–1791)

3. Play the following viola line from *Bassa imperiale*, then choose a partner and play as an ensemble.

Go to the PDM Web site for additional alto clef reading.

4. Think key signature as you play through these minor key examples.
   a.

b.

Andantino

p

c.

S. RAMAWY

Con Spirito

f

d.

Geschwindt

mp

e.

K. RICHMOND

Zierlich

2

1

2

1

KEYBOARD THEORY

1. The most basic type of authentic cadence is twofold: dominant to tonic. The dominant area is strengthened by preceding it with the subdominant or substituting another chord for the subdominant (such as the supertonic—ii).

   The ii–V7–I cadence appears frequently. For smooth voice leading (and because melodic content often dictates), the form is commonly ii6–V7–I.

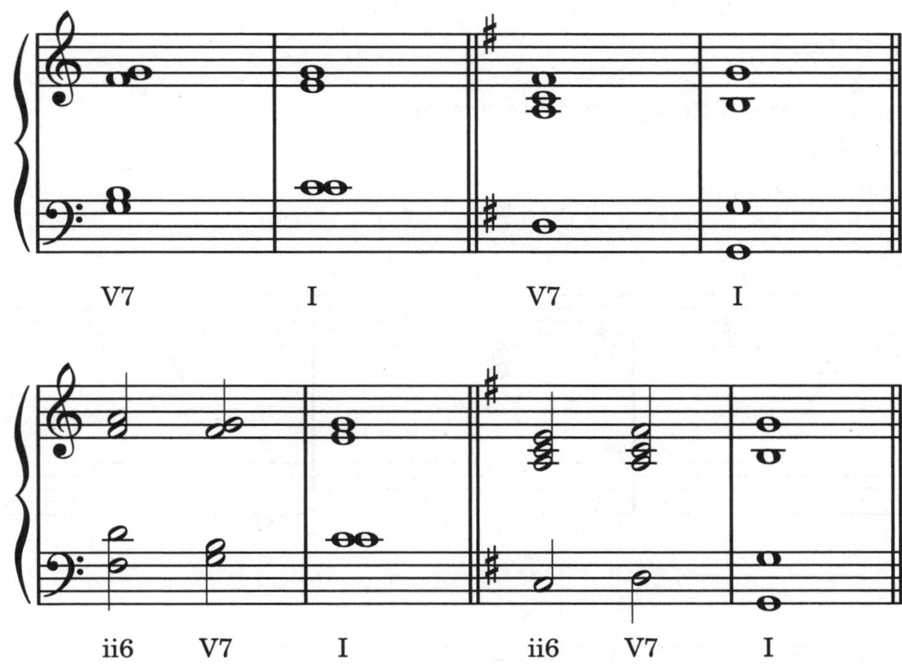

2. Play ii6–V7–I progressions in the following keys. Your teacher will set the tempo and give a measure of rest between each new key:

   A E♭ D A♭ G D♭

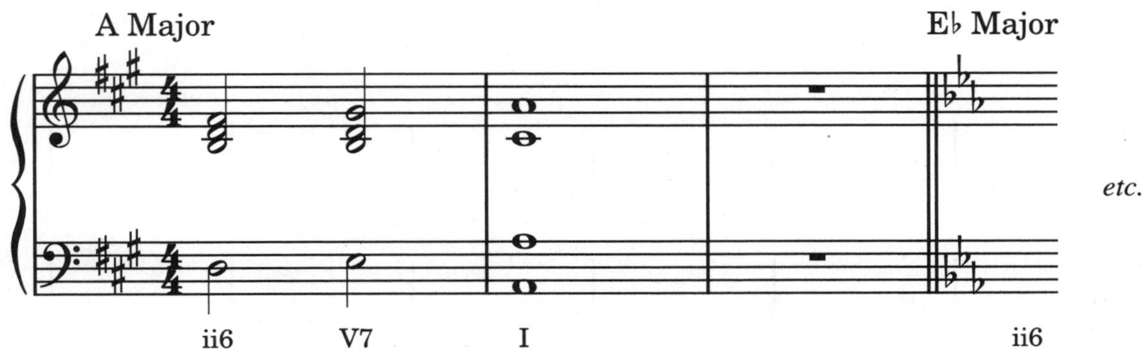

Go to the PDM Web site for additional drill of ii-V7–I.

3. As a class, create three minor key progressions. Play the progressions in keyboard style paying close attention to voice leading. Regardless of meter or choice of rhythm, you should demonstrate two four-bar phrases. Your choices will include:

   - remainder of harmonies
   - key signature
   - meter
   - beginning shape of right hand
   - tempo (choose a term you don't often see)

   Example: i | VI | iv | V7 | ii°6 | V7 | V$^6_5$ | i ||

   Key—C minor
   Meter—$\frac{3}{4}$
   Beginning shape of RH—second inversion
   Tempo Luftig

   Then you would play:

a. i | i6 | | | | | | ||

b. i | III | | | | | | ||

c. i | VI | | | | | | ||

HARMONIZATION

1. Follow the suggested styles.

c. Modified keyboard style

d. Left-hand chords with right-hand melody.

TRANSPOSITION

1. Play the following as a round in the key written. As the fourth group plays the last measure of the melody, the teacher will call for a new key. From that point on, at the downbeat of the last measure in each phrase, a new key will be called. Continue until the fourth group has played the melody two more times.

To Portsmouth!

2. With all transposing instruments, *think in concert key* rather than transposing each note. For clarinets in B♭, think down a whole step.

- In what key will you play the clarinet part?
- Play both parts.

Three Duos

(Excerpt)

LUDWIG van BEETHOVEN
(1770–1827)

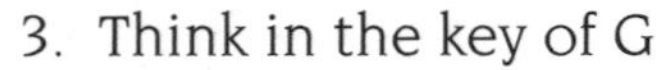

3. Think in the key of G.

4. In what key will you think?

5. The following will be transposed the interval of a tritone.

a. Transpose *up* to A minor.

C. BENSON

b. Transpose *up* to E minor.

K. RICHMOND

Go to the PDM Web site for more tritone transposition drill and transposing B♭ instruments.

IMPROVISATION

1. The ascending blues scale is formed by adding one note to the blues pentascale—flat 7.

Determine the best fingering and play the F blues scale several times.

2. A walking bass is characteristic in blues improvisation. Each harmony change should be started on bass root. Strong bass movement anticipates harmonic change by a step or half step above or below.

3. Choose a partner. One of you will play scat melody and the other will play walking bass. Use the bass above. Trade parts and play again.

COMPOSITION

1. Compose a piece in the style of E*tude* by Schytte (page 200). Think about:
   - imitation
   - sequence
   - easily defined harmonic structure
   - static rhythm

Be prepared to trade compositions on the due date and play what you receive. Therefore, "do unto others. . . !"

ENSEMBLE

1. Choose a partner and perform *Allegro in E Minor.*

Allegro in E Minor

ANTON DIABELLI
(1781–1858)

7
ff
p
ff
p
10
cresc.
cresc.
13
f
ff
f
ff

2. Perform the following once as written. Perform again with these options:

   - Parts 2 and 3 become one part.
   - On the repeat Part 1 should play a solo improvisation based on the harmonic structure; the second ending as written may be used for the close of the solo improvisation.

The ii–V Doodle

MARTHA HILLEY

SUBSEQUENT REPERTOIRE

1. Play the Bartók listening for the independent lines.

Mourning Song

from *For Children*, Vol. 2

BÉLA BARTÓK
(1881–1945)

2. A "brisk" tempo is essential.

Gigue

MONA MJOLSNES

17
p
21
25
p
poco
29
33
f
dim.

37
8va
a tempo
5
1 2
1
rit. pp
f
1
1
41
mf
45
dim.
49
pp
mf
53
8va
a tempo
5
1 2
pp rit.
f
1
1

3. Take the time to pencil in fingering shifts.

Menuett

DOMENICO ZIPOLI
(1688–1726)

10.

EXEMPLARY REPERTOIRE

TOPICS TO EXPLORE AND DISCUSS

RELATED SKILLS AND ACTIVITIES

SUBSEQUENT REPERTOIRE

Secondary Dominants/ Styles of Accompanying

EXEMPLARY REPERTOIRE **Sonatina, Op. 34, No. 3** Johann Anton André

INQUIRY

1. Scan *Sonatina*. Observe:
    - chord shapes within the Alberti bass
    - harmonic progression
    - form
    - clef changes
    - dynamic contrasts
2. Determine fingering.

   This sonatina movement is like a miniature opera. Where is the chorus making its declamatory statement? Where does the soprano step from behind a bush and give her somewhat shy reply?

PERFORMANCE

1. Block left-hand chord shapes.
2. Isolate the bass clef measures 9–12 and work hands separately until it is comfortable.
3. Choose a partner and play through, one with RH and one with LH, at performance tempo. Note the meter signature. Switch parts and play again.
4. Return to a steady "practice" tempo and put the hands together.

Sonatina

(Movement I)

JOHANN ANTON ANDRÉ, Op. 34, No. 3
(1775–1842)

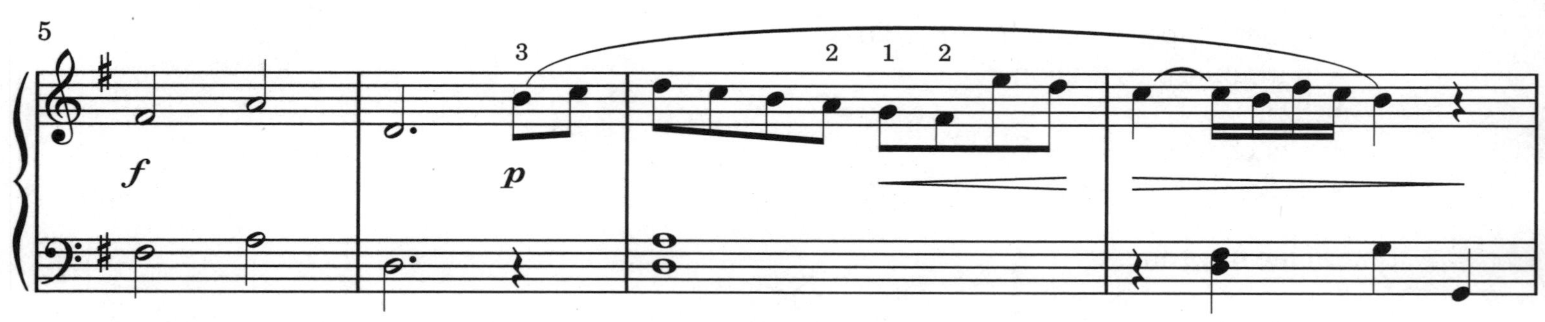

19
23
f
dim.
27
p
31
f
35
mf
f
39
dim.
p
pp

TOPICS TO EXPLORE AND DISCUSS

- Johann Anton André
- Alessandro Scarlatti
- Vincent Persichetti

RELATED SKILLS AND ACTIVITIES

TECHNIQUE

1. Review all minor scales (c, d, e, g, a), all forms.

RH:	1	2	3	1	2	3	4	1	2	3	1	2	3	4	5
LH:	5	4	3	2	1	3	2	1	4	3	2	1	3	2	1

2. Play the following broken-chord extensions.

3. Using traditional scale fingerings, mark the beginning and crossover fingerings for measures 5, 21, 23, and 25.

Etude in C

CORNELIUS GURLITT
(1820–1901)

READING

1. Determine chord shapes of arpeggios. What is the function of the dominant seventh chord in measure 7?

Wiedersehen

CORNELIUS GURLITT, Op. 117, No. 24
(1820–1901)

2. Play through these viola parts.

   a. Your teacher or a classmate should play the accompaniment.

Viola

mf

Piano

mp

5

   b. Notice the use of sequence in descending root position triads.

MOZART K. 424

   c. Which hand will play which part?

MOZART K. 563

3. Locate a singer in your class and accompany this excerpt from *Bist du bei mir*.

J. S. BACH

4. If there is a viola player in your class, accompany her/him in this Galliard *Sarabande* excerpt. If you have no string player in class use this as an opportunity for a classmate to practice reading alto clef.

GALLIARD

5. Be an efficient reader by noticing common tones.

Prelude

LUGWIG SCHYTTE

Go to the PDM Web site for additional reading material.

KEYBOARD THEORY

Play the chord of resolution for each secondary dominant. Thinking of each key in parentheses as the tonic, analyze and play the secondary dominant and its chord of resolution.

Example:

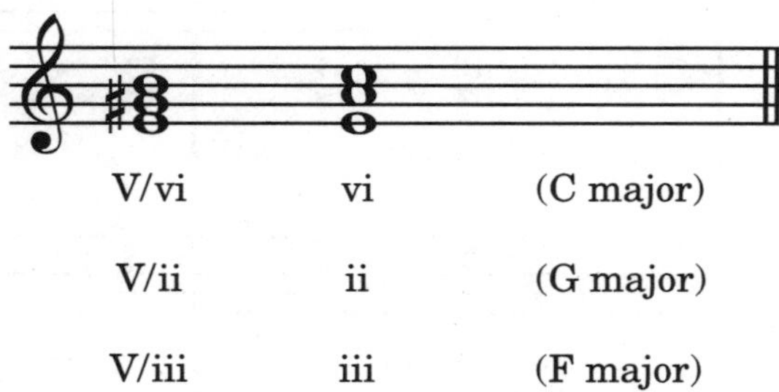

V/vi	vi	(C major)
V/ii	ii	(G major)
V/iii	iii	(F major)

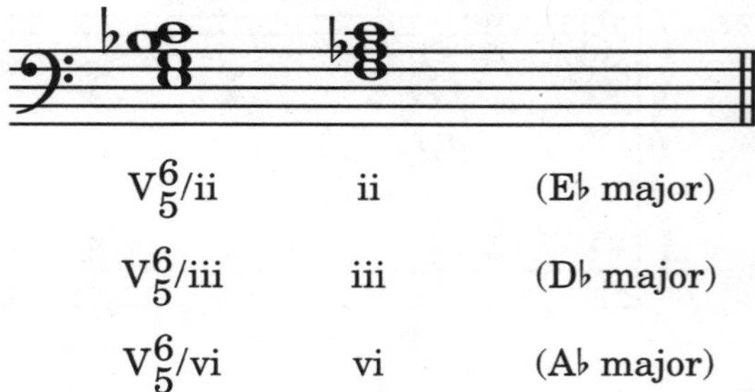

V^{6}_{5}/ii	ii	(E♭ major)
V^{6}_{5}/iii	iii	(D♭ major)
V^{6}_{5}/vi	vi	(A♭ major)

V/____	____	(C minor)
V/____	____	(G♭ major)
V/____	____	(D♭ major)
V/____	____	(A♭ major)

V^{4}_{2}/____	____	(D major)
V^{4}_{2}/____	____	(E major)
V^{4}_{2}/____	____	(C♯ minor)

V^{4}_{3}/____	____	(B♭ major)
V^{4}_{3}/____	____	(E♭ major)
V^{4}_{3}/____	____	(A♭ major)
V^{4}_{3}/____	____	(F major)
V^{4}_{3}/____	____	(G major)

Go to the PDM Web site for extensive drill on secondary dominants within harmonic progressions.

HARMONIZATION

1. Develop ostinato patterns that reinforce the AABA form and harmonize the following.

Southern Harmony, 1855

Simply

p

Transpose to one other pentatonic scale.

2. Harmonize the following melodies, using secondary dominants when appropriate.

   a. Use closest-position left-hand chords.

b. An accompaniment should compliment the melody and support the harmonic rhythm. The following item has been harmonized for you. Do the choices, both harmonically and rhythmically, make sense?

d. Two-handed accompaniment

mp

p

I I I V7 I

HENRI A. CESAR MALAN
(1787–1804)

Moderato

mp

6

11

16

e. Use a two-handed accompaniment style as your teacher plays the melody.

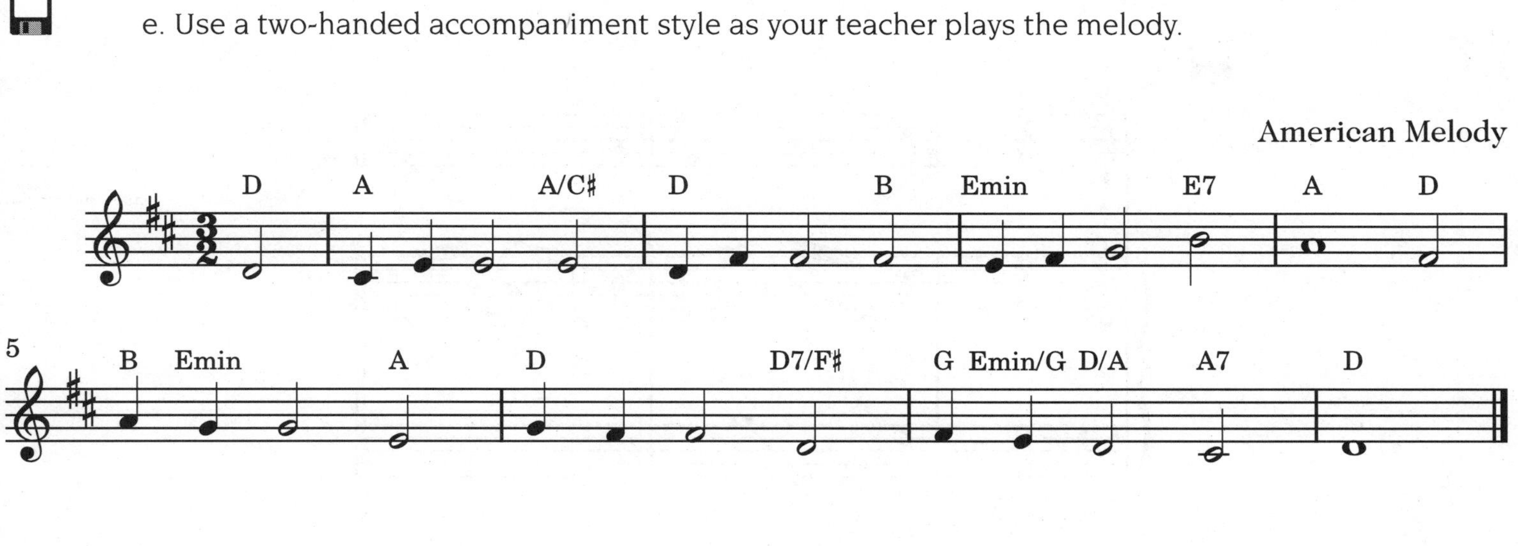

3. Complete the harmonization in the three styles indicated.

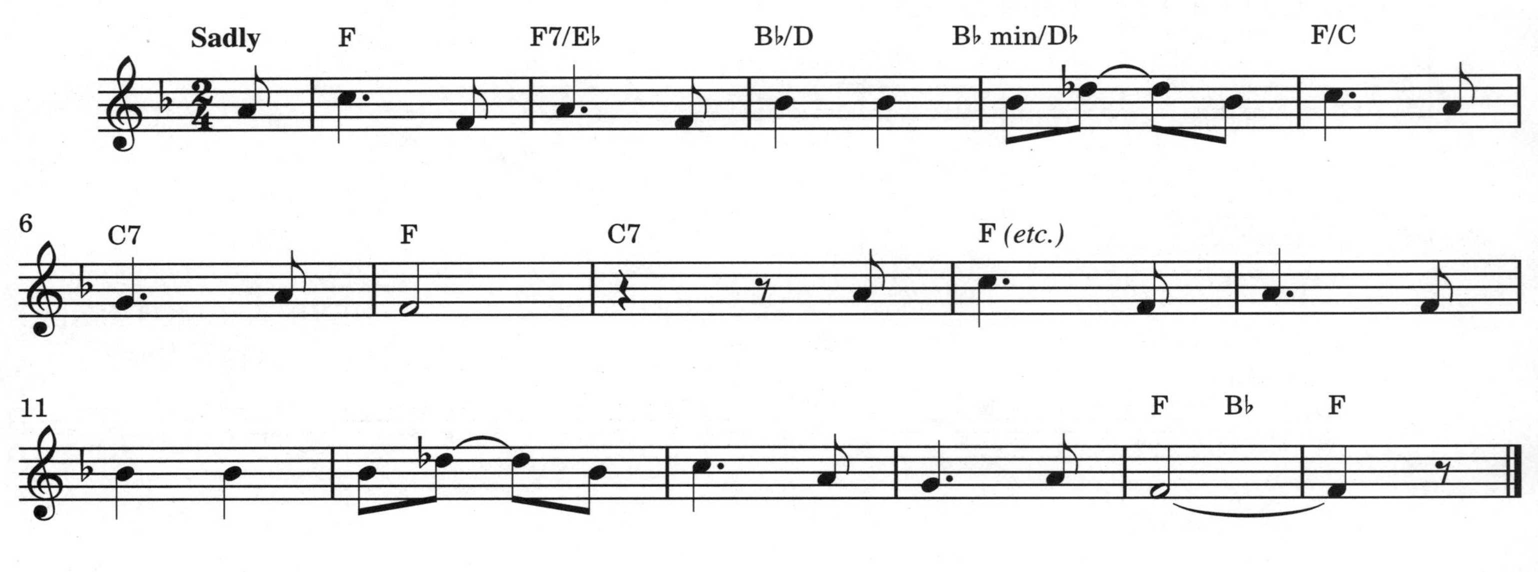

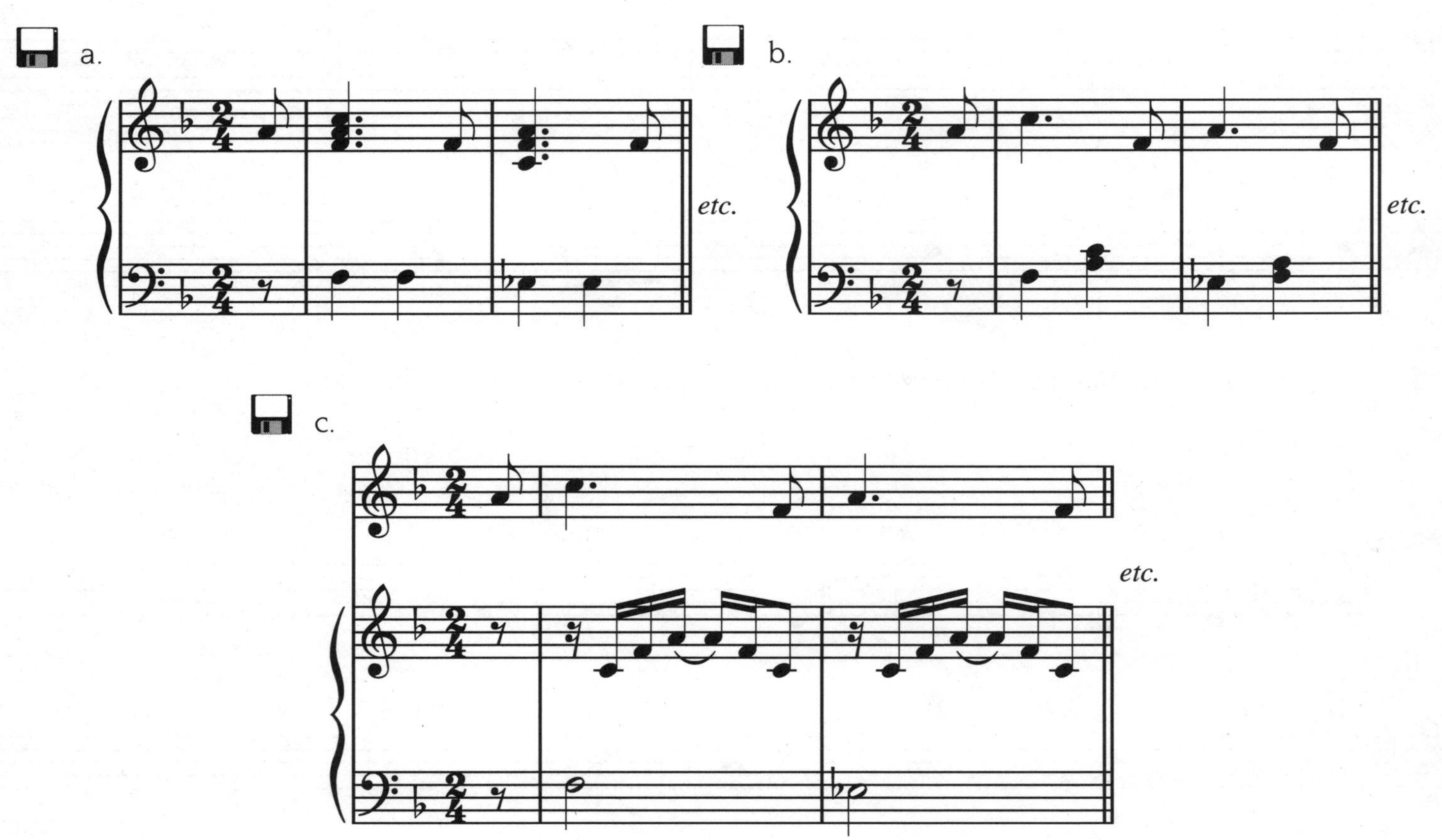

Go to the PDM Web site for practice tips on some of the harmonization items in this chapter.

TRANSPOSITION

1. Discover as a group why this etude will be easy to transpose. Transpose to at least three other major keys.

Etude

CORNELIUS GURLITT
(1820–1901)

2. Transpose to begin on C. What key signature must be used to retain the original tonal quality?

3. The following are to be transposed the interval of a tritone.

a. Transpose *up* to A major.

b. Transpose *up* to B♭ major. Think about key and function before you start.

K. RICHMOND

c. Label with Roman numerals, then transpose *down* to E♭.

4. Play both parts.

a. Think B♭ major.

BEETHOVEN

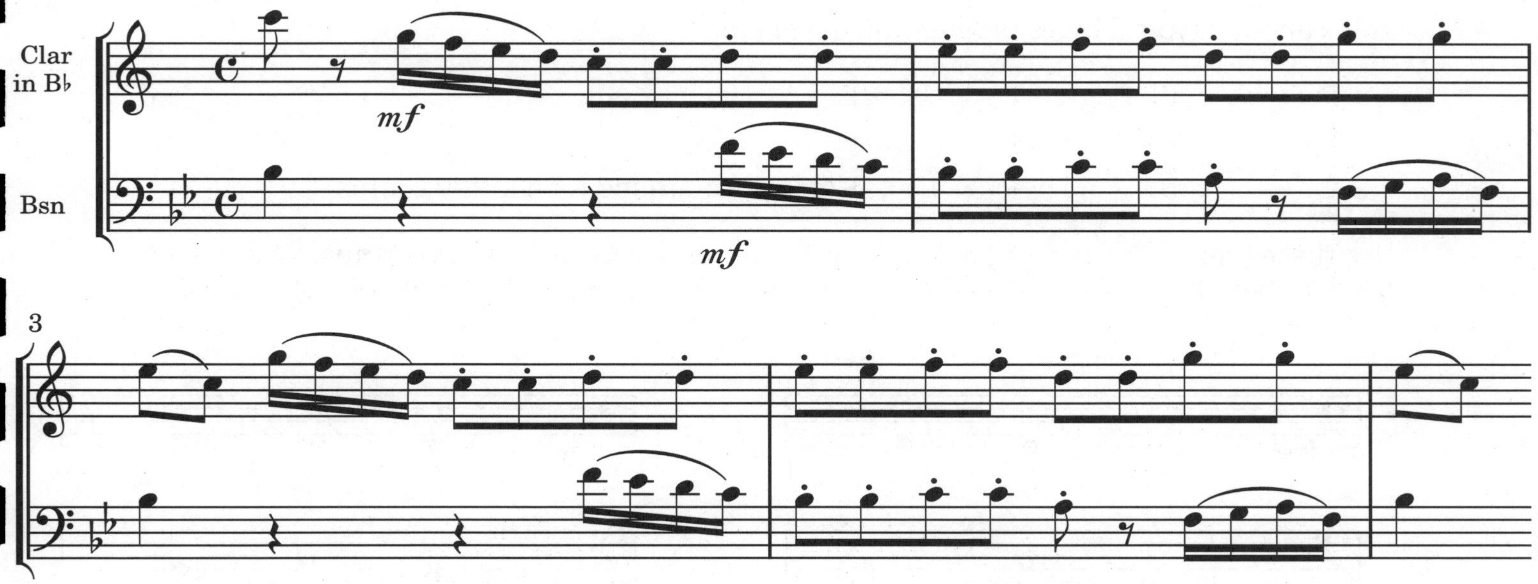

b. Think G major.

IMPROVISATION

1. Creating a bass line for a chorus of blues can be the simple process of putting together one- and two-measure ideas. The catch is that the ideas have to be there to draw upon!

   Think about a typical blues progression in F major:

F	B♭	F	F
B♭	B♭	F	F
C	B♭	F	F (or C turn-around for another chorus)

   Use these one bar ideas for bars 1, 2, 9, or 10. In the case of playing two choruses these could be used for bars 11 and 12 as well. Simply transpose the idea(s) to the harmonies of C and B♭.

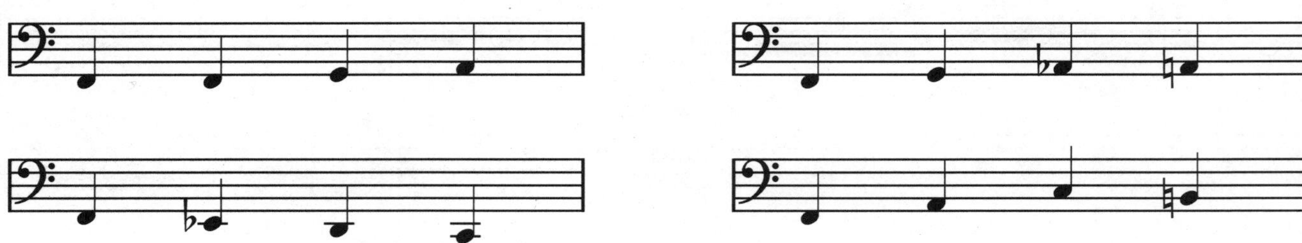

   Use two-bar ideas for measures 3–4, 5–6, 7–8, and the "final" 11–12. Again, transpose to the appropriate harmony. These are nothing more than ascending and descending Mixolydian modes.

2. Play two choruses of blues in your choice of F or G. In the first chorus, improvise on the blues scale while playing left-hand tritones. In the second chorus, improvise a walking bass while playing right-hand tritones. *The octave placement of your tritones should not change—always mid-range.*

3. It was fairly common practice in eighteenth-century music to vary recurring materials by adding figuration to the written score. In addition to increased ornamentation of the trill and mordent variety, it was natural for the performer to "fill in" tones, especially in the small skips. On a repeat, for example:

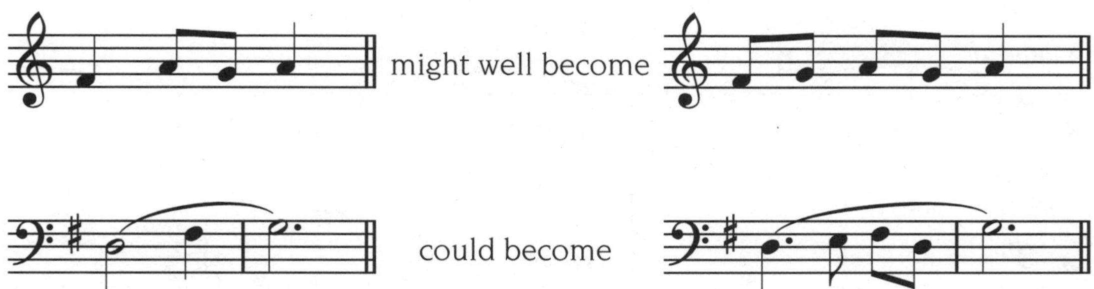

Rhythmic variations were common also. A single held chord or tone could be given new vigor through repetition

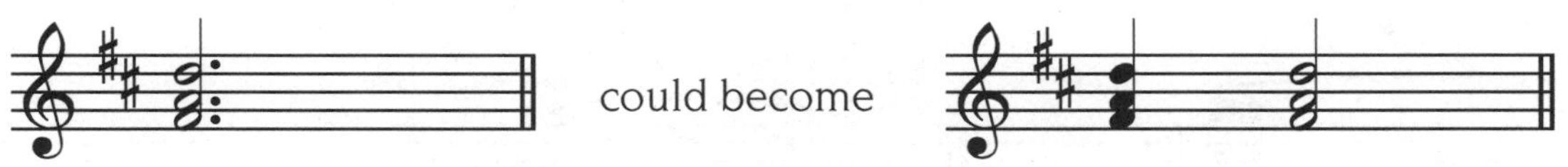

and "straight" rhythms could be "bent" to provide a new buoyancy. In many cases, these dotted rhythms were played in a "lazy" or rounded manner when a gentle lilt was appropriate.

Following the original version of the Krieger M*inuet*, we have suggested some ways to ornament the patterns. Use these ideas and vary them. This practice is called "melodic ornamentation," and, as in all such matters, your own sense of style and taste should be your main guide.

(The balance of this page has been left blank to avoid a difficult page turn.)

Minuet

JOHANN KRIEGER
(1651–1738)

Possible melodic ornamentation for the A section:

Possible melodic ornamentation for the B section:

ENSEMBLE

1. Combine parts as follows for an "open score" reading experience.
   - Parts 1 and 2
   - Parts 2 and 3
   - Parts 2 and 4
   - Parts 1 and 3
   - Parts 3 and 4
   - Parts 1 and 4

Greensleeves

English
Arr. Robert D. Vandall

Did you "anticipate" measure 15 when playing Parts 2 and 3?

2. Note that the two middle staves are to be played as one part.

Alexander's Ragtime Band

IRVING BERLIN
(1888–1988)
Arr. S. Ogilvy

13
f
17
21
mf

25
29
33
f

COMPOSITION

Compose an original minuet in Baroque style (refer to *Minuet* by Krieger, page 264). At the time of performance, add melodic ornamentation to the repetition of the A and B sections.

SUBSEQUENT REPERTOIRE

1. Notice repetition in the left-hand extensions.

Basic principles of chromatic scale fingering are necessary for a successful performance of *Chromatizone Rag*. Do Not Swing the Eighth Notes!

ANN COLLINS

17
21
25
29
8va

3. As a class determine a fingering that will support a "seamless" effect.

Aria

ALESSANDRO SCARLATTI
(1660–1725)

4. Pay careful attention to accents and the effect they have on a feel for meter.

Fanfare

VINCENT PERSICHETTI
(1915–1987)

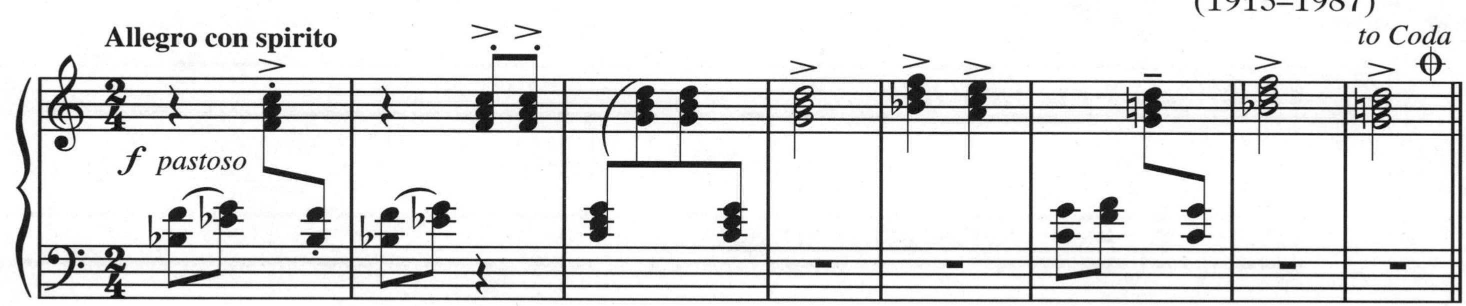

11.

EXEMPLARY REPERTOIRE

TOPICS TO EXPLORE AND DISCUSS

RELATED SKILLS AND ACTIVITIES

SUBSEQUENT REPERTOIRE

Harmonic Implications of Common Modes

EXEMPLARY REPERTOIRE	**Little Fable, Op. 27, No. 9**	Dmitri Kabalevsky

INQUIRY

1. Scan the *Little Fable*. Observe:
   - melodic motion between the hands
   - chordal outlines
   - tonality
   - staccato throughout

PERFORMANCE

1. Fingering is critical to your success. The fingering suggested is from the composer. If something different fits your hand better, please change the fingering. The key is that you find a fingering that works and maintain it.
2. Start practice with measures 12–18.
3. The persistent staccato touch can easily cause tension. It must be a light action, never punched or jabbed. The wrist must remain loose.
4. Play as written.

Little Fable

DIMITRI KABALEVSKY, Op.27, No. 9
(1904–1987)

TOPICS TO EXPLORE AND DISCUSS

- Dmitri Kabalevsky
- Frank Lynes
- Carl Orff
- Johann Pachelbel

RELATED SKILLS AND ACTIVITIES

TECHNIQUE

1. The following is traditional F major/minor scale fingering (2 octaves)

RH:	1	2	3	4	1	2	3	1	2	3	4	1	2	3	4
LH:	5	4	3	2	1	3	2	1	4	3	2	1	3	2	1

Away from the keyboard on a flat surface, play the scale upward and downward. Say "1's" when thumbs play together. Now play on the keyboard, slowly and steadily.

Play the F major and three forms of F minor scales.

Go to the PDM Web site for further drill in F major scales.

2. Observe clef changes and sequence before playing.

Prelude in C Minor

GIUSEPPE CONCONE, Op. 37
(1801–1861)

READING

1. Play violin II and viola together. Notice parallel and oblique motion.

String Quartet in E-Flat Major

(Violin II and viola excerpt)

WOLFGANG AMADEUS MOZART
(1756–1791)

2. Play both parts.

Duo in C Major

(Excerpt)

JOHANN GEORG ALBRECHTSBERGER
(1736–1809)

3. Before playing, look for parallel and contrary motion between the parts.

String Quartet in G Major

(Viola and cello excerpt)

WOLFGANG AMADEUS MOZART
(1756–1791)

4. Even though there are three staves, reading will be more efficient if you place all three parts in your RH and think chord shapes.

JEAN SIBELIUS

5. Probably best suited for two hands.

6. What grouping do you feel is appropriate? RH—Sopr I and II, or LH—Sopr II and Alto?

7. Look for chord shapes, common tones, and parallel movement.

8. This example has rhythmic challenges.

9. Open score reading can have the effect of making "ordinary" sight reading seem less challenging.

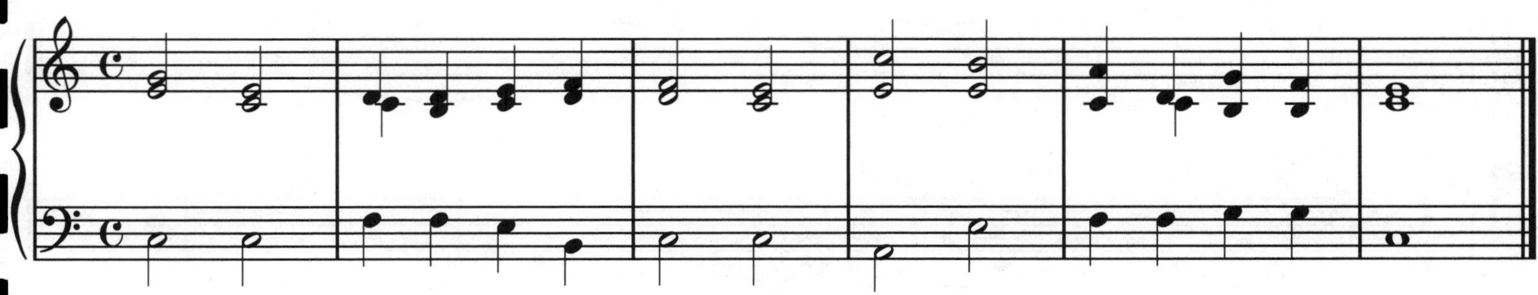

Go to the PDM Web site for additional open score reading.

KEYBOARD THEORY

1. The harmony in modal music is diatonic to the particular scale. Modes can be divided into major and minor categories.

Major	**Minor**
Ionian	Dorian
Lydian	Phrygian
Mixolydian	Aeolian

The harmonies resulting from building triads on modal scale tones tend to diffuse the strong traditional sense of tonic. For example, in Dorian, Mixolydian, and Aeolian modes, the dominant is a minor triad; in Phrygian, the dominant is diminished.

Play diatonic triads for the following modal scales.

Example:

D Phrygian:

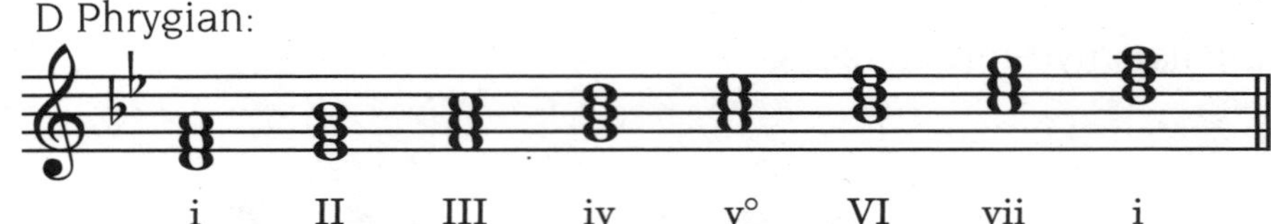

A Dorian

B♭ Mixolydian

E Lydian

C Phrygian

2. In the following examples, indicated harmonies represent progressions characteristic of the mode. Complete each harmonization using chords that will highlight the mode.

It is occasionally appropriate to harmonize modal melodies in ways not associated with eighteenth-century common practice because of the special characteristics of certain modes. Although modal harmonies should use only pitches from the mode in question, occasional accidentals (such as a raised 7th or a lowered 6th) may occur as the tasteful choice.

HARMONIZATION

1. Use left-handed broken-chord accompaniment.

Irish

Gently

p

4

8

cresc. *mp*

12

p

2. On what mode is the following American melody based?

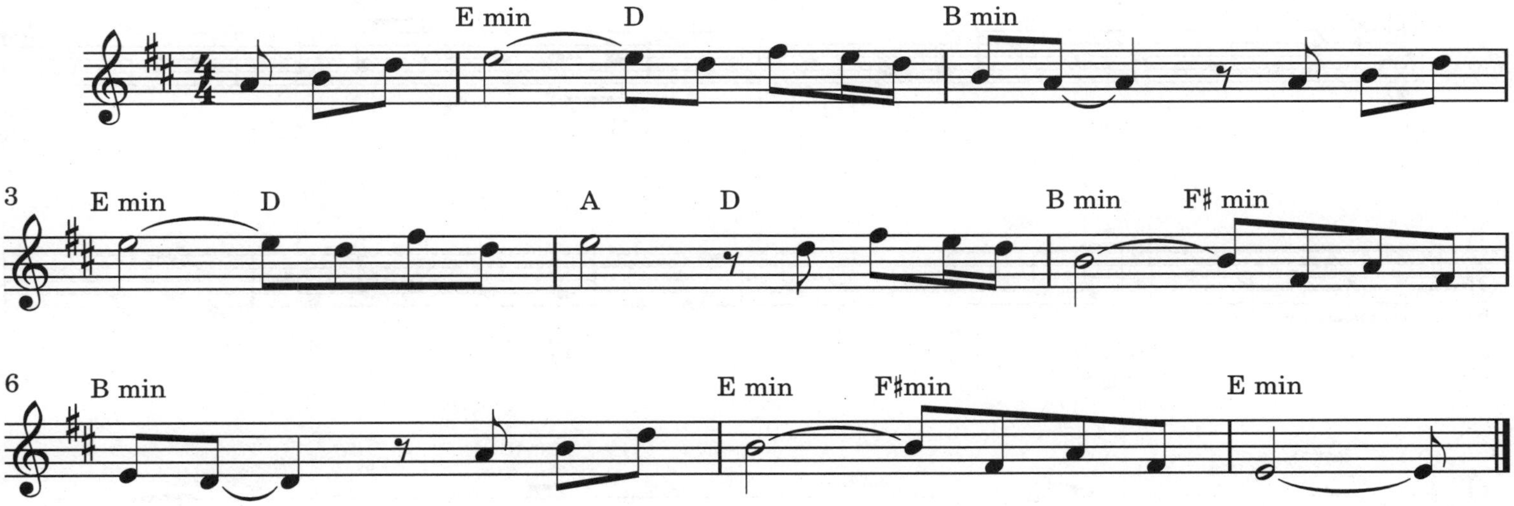

E min D B min

3 E min D A D B min F♯ min

6 B min E min F♯min E min

Harmonize using a "strumming" style of accompaniment:

3. Use keyboard style.

FRANZ SCHUBERT
(1797–1828)

4. Choose an appropriate style.

American

5. Complete in the style indicated. Plan carefully for measures 7 and 15.

AMILCARE PONCHIELLI
(1834–1886)

Moderato con grazia

p

C

4

etc.

B/F♯

E min

7 G/D

D7

G7

a tempo

C

rit.

G7/D

G7

C

10

E7

F

C/G

G7

C

13

TRANSPOSITION

1. The clarinet part must be transposed down a whole step in order to be played on a keyboard. Simply think in the key of B-flat and read intervals.
    - Play the clarinet line
    - Play the accompaniment
    - Choose a partner and play as an ensemble

Sonata for B-Flat Clarinet

(Excerpt)

JOHANN BAPTIST WANHAL
(1739–1813)

Allegro moderato

Clarinet in B♭

Piano

f *tr* *p* *f*

5

p

Go to the PDM Web site for more B♭ transposing instruments.

2. The following examples are to be transposed the interval of a tritone.

a. Transpose *down* to A major.

K. RICHMOND

b. Transpose *up* to D major.

K. RICHMOND

c. Transpose *down* to C major.

3. A horn in F transposes down a perfect fifth. Work through the following examples. Transposing individual pitches makes this a daunting task. Think in the transposed or new key and then simply read intervals.

a. Think the key of A major.

b. Think in the key of F major. Ask a classmate to accompany you, then trade parts.

c. In what key should you think?

d. Prepare for larger intervals in the trombone part.

Go to the PDM Web site for additional horn in F materials.

IMPROVISATION

1. Determine the tonal center for each of the following and improvise melodically above the given bass.

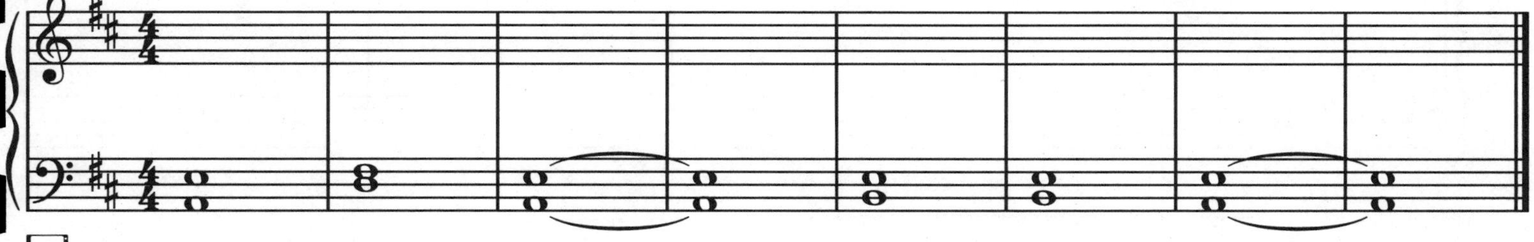

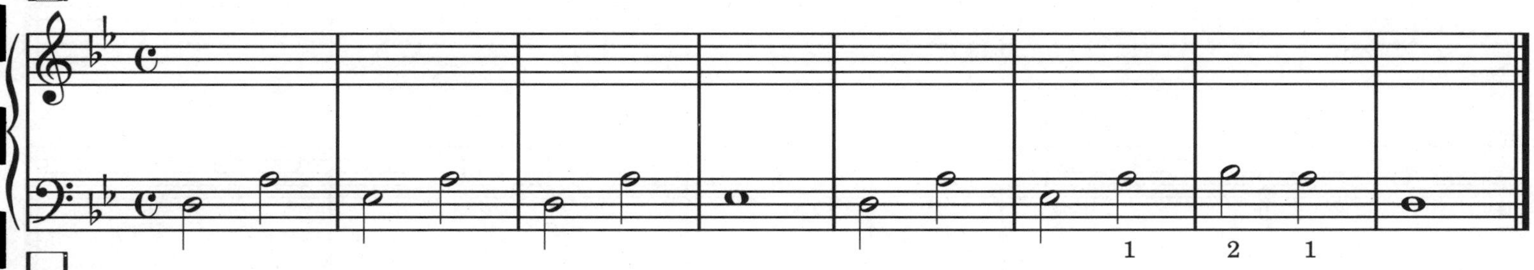

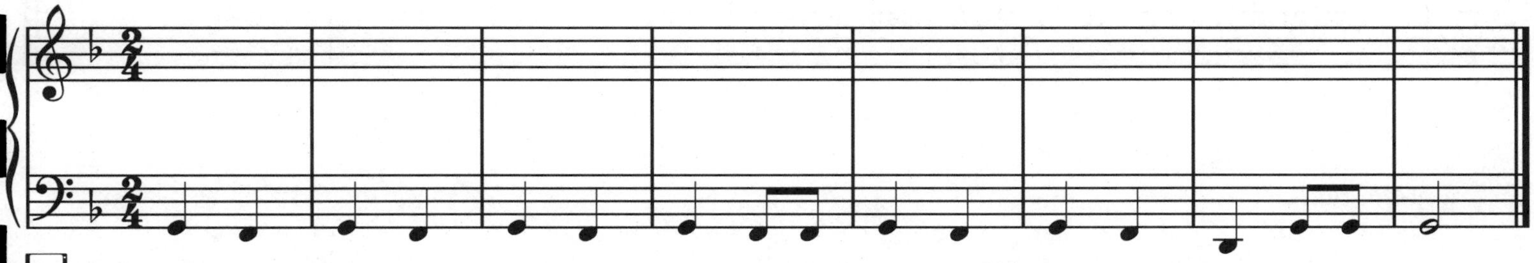

2. In Chapter 9 (Keyboard Theory, page 230) your class created minor progressions. With these progressions you were to demonstrate harmonic content, rhythm, and two four-bar phrases. Return to those progressions and alter them to represent one Dorian, one Phrygian, and one Aeolian progression. Choose a partner and create an improvisation duet—one plays the progressions as a two-handed accompaniment demonstrating harmonic content and rhythm while the other plays a melodic improvisation representing the particular mode.

   For instance, the C minor example could become C Dorian resulting in a diminished vi, a major IV, a minor v, and a minor ii. You should probably retain the accompaniment as shown with the exception of changing the bass note of the vi° to "C" to eliminate doubling of a member of the tritone. A possible melodic improvisation has been added to serve as an example.

COMPOSITION

1. Compose an ensemble "in the style" of *Allegretto* (page 296). You may wish to do a harmonic analysis of the Czerny and then pick an alternate key in which to compose your own ensemble. This *is not* simply a transposition of *Allegretto*.

   Notice the following characteristics in the original score:

   - broken chords
   - melodic passing tones and neighbor tones
   - pedal tones
   - closest-position implied harmonies

   Choose a classmate as your duet partner and perform your composition.

ENSEMBLE

1. Practice skipping around the score without stopping. Throughout, at the *'s, each player skips to the next part in order, reading downward (Part 1 to Part 2 to Part 3, etc.). When you have mastered the idea, try skipping two parts at each *.

Observe that Part 3 is notated the way most Tenor parts appear in choral music. It is to be played one octave lower than written.

Gavotte

SAMUEL WESLEY
(1766–1837)
Arr. Lynn Freeman Olson

12
1
2
3
4
16
mp
mp
mp
mp
3
20
*

24
28
f sub.
32
(2nd time cresc.)
(2nd time rall. & ff)

2. Trade parts at each repeat.

Allegretto

Secondo

CARL CZERNY, Op. 824, No. 18
(1791–1857)

Allegretto

Primo

CARL CZERNY, Op. 824, No. 18
(1791–1857)

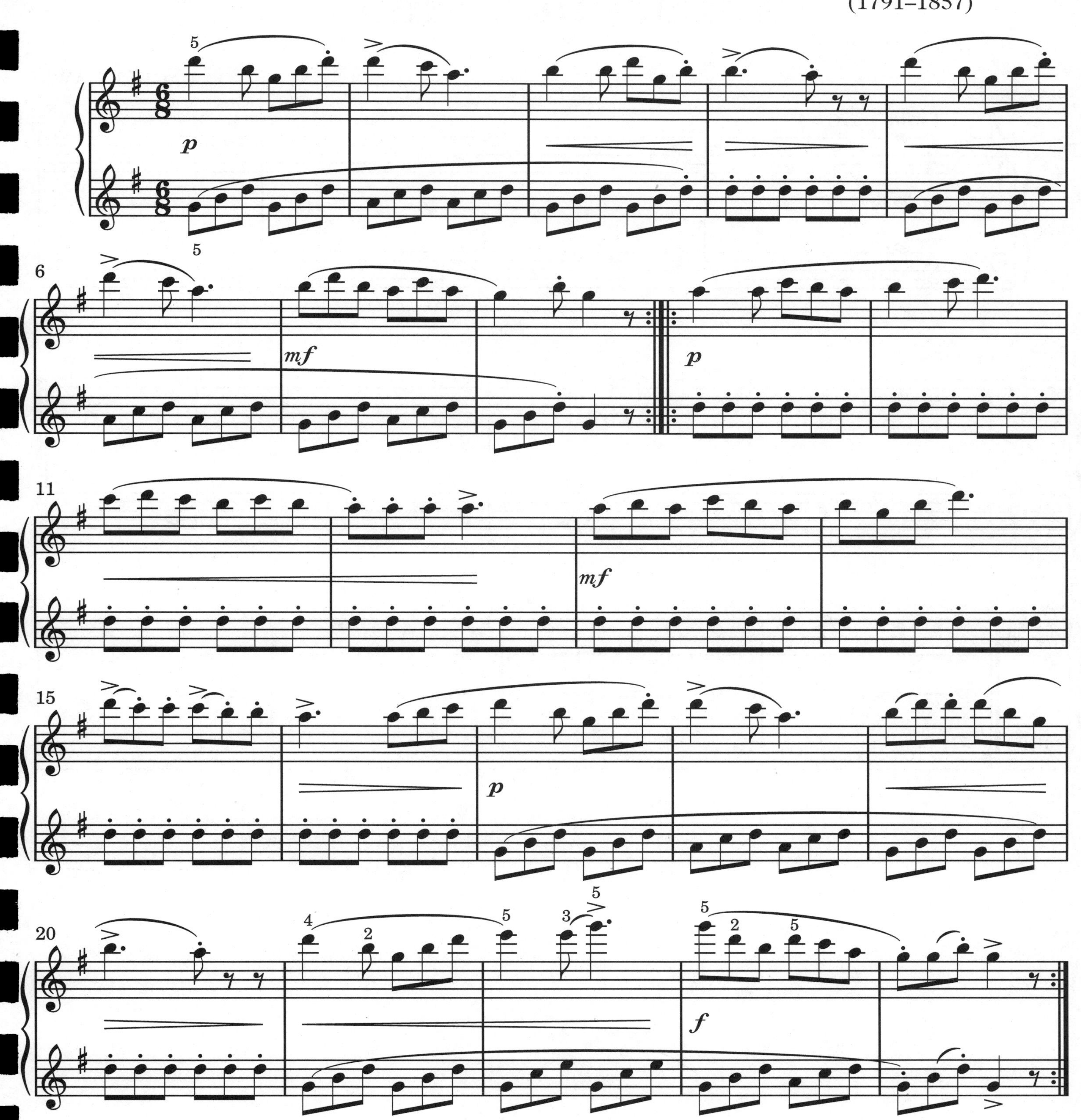

1. This was composed by a group piano student.

Minuet in B Minor

RACHEL HAWN

13
17
f
21
rit.

2. Locate all examples of broken chords, sequential patterns, scale passages, and repetition in this sonatina movement.

Sonatina

from *Analytical Sonatinas*

FRANK LYNES, Op. 39, No. 1
(1858–1913)

17
p
22
27
mf
32
mf
p
36
cresc.
f

3. Discuss variable meters and tonal basis before playing. Your tempo must compliment the meter and a feel for one pulse to a bar.

Dance Piece

(1933)

CARL ORFF
(1895–1982)

4. Practice the "layering" effect of the left hand.

Sarabande

JOHANN PACHELBEL
(1653–1706)

12.

EXEMPLARY REPERTOIRE

TOPICS TO EXPLORE AND DISCUSS

RELATED SKILLS AND ACTIVITIES

SUBSEQUENT REPERTOIRE

Diatonic Seventh Chords in Major and Minor/ Secondary Seventh Chords

EXEMPLARY REPERTOIRE **Prelude in C Major** Muzio Clementi

INQUIRY

1. Scan *Prelude in C Major*. Observe:

   - chordal outlines
   - bass motion
   - roulade effects

PERFORMANCE

1. Block the chordal outlines in the first eight measures, maintaining the pulse—

2. Practice the written roulade (measures 9–12)

3. Play as written at a slow tempo.

4. In *An Introduction to the Art of Playing on the Pianoforte*, Clementi states, "The pause 𝄐 renders the note longer at pleasure; and in certain cases, the composer expects some embellishments from the performer; but the pause on a rest only lengthens, at pleasure, the silence." In bar 14, improvise a right-hand roulade while sustaining the left-hand harmony.

5. Play as written, including your improvisation.

Prelude in C Major

MUZIO CLEMENTI
(1752–1832)

TOPICS TO EXPLORE AND DISCUSS

- Muzio Clementi
- Lead sheets
- William Schuman

RELATED SKILLS AND ACTIVITIES

TECHNIQUE

1. Play the following arpeggio drills.

a.

Allegretto

mf

b.

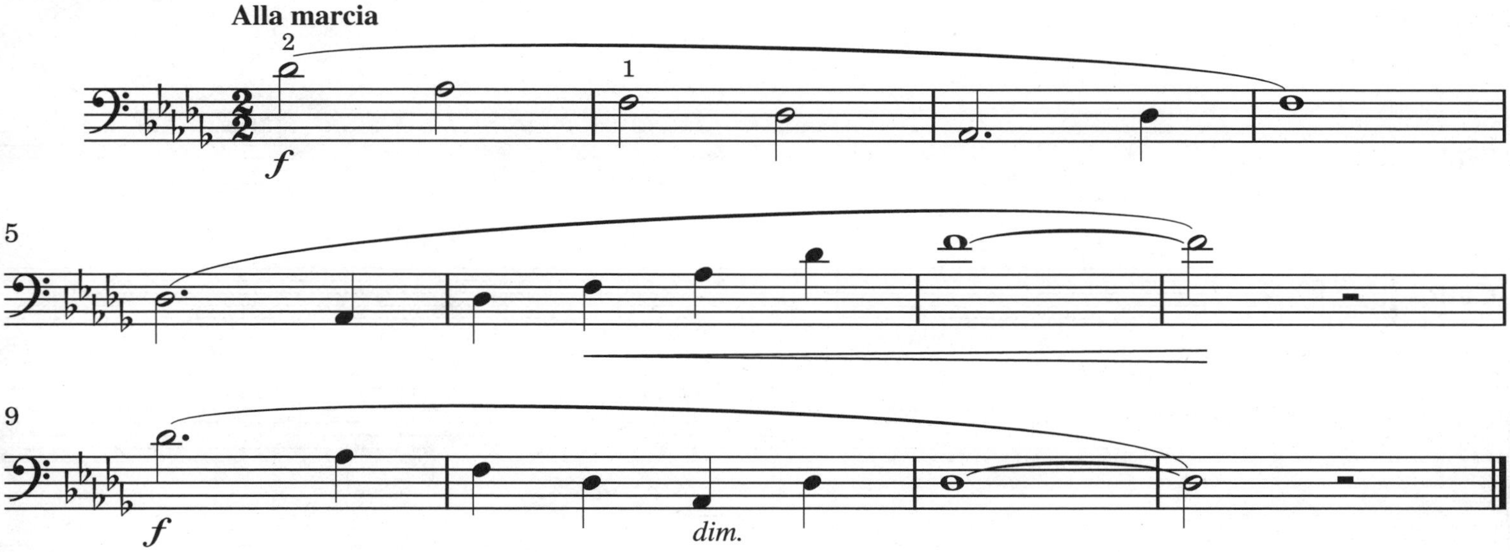

Alla marcia

f

f *dim.*

2. A♭/G♯ minor, B♭/A♯ minor, and E♭/D♯ minor scales use the same fingering combinations as their relative majors:

G♭ major

RH: 2 3 4 1 2 3 1 2 3 4 1 2 3 1 2
LH: 4 3 2 1 3 2 1 4 3 2 1 3 2 1 4

E♭ minor

RH: 3 1 2 3 4 1 2 3 1 2 3 4 1 2 3
LH: 2 1 4 3 2 1 3 2 1 4 3 2 1 3 2

Try each of the scales in all three forms, two hands, two octaves.

READING

1. Play the following viola and cello excerpts.

a. Set a reasonable tempo.

6

b.

Viola

Cello

4

Go to the PDM Web site for additional two-part viola excerpts.

2. Play these combinations: Violin I and violin II or violin I and viola.

WOLFGANG AMADEUS MOZART
(1756–1791)

3. Before playing, look for parallel and contrary motion between the parts. Play all three parts *very slowly*!

WOLFGANG AMADEUS MOZART
(1756–1791)

Molto Allegro

Violin II

Viola

Cello

5

p

p

p

9

4. Play the vocal lines of the Mozart excerpt as your teacher plays the accompaniment.

Die Zauberflöte

(Excerpt)

WOLFGANG AMADEUS MOZART, K. 620
(1756–1791)

5. Look for chord shapes.

Cantata No. 27

J. S. BACH

Sopr I

Sopr II

Alto

5

6. Notice parallel motion in Baritone parts.

7. Look for chord shapes and common tones.

a.

b.

KEYBOARD THEORY

1. In a major key, diatonic 7th chords fall into one of four categories.

Major 7th	Minor 7th	Major-Minor 7th	Half-Diminished 7th
I7	ii7	V7	vii°7
IV7	iii7		
	vi7		

Play the diatonic 7th chords in each white-key major scale as shown. Use the keys of C, D, E, F, G, and A.

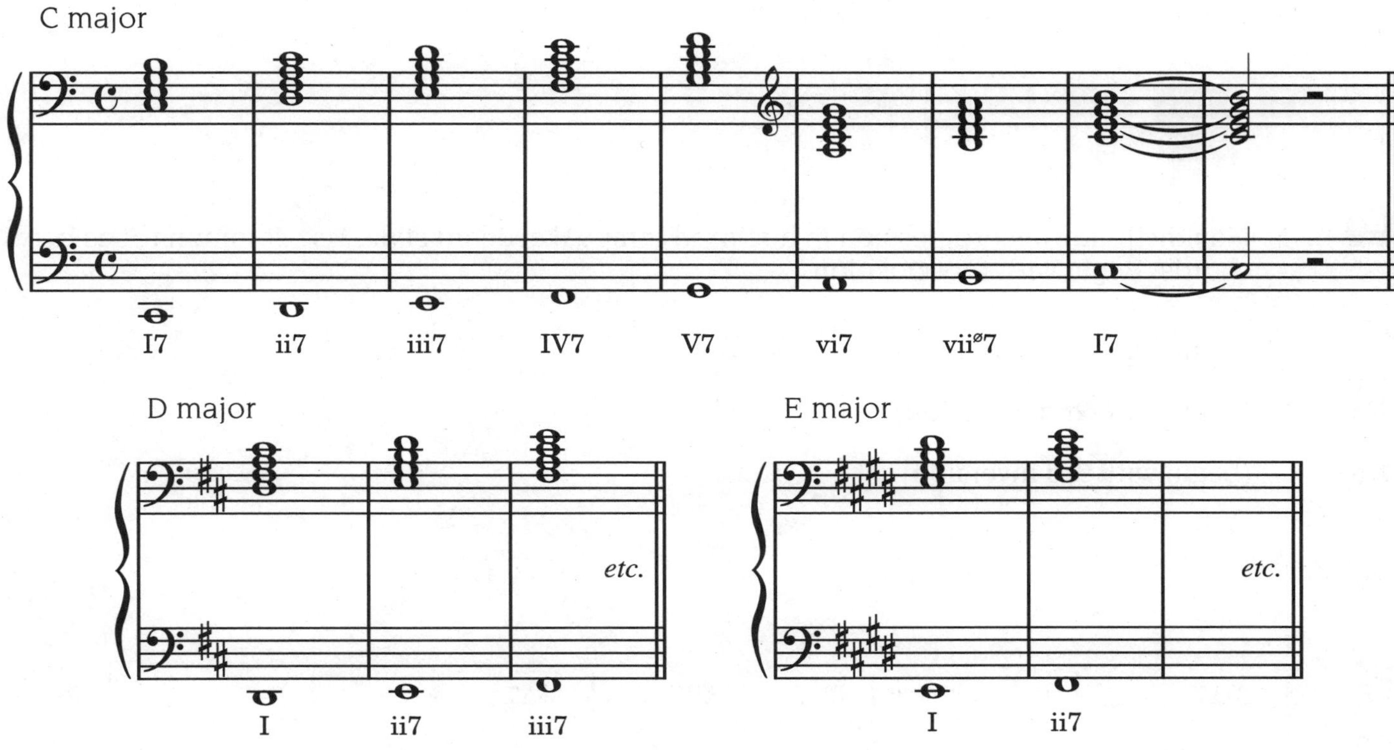

2. Play the following 7th chords in C minor. Notice the raised 7th degree in the i7 (creating a minor-major 7th chord).

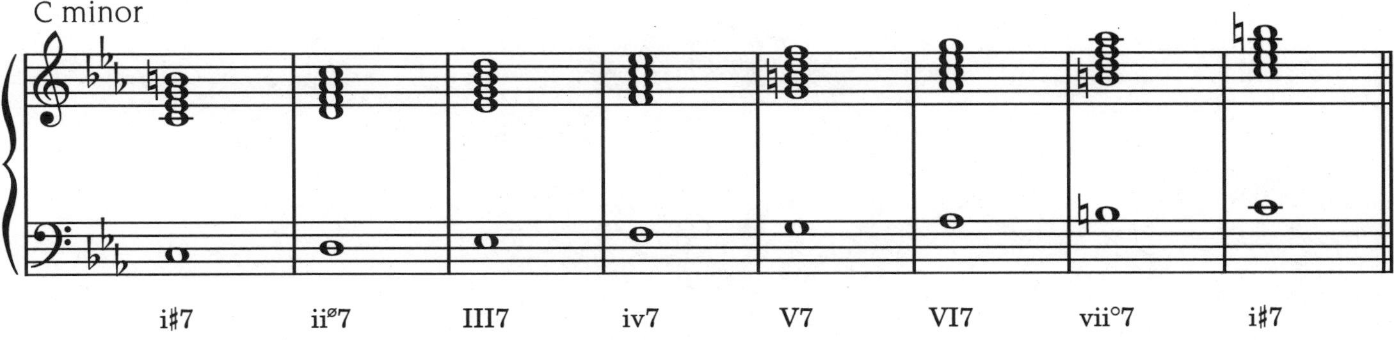

4. There are many ways to write lead sheet notation of 7th chords.

Key of C:	I7	C Δ7 or C maj 7
	ii7	D-7 / D min 7
	iii7	E-7 / E min 7
	IV7	F Δ7 / F maj 7
	V7	G7
	vi7	A-7 / A min 7
	vii^{ø}7	B-7♭5 / B min 7♭5

A designation of G^{sus} or G^{sus}C is a suspended 4th above the root. A triad with an added 6th is shown as C6 (CEGA).

5. Play the following progression in a relaxed tempo, keyboard style. Use common tones between chords. Begin with root position.

(begin with 1st inversion)

(begin with 2nd inversion)

(begin with 3rd inversion)

Ballad

4/4 E♭Δ7 | C-7 | B♭-7 E♭7 | A♭Δ7 F-7 | F-7 | B♭7 |

C-7 C-7/B♭ | A♭Δ7 A♭Δ7/G | F-7 | B♭7 | E♭Δ7 | E♭6 ||

HARMONIZATION

1. Accompany *Myrtilla* in a similar manner, varying the pattern as necessary for faster harmonic changes. Furnish missing harmonies before playing.

Myrtilla

THOMAS ARNE
(1710–1778)

2. Complete in the style indicated.

Take Me Out to the Ball Game

ALBERT VON TILZER
Words by Jack Norworth

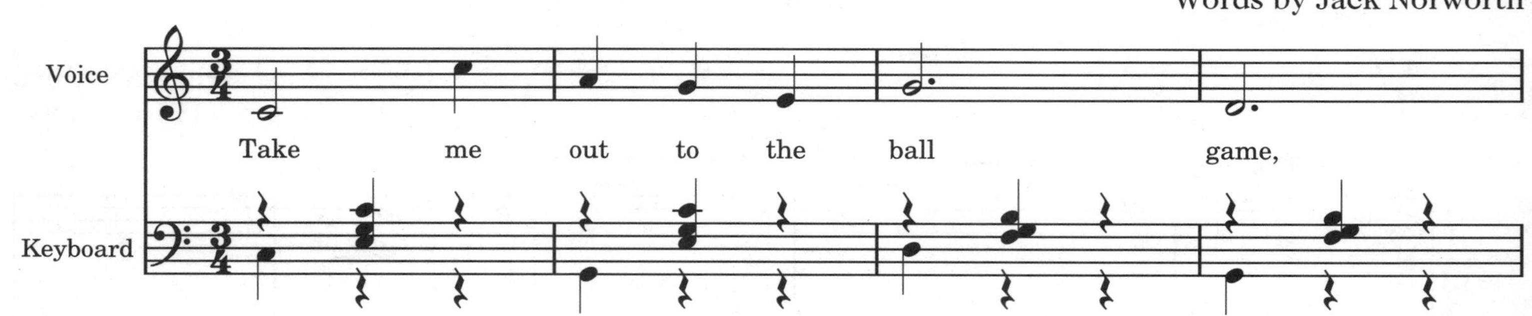
Voice
Keyboard
Take me out to the ball game,

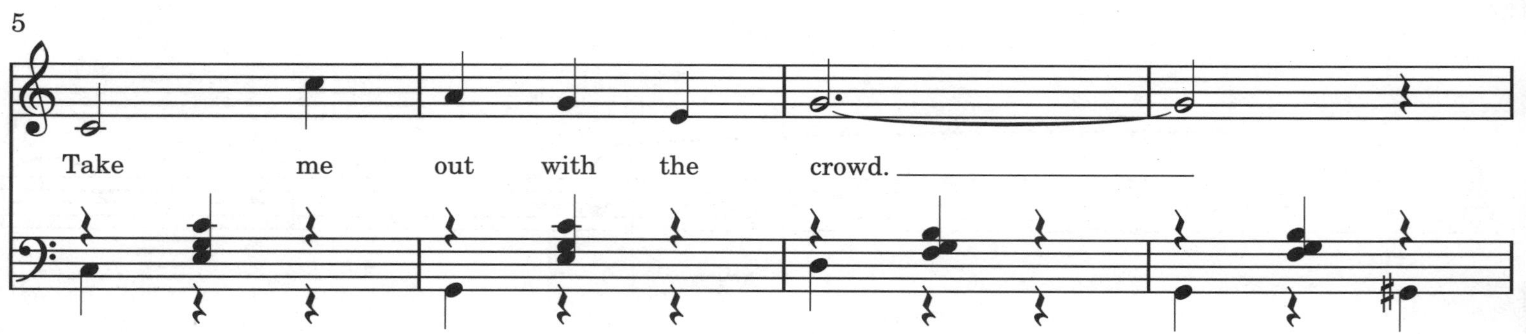
5
Take me out with the crowd.

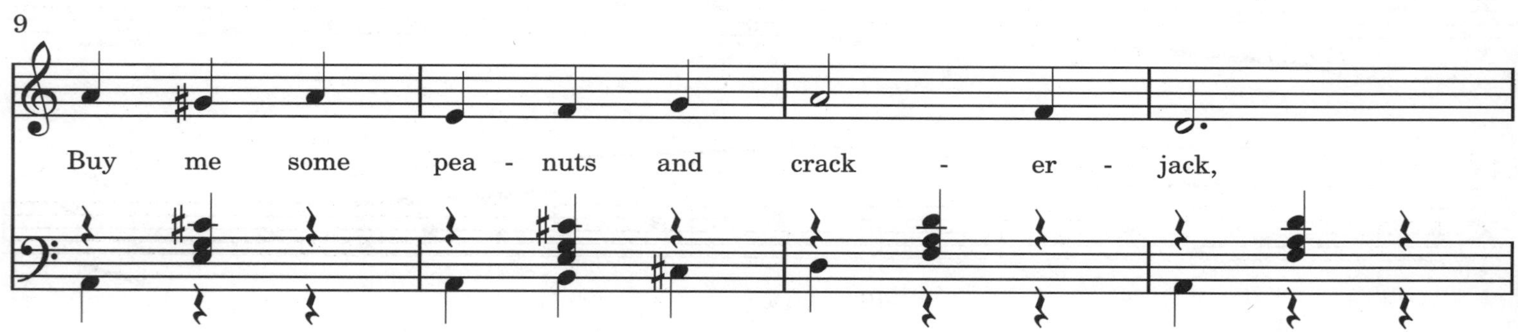
9
Buy me some pea - nuts and crack - er - jack,

13
I don't care if we nev - er get back, Let me

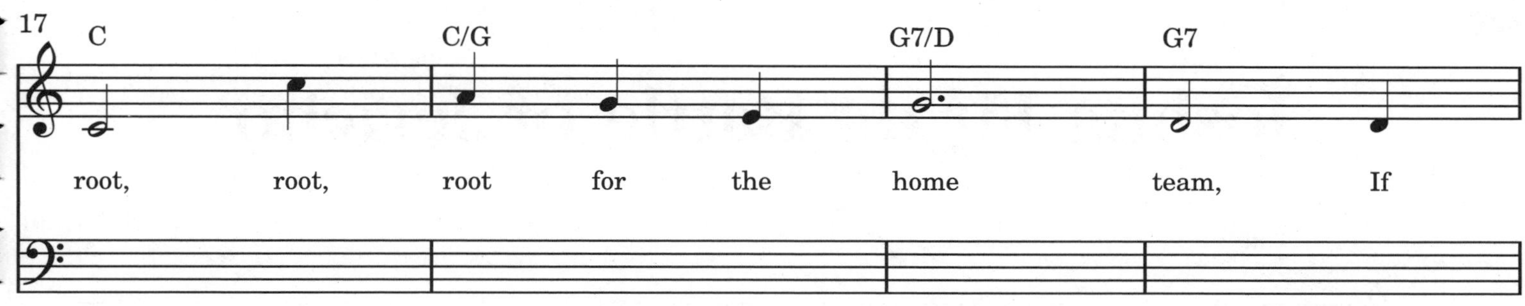
17
C
C/G
G7/D
G7
root, root, root for the home team, If

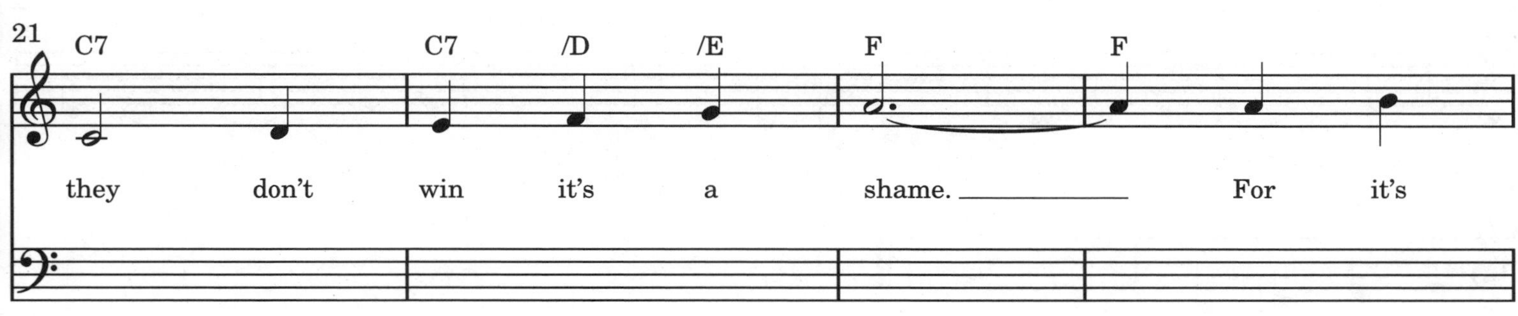
21
C7
C7
/D
/E
F
F
they don't win it's a shame. For it's

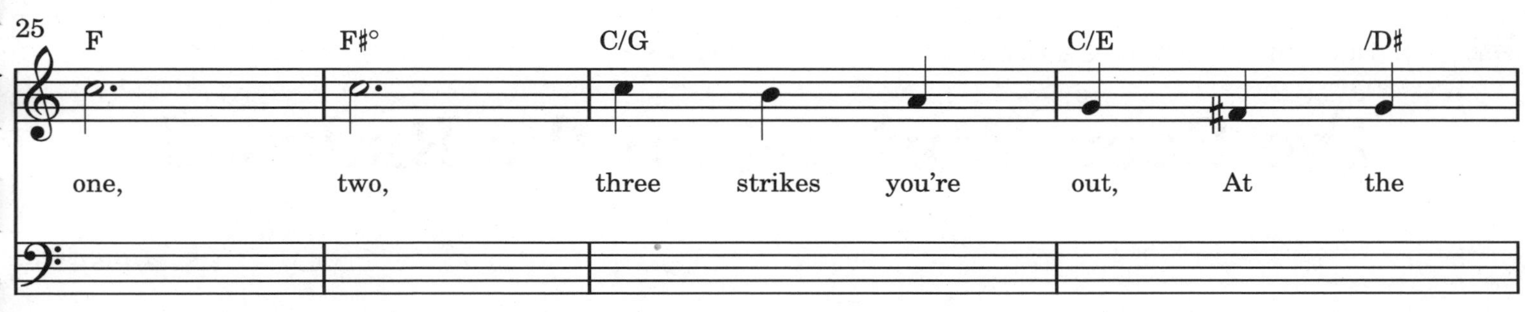
25
F
F#°
C/G
C/E
/D#
one, two, three strikes you're out, At the

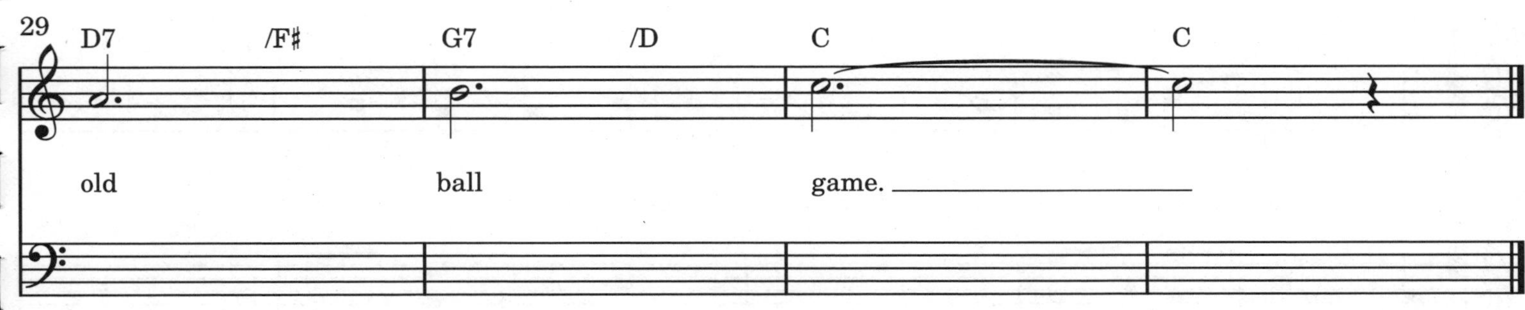
29
D7
/F#
G7
/D
C
C
old ball game.

3. Play verse by ear. Use modified keyboard style throughout.

Joshua Fit da Battle of Jericho

Spiritual

4. Determine harmonies and play in an appropriate style.

I've Been Working on the Railroad

American

5. A two-handed "root-chord" accompaniment works nicely.

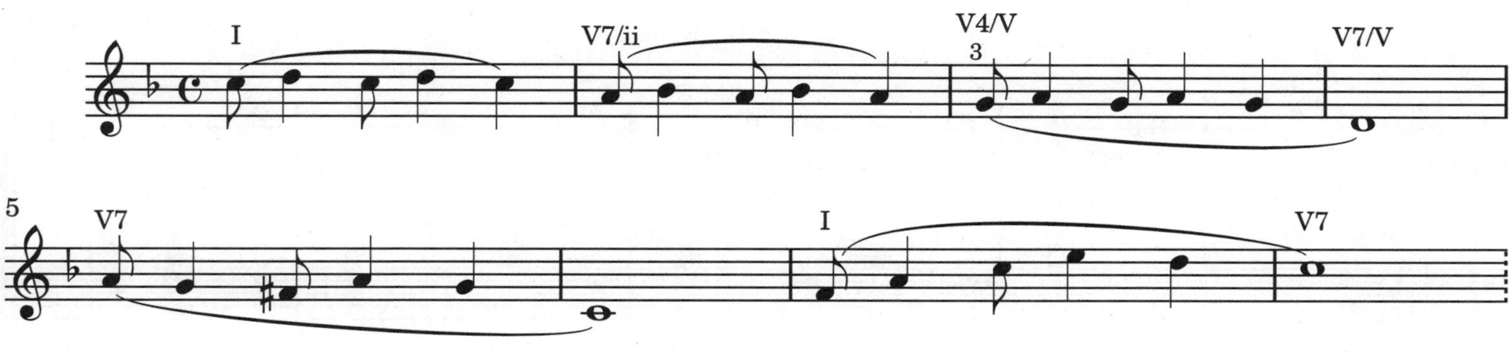

6. Use modified keyboard style with chords mostly on downbeats.

TRANSPOSITION

1. The following examples are to be transposed the interval of a tritone.

a. Transpose *up* to B♭ major.

b. Transpose *down* to G major.

K. RICHMOND

c. Transpose *down* to F major.

S. RAMAWY

2. Your singer has a cold—play this down a 4th in the key of D major.

Salti de terza

NICOLA VACCAJ
(1790–1848)

Andantino
Voice
Sem - pli - cet - ta tor - to - rel - la, che non ve - de il suo pe -
Piano
p

5

ri - glio, per fug - gir dal cru - do ar - ti - glio vo - la in grem - bo al cac - cia -

9

tor per fug - gir dal cru - do ar - ti - glio, per fug - gir dal cru - do ar -

13

ti - glio vo - la in grem-bo al cac - cia - tor, vo - la in grem-bo al cac - cia - tor.

Go to the PDM Web site for tutorial help with this transposition.

3. Ask a classmate to accompany you. Then switch parts.

a. Think the key of F major.

b. Think the key of E♭ major.

IMPROVISATION

1. Return to the Pachelbel *Sarabande* (page 303). Improvise a countermelody as your teacher or a partner plays the printed score. Use the following plan:

   Bars 1–8 Based on chord tones only. Countermelody should move in contrary motion to upper voice of printed score.

   Bars 9–12 Add passing tones and lower and/or upper neighbor tones.

   Bars 13–16 You are "on your own."

2. Improvise a two-handed accompaniment for each basic movement.

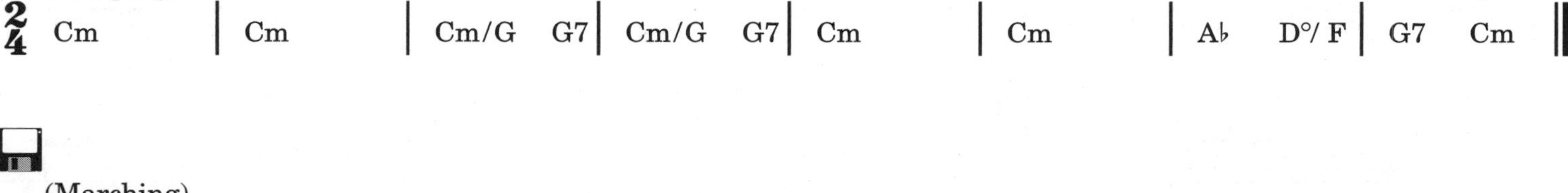

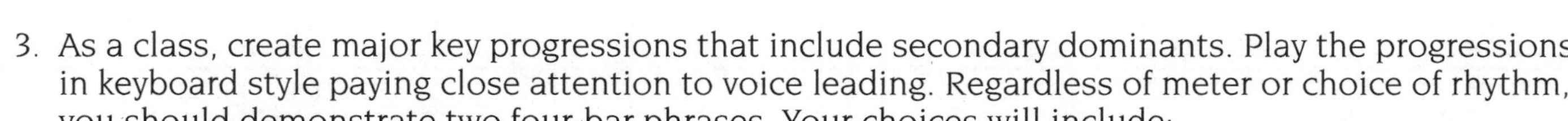

3. As a class, create major key progressions that include secondary dominants. Play the progressions in keyboard style paying close attention to voice leading. Regardless of meter or choice of rhythm, you should demonstrate two four-bar phrases. Your choices will include:

   - remainder of harmonies
   - key signature
   - meter
   - beginning shape of right hand
   - tempo (choose a term you don't often see)

   Example: I | V^4_3/vi | vi | IV | V^6_5/ii | ii | V7 | I |

   - Key— E♭ Major
   - Meter—$\frac{2}{4}$
   - Beginning shape of RH—first inversion
   - Tempo—Vite

   Then you would play:

COMPOSITION

1. Using diatonic seventh chords, arrange one of your favorite folk songs. The arrangement should be completely notated. Trade compositions with your classmates.

ENSEMBLE

1. Each part has some challenging "moments" but the end product is worth the effort.

Secondo
19
23
27
30
rit.
34
rit. ed ad lib al fine
rit.

Amazing Grace

Primo

Traditional
Arr. Leigh Kaplan

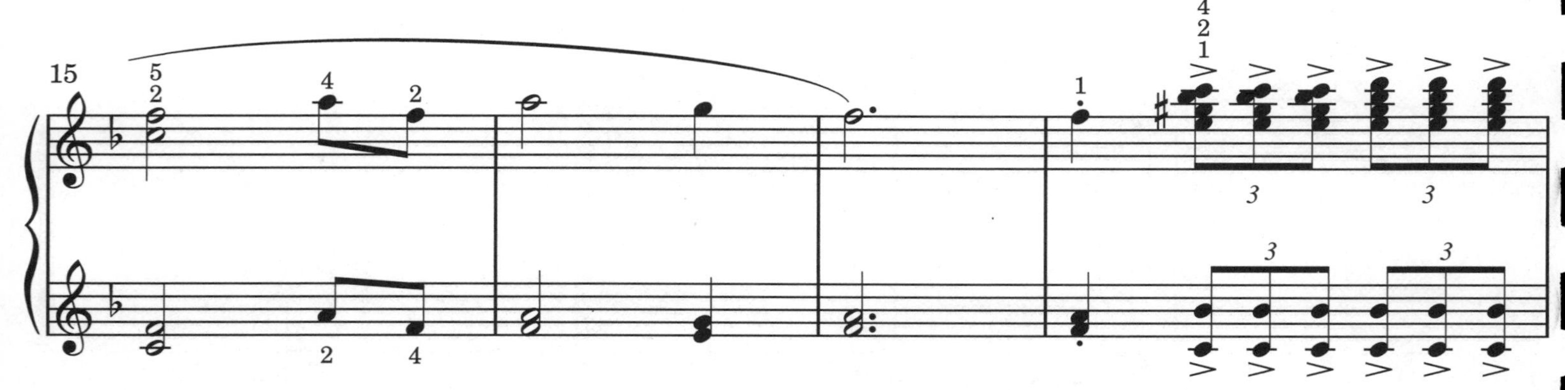

Primo
rit.
rit. ed ad lib al fine
R.H.
L.H.
rit.

SUBSEQUENT REPERTOIRE

1. Syncopation reigns! The eighth notes are even.

Carnival in St. Thomas

GLENDA AUSTIN

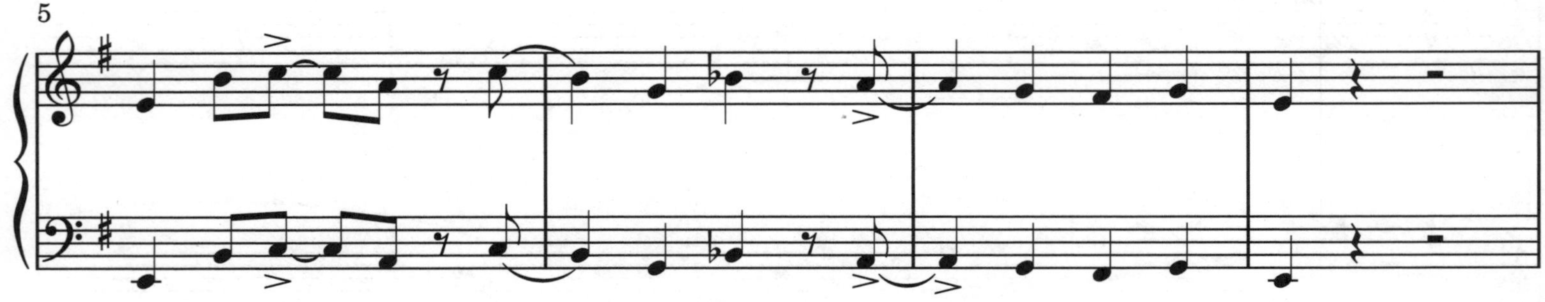

29
f

33
f

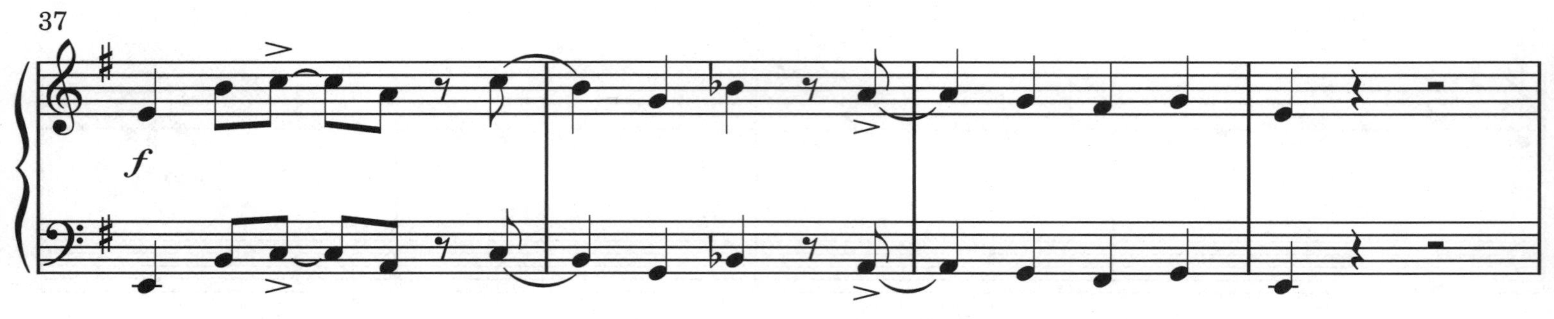
37
f

41
mp
mp

45
p
ff

2. Plan chord shapes silently. Note that the pedal is generally used throughout when performing.

II

from *Three-Score Set*

WILLIAM SCHUMAN
(1910 – 1992)

3.

Lydian Nocturne

ROBERT D. VANDALL

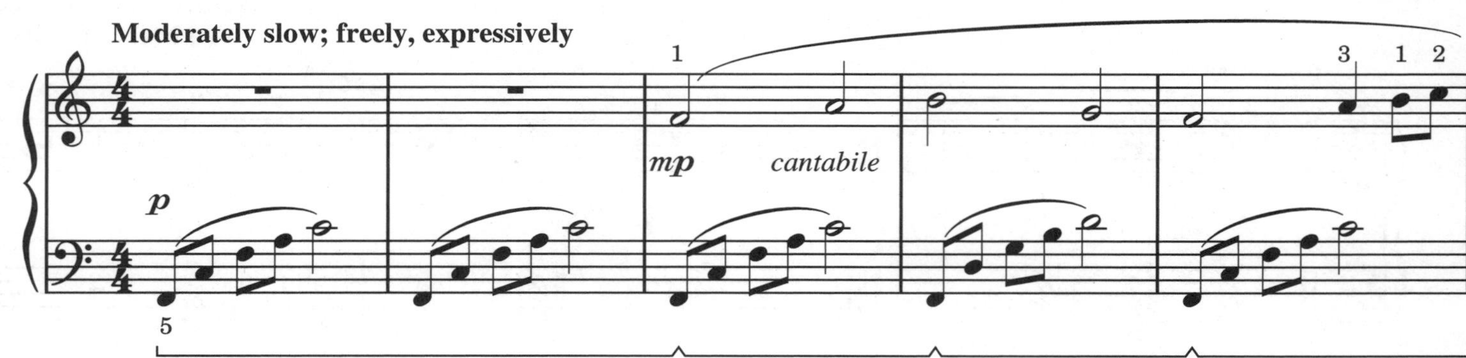

8va
p
cresc.
f
mf
dim.
(8va)
rit.
a tempo
mp
loco
rit.

13.

EXEMPLARY REPERTOIRE

TOPICS TO EXPLORE AND DISCUSS

RELATED SKILLS AND ACTIVITIES

SUBSEQUENT REPERTOIRE

Altered/Borrowed Triads

EXEMPLARY REPERTOIRE **Adagio** Daniel Steibelt

INQUIRY

1. Scan *Adagio*. Observe:

   - form
   - nonpivot modulation
   - ♯iv$^6_3$—Italian augmented 6th chord

   This triad is built on the raised 4th scale degree of the key. It consists of ♯4, ♭6, and an unaltered tonic. The triad usually occurs in first inversion, forming the augmented 6th between the bass and another voice. This interval resolves outward to the dominant octave.

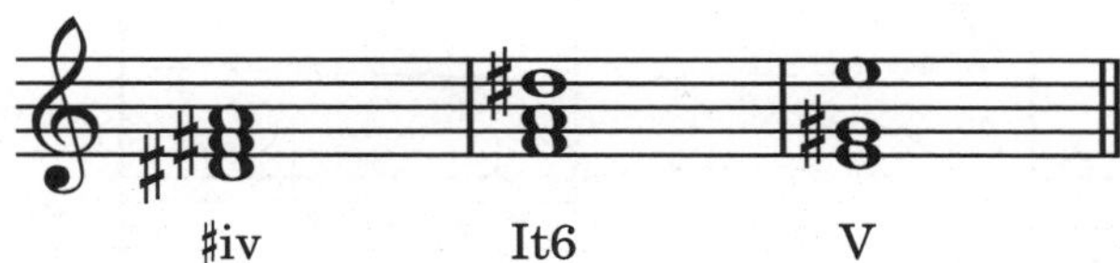

   - use of appoggiaturas

PERFORMANCE

1. Play the melodic line of the A section. Pay particular attention to the use of two-note slurs for appoggiaturas and notes of resolution.
2. Play the A section as written.
3. Play the B section. Listen carefully for proper voicing.
4. Play *Adagio* as written.

Adagio

DANIEL STEIBELT
(1765–1823)

TOPICS TO EXPLORE AND DISCUSS

- Daniel Steibelt
- Franz Anton Hoffmeister
- Karol Kurpinski
- Pandiatonicism

RELATED SKILLS AND ACTIVITIES

TECHNIQUE

1. C♯ minor and F♯ minor scales may use two different sets of fingerings. One of these uses the same fingering *combinations* as the relative major scale:

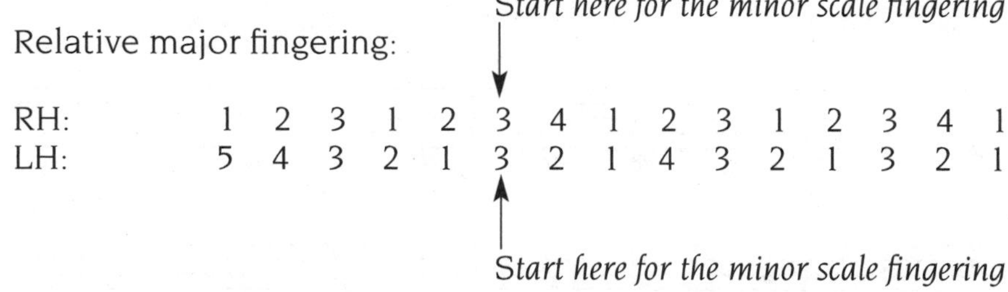

The other choice of fingering is related to the black-key-group principle:

For C♯ minor

RH:	2	3	1	2	3	4	1	2	3	1	2	3	4	1	2
LH:	3	2	1	4	3	2	1	3	2	1	4	3	2	1	3

For F♯ minor:

2	3	4	1	2	3	1	*etc.*
4	3	2	1	3	2	1	

2. Play the following scale in rhythm. Then play the scale in the key of B major.

3. Tap the rhythm before playing. Also play the scale in the key of G♭ major.

READING

1. The tenor clef positions middle C on the fourth line of the staff. Play the following violoncello excerpt.

2. [vocal tenor clef] is a vocal tenor clef. The actual sound is an octave lower than written.

a.

b.

3. Play all three parts of the Haydn *Psalm* 31.

Psalm 31

(Excerpt)

FRANZ JOSEPH HAYDN
(1732–1809)

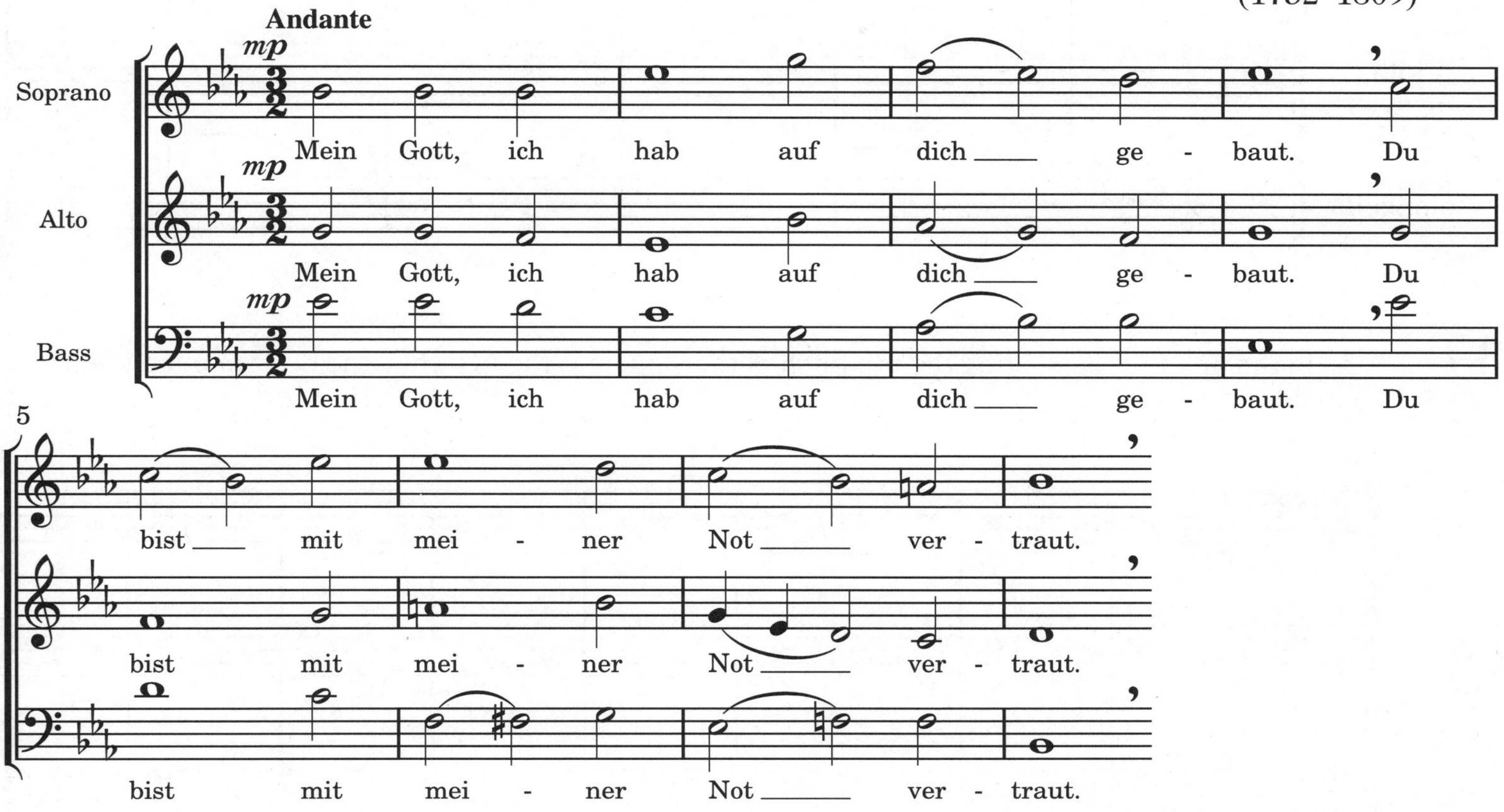

Andante

Soprano — *mp* — Mein Gott, ich hab auf dich ___ ge - baut. Du

Alto — *mp* — Mein Gott, ich hab auf dich ___ ge - baut. Du

Bass — *mp* — Mein Gott, ich hab auf dich ___ ge - baut. Du

5

bist ___ mit mei - ner Not ___ ver - traut.

bist mit mei - ner Not ___ ver - traut.

bist mit mei - ner Not ___ ver - traut.

4.

Soprano

Alto

Bass

5

Go to the PDM Web site for additional SAT and SAB examples.

5.

a. Look for chord shapes.

b. In the first four bars, bring the top pitch of the viola into the RH while the bottom pitch joins the cello in the LH.

c. Be careful of octave placement in the viola part.

Go to the PDM Web site for additional three-part open score with alto clef exercises.

6. Scan each example quickly. Look for:

- common tones
- chord shapes
- consecutive intervals (3rds, 6ths)
- key signatures
- rhythmic challenges

KEYBOARD THEORY

1. Borrowed chords use notes that are accidentals in the major key but would be diatonic in a minor key. The following example shows the borrowed triads most often used in a major key.

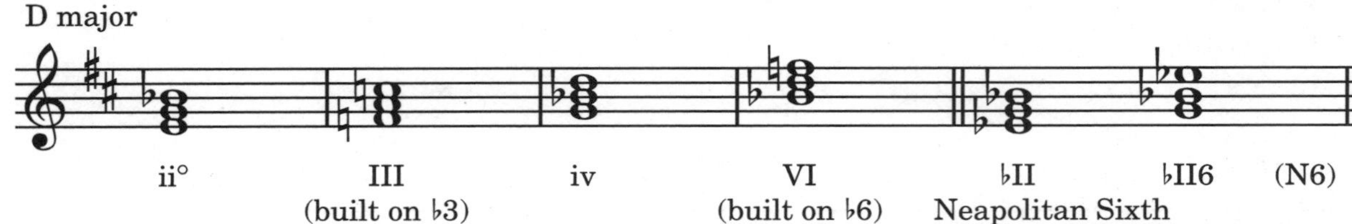

2. Play the following progressions using borrowed triads.

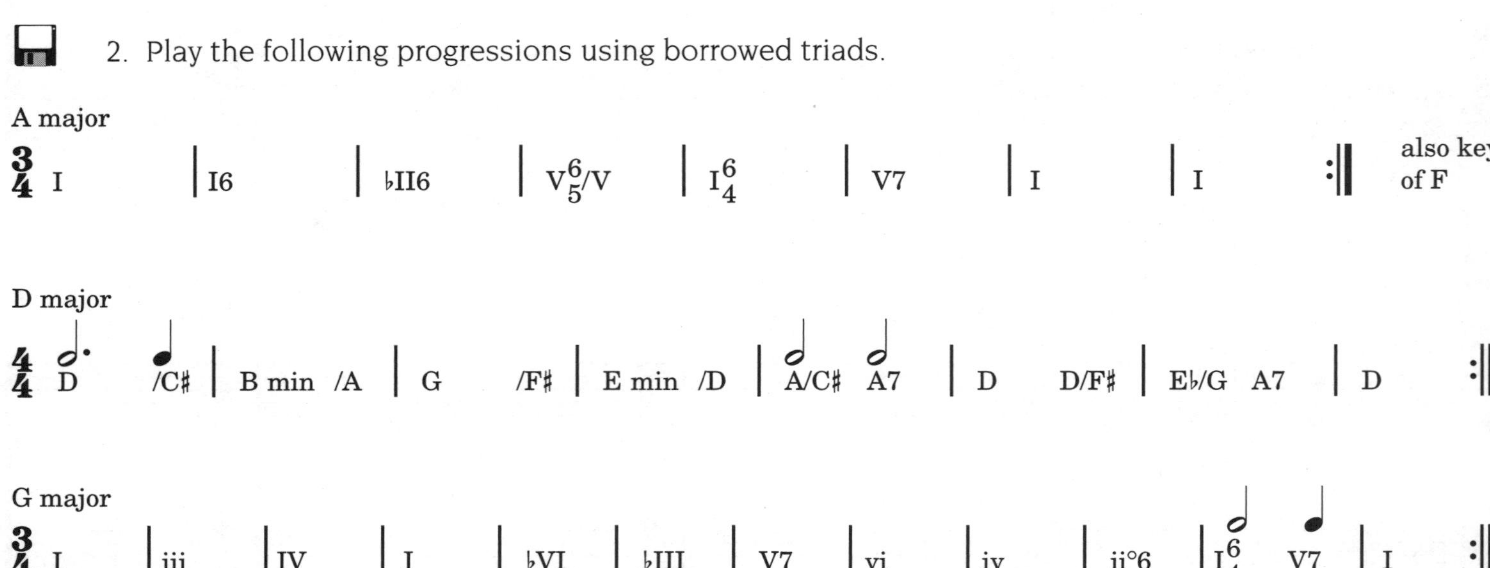

Go to the PDM Web site for a tutorial on these progressions.

HARMONIZATION

1. Use a two-handed "boom-chick-chick" accompaniment.

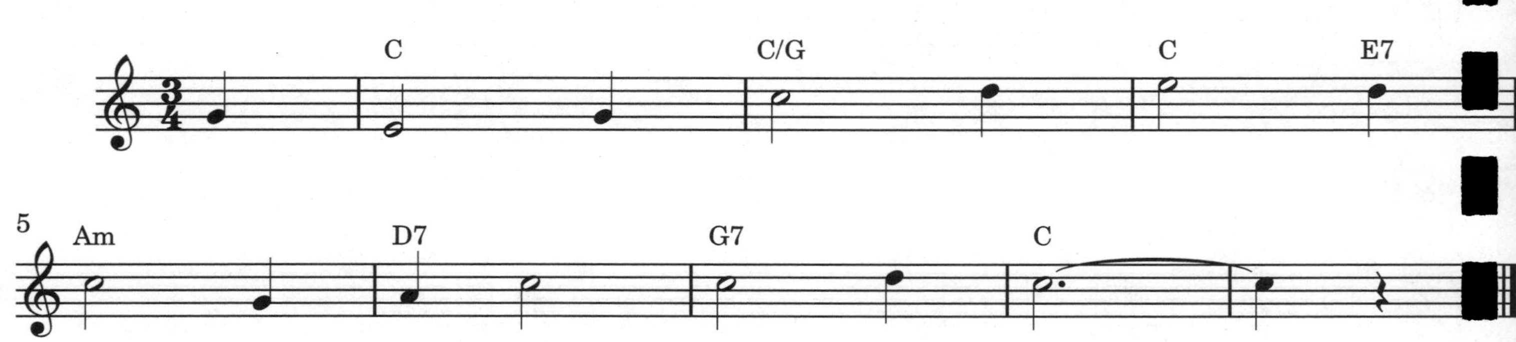

2. Use keyboard style.

3. Use keyboard style.

4. Use a traditional two-handed "root-chord" style.

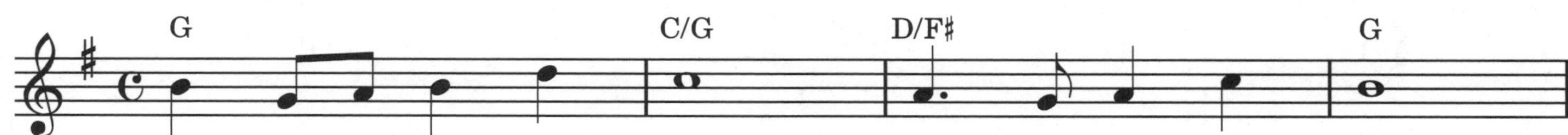

5. Harmonize the following and include vi, V7/IV, V7/V, and III. Play the verse by ear. Use keyboard style.

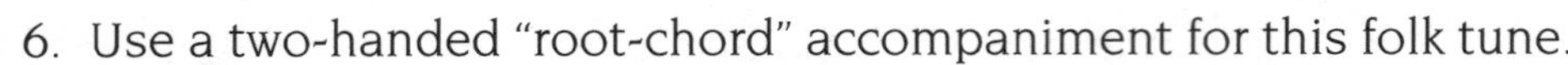

6. Use a two-handed "root-chord" accompaniment for this folk tune.

American

7. Play a two-handed accompaniment using the following progression.

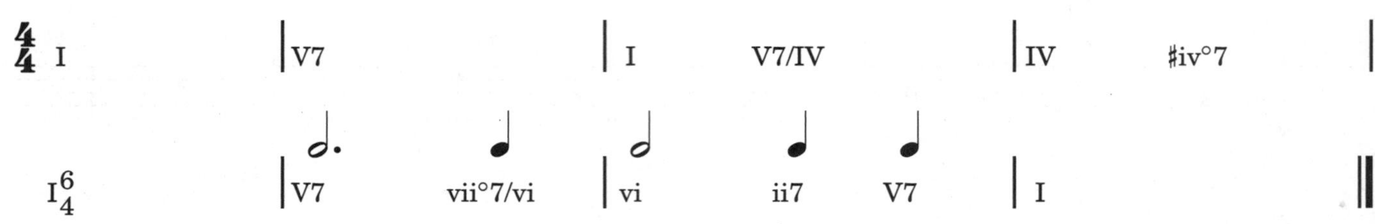

8. Add the melody to *Auld Lang Syne* and play in keyboard style.

Go to the PDM Web site for additional help with items 6 and 8.

TRANSPOSITION

1. The following examples are to be transposed an interval of a tritone.
   a. Transpose *up* to A major.

C. MORENUS

b. Transpose *up* to E♭ major.

C. MORENUS

2. Play the following B♭ clarinet. Even played as a duet, this is a challenge!

Scherzo

FRANZ ANTON HOFFMEISTER
(1754–1812)

3. Note clef changes in bassoon. Choose a partner and play as a duet. Don't forget to trade parts.

Paysage Musical

(Excerpt)

KAROL KURPINSKI
(1785–1857)

4. Transpose the *Etude in* D to A♭ major.

Etude in D

LUDVIG SCHYTTE, Op. 108, No. 7
(1848–1909)

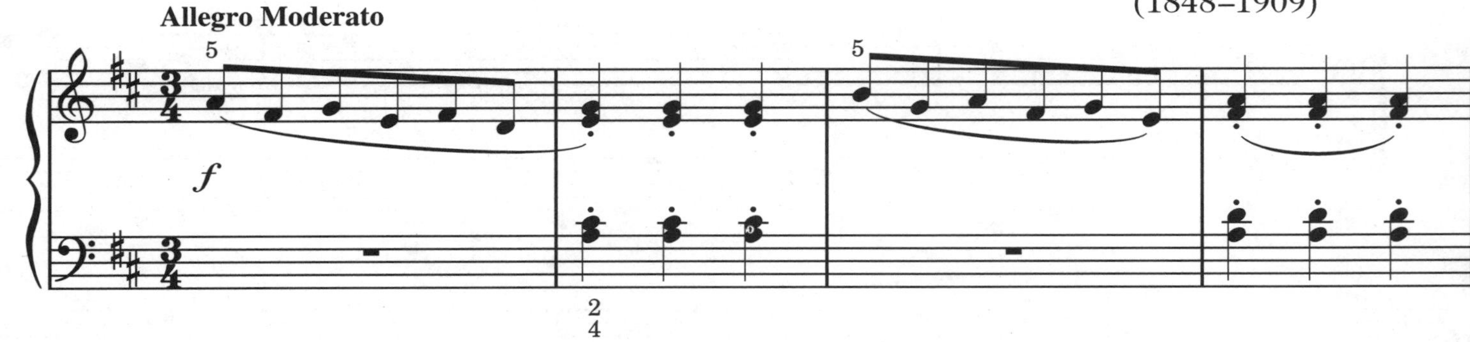

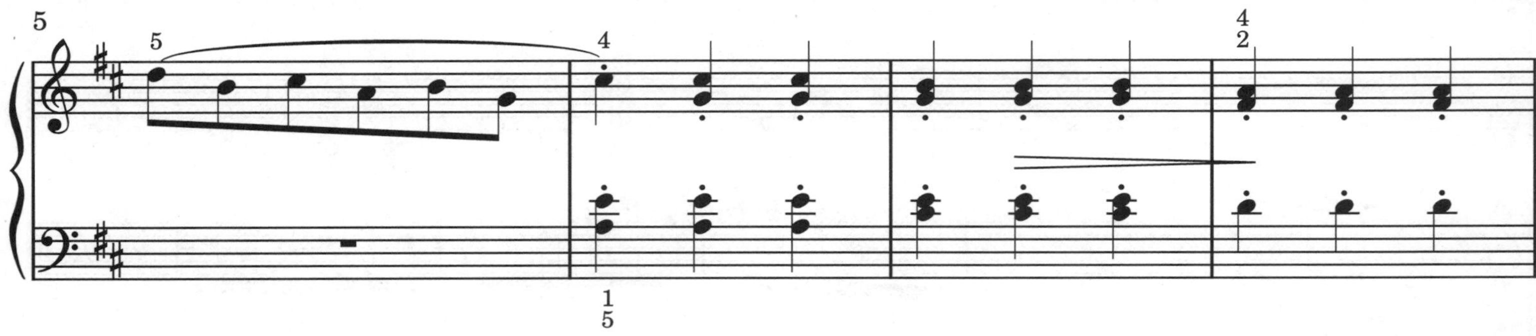

Go to the PDM Web site for extra assistance with this transposition.

IMPROVISATION

1. Create improvised music for the following technique exercises in classical ballet.

   a. At the barre: *Petite battements sur le cou-de-pied* (moderately fast $\frac{4}{4}$ meter; 2-bar introduction and 32 bars of exercise).

   b. In centre floor: *Port de bras* and *révérence* (slow $\frac{3}{4}$ meter; 2-bar introduction and 32 bars of exercise with the appropriate *révérence* conclusion).

Use the following form for each:

Intro.	—	2 bar
A	—	8 bar
A	—	8 bar
B	—	8 bar
A	—	8 bar
Révérence	—	2 bar

2. Return to the progressions you created in Chapter 12 (page 323). Choose a partner and create improvisation duets—one plays the progression, the other improvises a melody. As before, clearly demonstrate harmonic content, meter, and two four-bar phrases.

ENSEMBLE

Rondeau

from *First Suite*, first movement
(The PBS "Masterpiece Theatre" Theme)

JEAN JOSEPH MOURET
(1682–1738)
Arr. Weekley and Arganbright

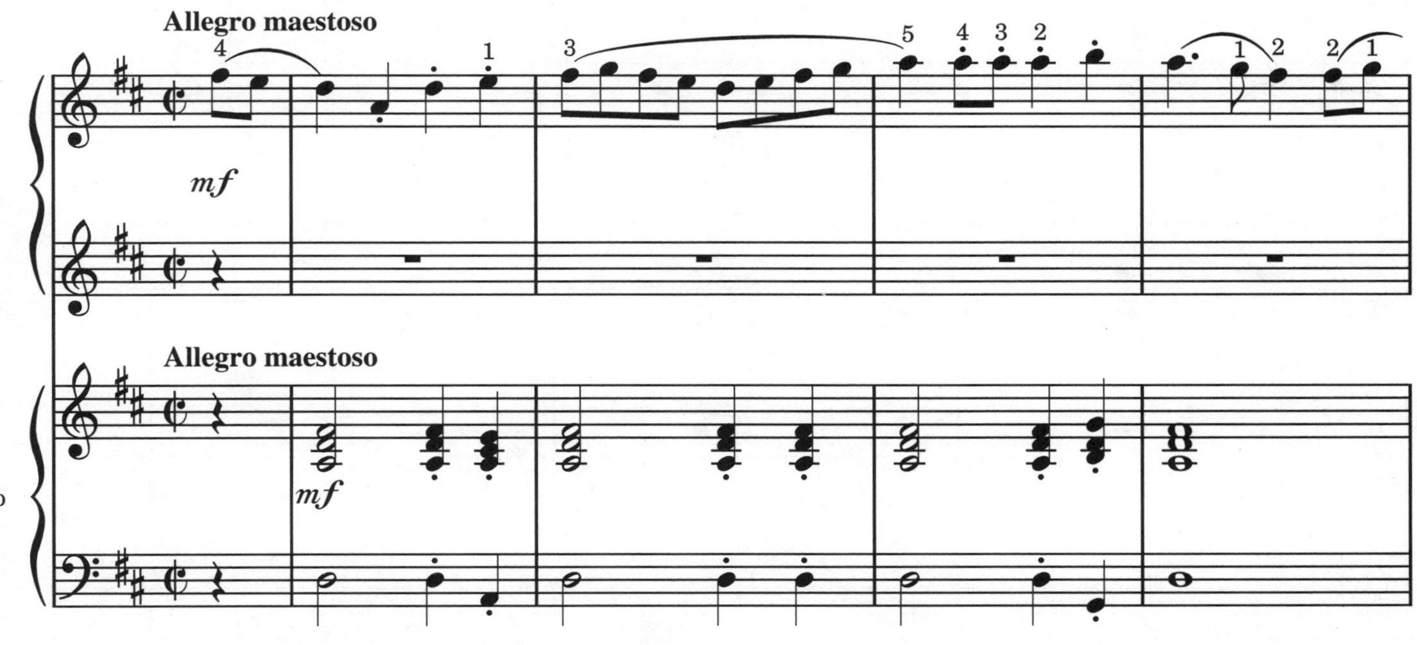

8va
(8va)
(8va)
mp

17
mp
21
mf
25
mf

Meno mosso
8va
ff
Meno mosso

COMPOSITION

Create a rhythmic invention. In the composition, have at least two voices with clear entrances of the "subject." Assign particular sounds (clicking a pair of pencils together, dragging a bench, slamming a book on a desk, rattling a set of keys, etc.) to particular note values. You might refer to the rhythm drill on page 66 for sound ideas. Your title might include the word "invention" if written for two parts or the word "sinfonia" if written for three parts.

After distribution to your classmates, become the composer/conductor and lead the class in a performance.

SUBSEQUENT REPERTOIRE

1. The A section of *Bright Orange* is divided into the following groups of measures: 3 + 3 + 3 + 6.

   - Divide the class into four groups and *patsch* the rhythm of this section in a round-robin fashion.
   - Determine the sections and groups of measures for the balance of the piece. *Patsch*.
   - Play left-hand triads while tapping the right-hand rhythm patterns on a flat surface.
   - Play as written.

Bright Orange

from *Sketches in Color*

ROBERT STARER
(1924–2001)

21
1
2
27
3
f
32
ff
mf
38
f
43
1
8va
ff
sfz

2. This piece has been labeled as pandiatonic. Do you agree? Why or why not?

Chartreuse

ELOISE RISTAD

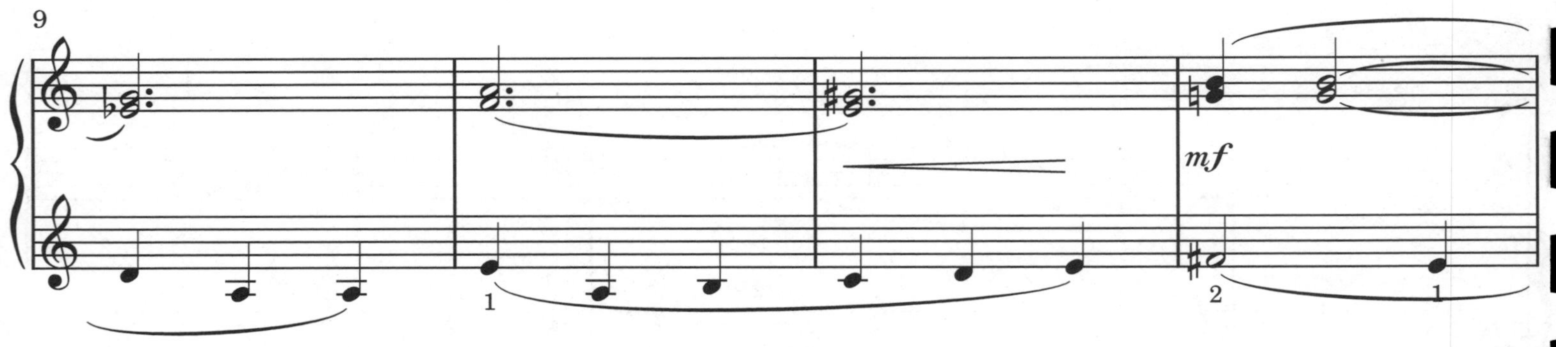

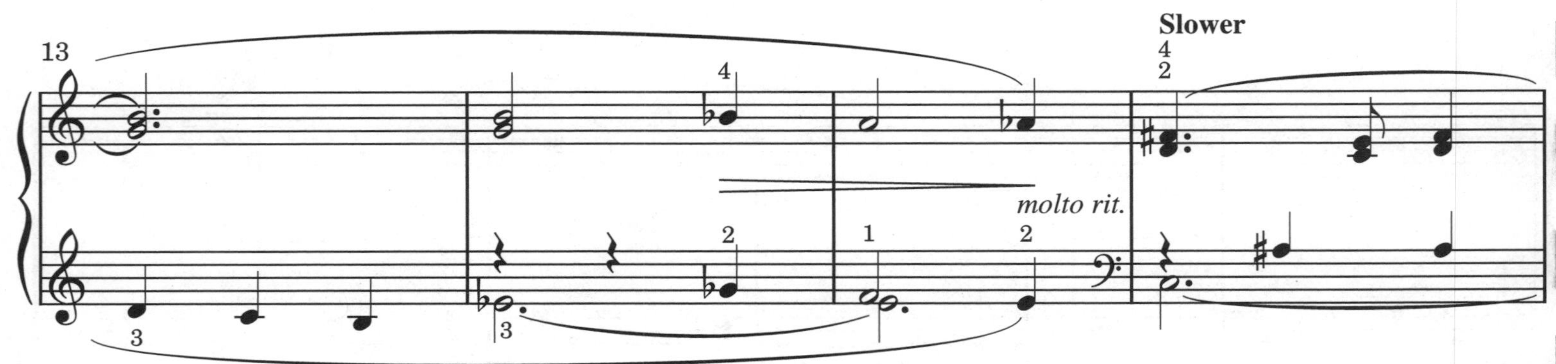

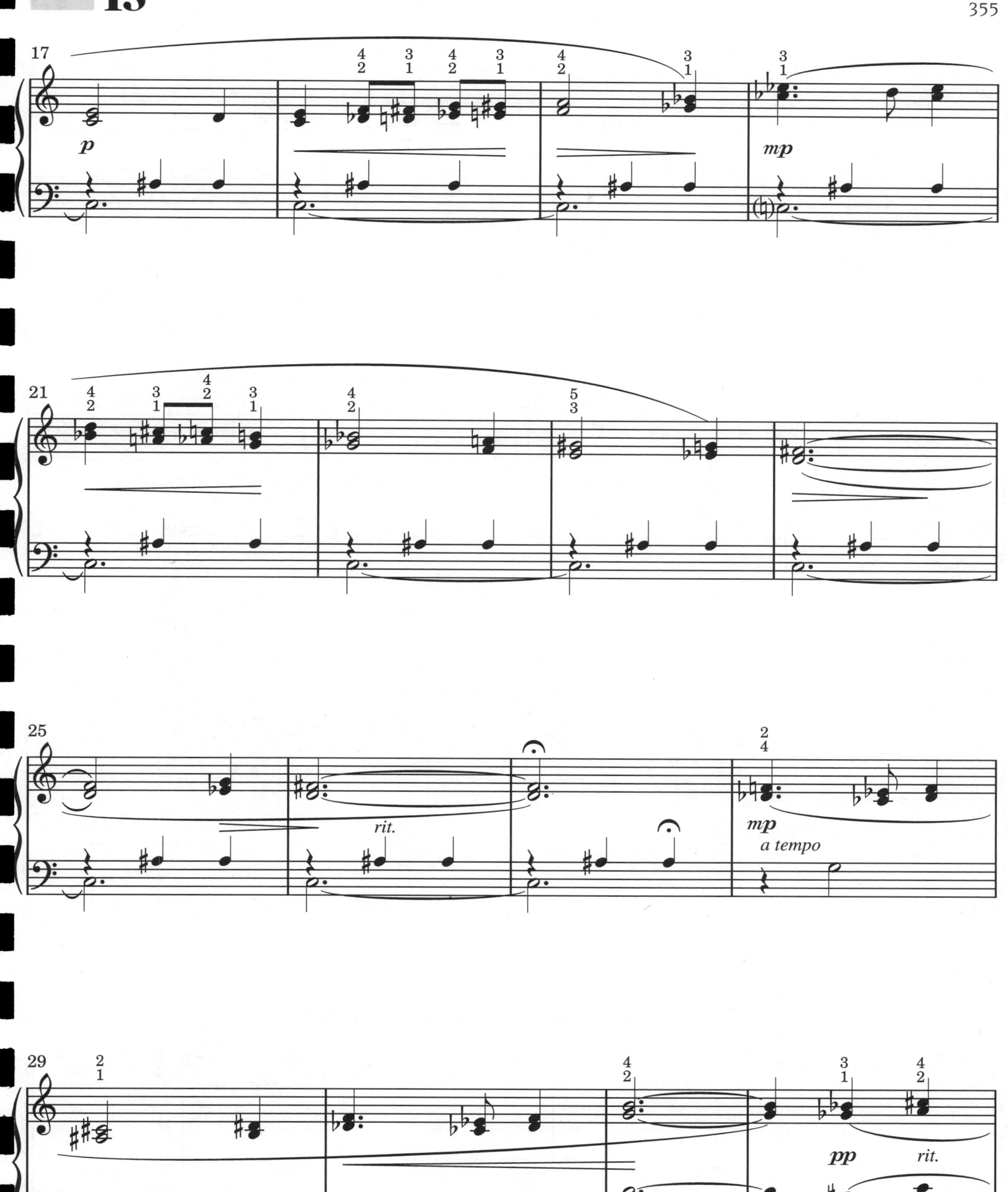
17
p
mp
21
25
rit.
mp
a tempo
29
pp
rit.

33
rit.
mp
a tempo

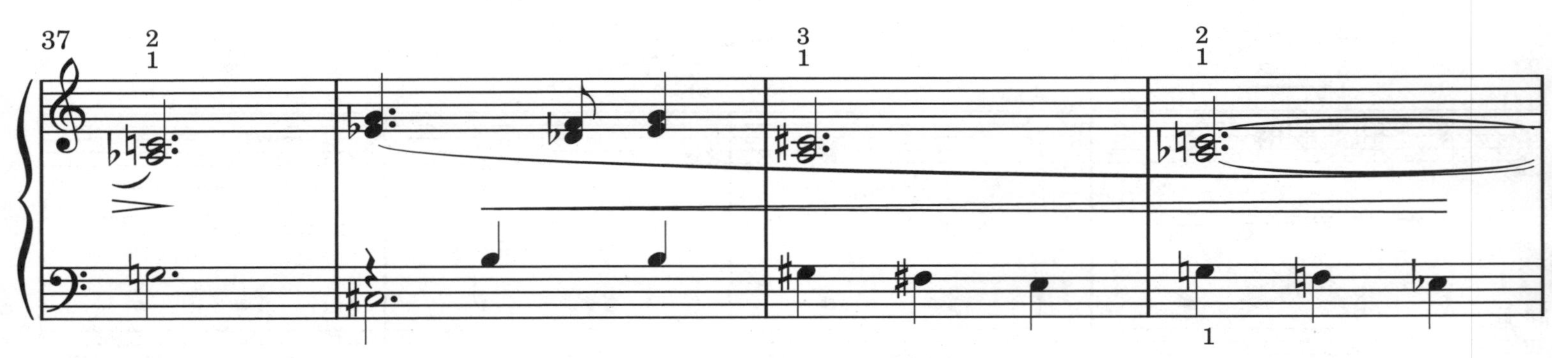
37

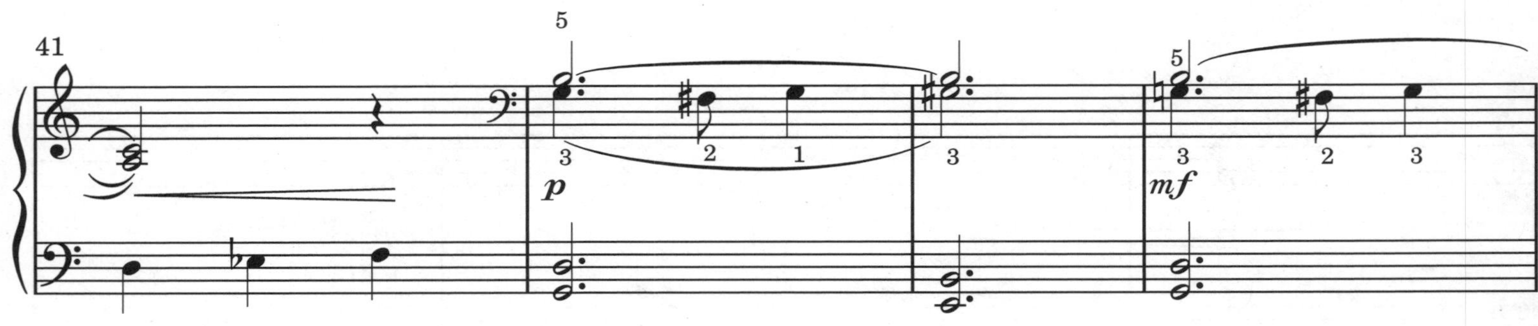
41
p
mf

45
rit.
mp
mf
p
8va

3. Carefully mark shifts, cross-overs, etc., in your score. A workable fingering doesn't "work" if it is constantly changing!

Progress

JOHANN FRIEDRICH BURGMÜLLER
(1806–1874)

14.

EXEMPLARY REPERTOIRE

TOPICS TO EXPLORE AND DISCUSS

RELATED SKILLS AND ACTIVITIES

SUBSEQUENT REPERTOIRE

Altered Seventh Chords/ Extended Harmonies (Ninth, Thirteenth)

EXEMPLARY REPERTOIRE **Prelude in A-flat Major, Op. 43** Muzio Clementi

INQUIRY

1. Scan *Prelude in A-flat Major.* Observe:

   - chord shapes within arpeggios
   - a type of "sigh" motive in bars 2, 4, 6, and 8
   - harmonic analysis
   - augmented sixth chord

PERFORMANCE

1. Block the arpeggiated chords throughout:

2. Add the written LH to the blocked chords.

3. Play as written.

Prelude in A-Flat Major

MUZIO CLEMENTI, Op. 43
(1752–1832)

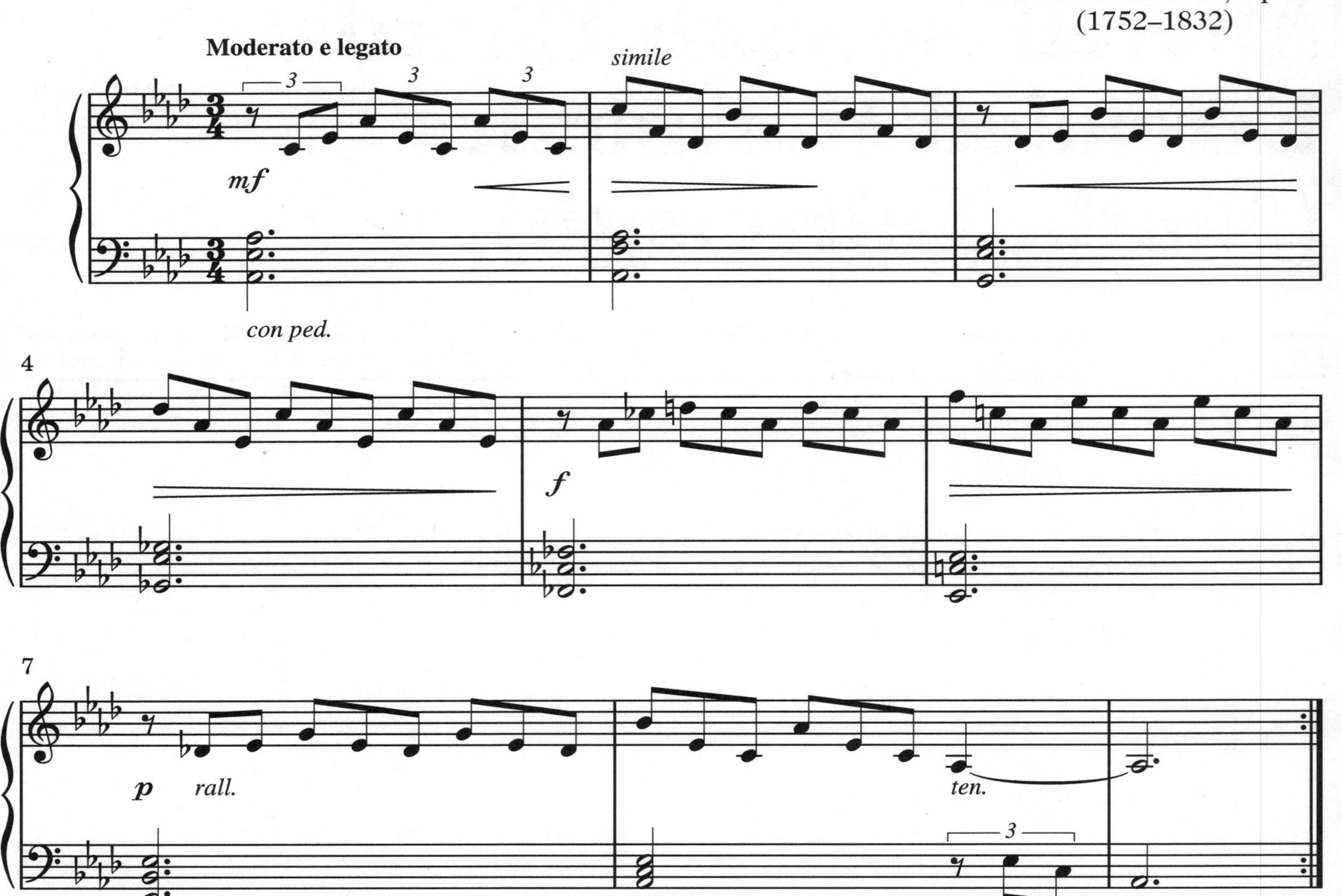

TOPICS TO EXPLORE AND DISCUSS

- François Devienne
- Arletta O'Hearn
- John Funkhouser
- Lynn Freeman Olson

RELATED SKILLS AND ACTIVITIES

TECHNIQUE

1. The following are traditional fingerings for B♭ and E♭ major scales. Note the left hand.

B♭ Major
RH: 4 1 2 3 1 2 3 4 1 2 3 1 2 3 4
LH: 3 2 1 4 3 2 1 3 2 1 4 3 2 1 3

E♭ Major
RH: 3 1 2 3 4 1 2 3 1 2 3 4 1 2 3
LH: 3 2 1 4 3 2 1 3 2 1 4 3 2 1 3

Away from the keyboard on any flat surface, play these scales ascending and descending. Then play slowly on the keyboard as you watch the finger numbers.

2. Review the white-key major scales. Start with C and repeat in the keys of D, E, F, G, A, and B major.

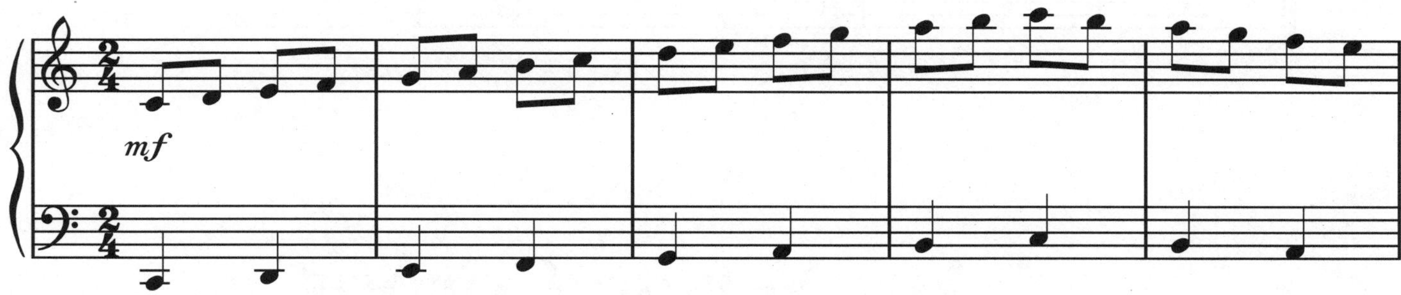

3.

Prelude in G Minor

MUZIO CLEMENTI, Op. 43
(1752–1832)

READING

1. Play different combinations of the SATB excerpts (SAT, ATB, STB, SATB).

a.

b.

Ave Verum Corpus

W. A. MOZART

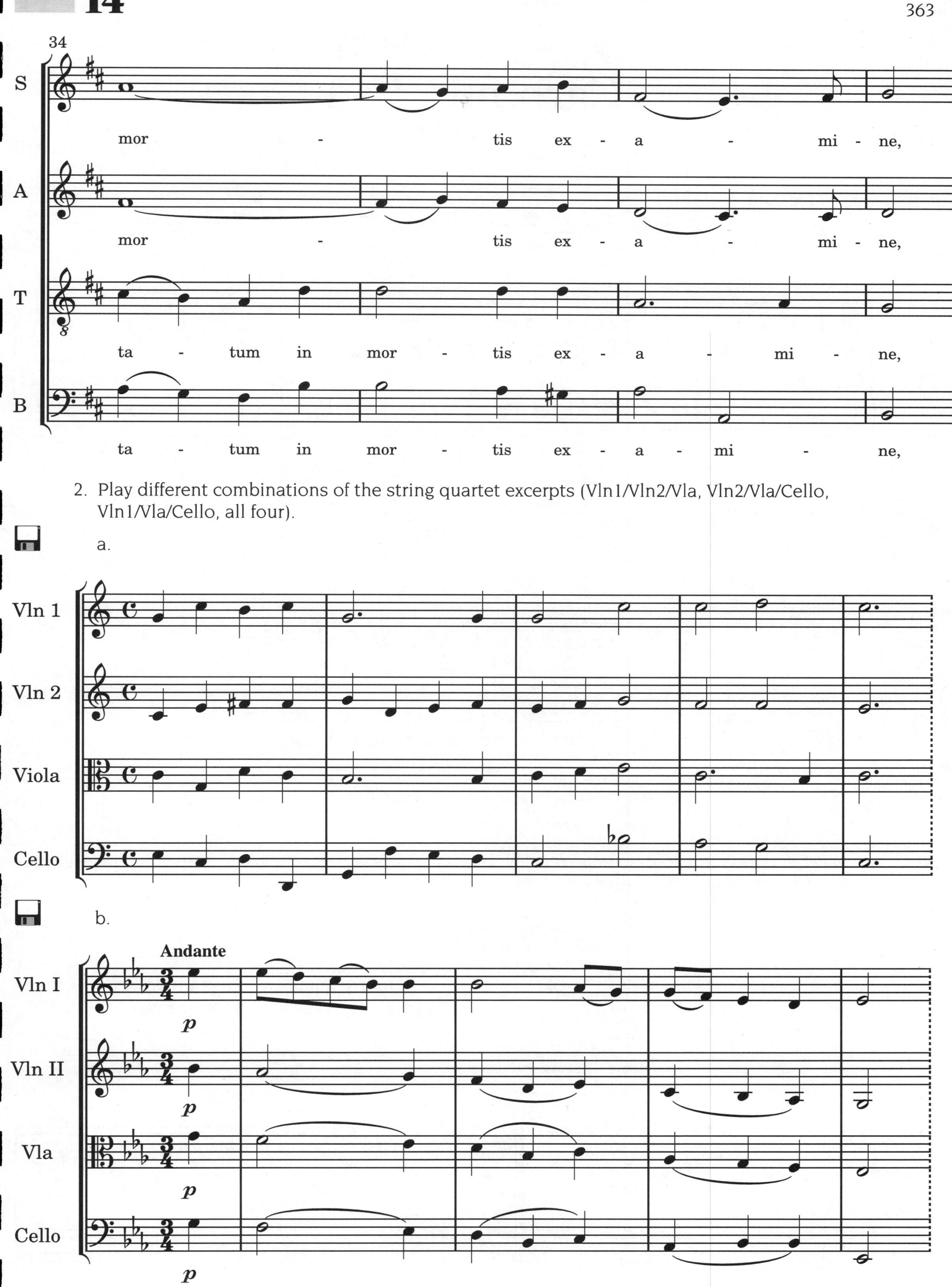

2. Play different combinations of the string quartet excerpts (Vln1/Vln2/Vla, Vln2/Vla/Cello, Vln1/Vla/Cello, all four).

a.

b.

3. Determine fingering before playing these accompaniment excerpts.

Caro mio ben

(Excerpts)

GIUSEPPE GIORDANI
(1753–1798)

4. Play the right-hand accompaniment as blocked chords first. Then choose a partner and play as written. Don't forget to switch parts.

Sonate

(Excerpt)

LUDWIG van BEETHOVEN, Op. 24, No. 5
(1770–1827)

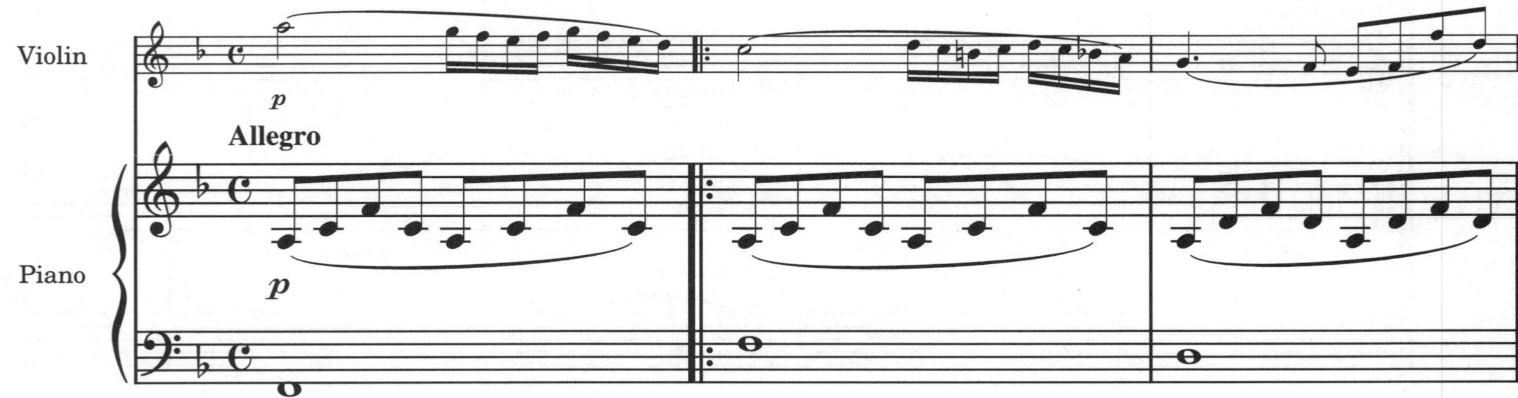

Go to the PDM Web site for many more reading examples.

KEYBOARD THEORY

1. Altered 7th chords fall into one of two categories—those that are borrowed from the parallel minor and those that tonicize a chord diatonic to the key (secondary dominants—V7 of iii and so on). The following example shows both types.

Play the following progression in the key indicated. Move to the closest chord possible.

D major

$\frac{3}{4}$ I | V7/IV | iv | iiø7 | I^{6}_{4} | V7 | vii°7 | I ‖

2. Augmented 6th chords fall into a category of altered 7ths. The Italian is actually a triad, but in first inversion the sound is that of a dominant 7th chord. The German, Italian, and French augmented 6ths all contain a ♯4 of the key, and this tone acts as leading tone to the dominant.

♯iv	Italian	(♯6)	contains ♯4, ♭6, tonic
♯iv7	German	$(^{\sharp 6}_{5})$	contains ♯4, ♭6, tonic, ♭3
ii7	French	$(\begin{smallmatrix}\sharp 6\\4\\3\end{smallmatrix})$	contains 2, ♯4, ♭6, tonic
♯ii7	German	$(\begin{smallmatrix}\sharp 6\\\sharp 4\\3\end{smallmatrix})$	contains ♯2, ♯4, ♭6, tonic (doubly augmented resolves to I^{6}_{4})

Spell augmented 6th chords in the keys given; then play in the proper inversion and resolve. The doubly augmented 6th is the only one resolving to I $^6_4$; the others resolve to V.

Example: Key of F, German

Spell: B♮ D♭ F A♭ / Play:

or

Spell: G♯ B♮ D♭ F / Play:

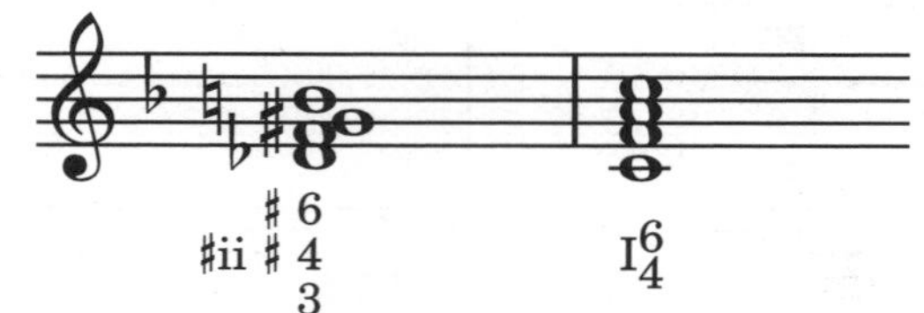

The sound is identical until the chord of resolution.

Key of A major—German | Key of D major—French | Key of G major—French

Key of B♭ major—Italian | Key of E♭ major—German | Key of A♭ major—Italian

Go to the PDM Web site for more drill on augmented 6th chords.

3. Extended harmonies add a new dimension to blues improvisation. In the example below, notice which chord members are included with each harmony. This voicing is standard for blues when using harmonies that go beyond triads and 7ths.

Keyboard players often omit roots of chords when improvising in a blues style. The following chords are referred to as "non-root" voicing.

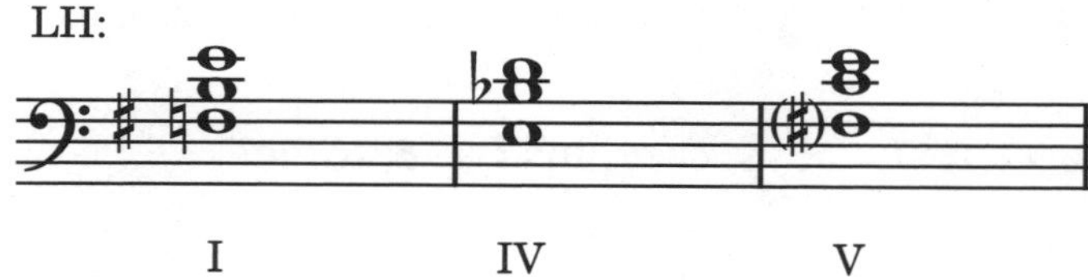

HARMONIZATION

1. For each of the melodic excerpts below choose what you feel would be an appropriate accompaniment style. Plan for changes in harmonic rhythm.

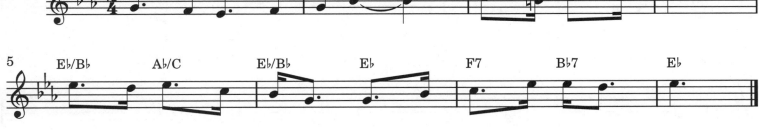

2. Use non-root chords to harmonize. Refer back to page 366 if necessary.

St. Louie Blues

W. C. HANDY
(1873–1958)

3. Use a two-handed accompaniment as you sing.

My Wild Irish Rose

CHAUNCEY OLCOTT
(1858–1932)

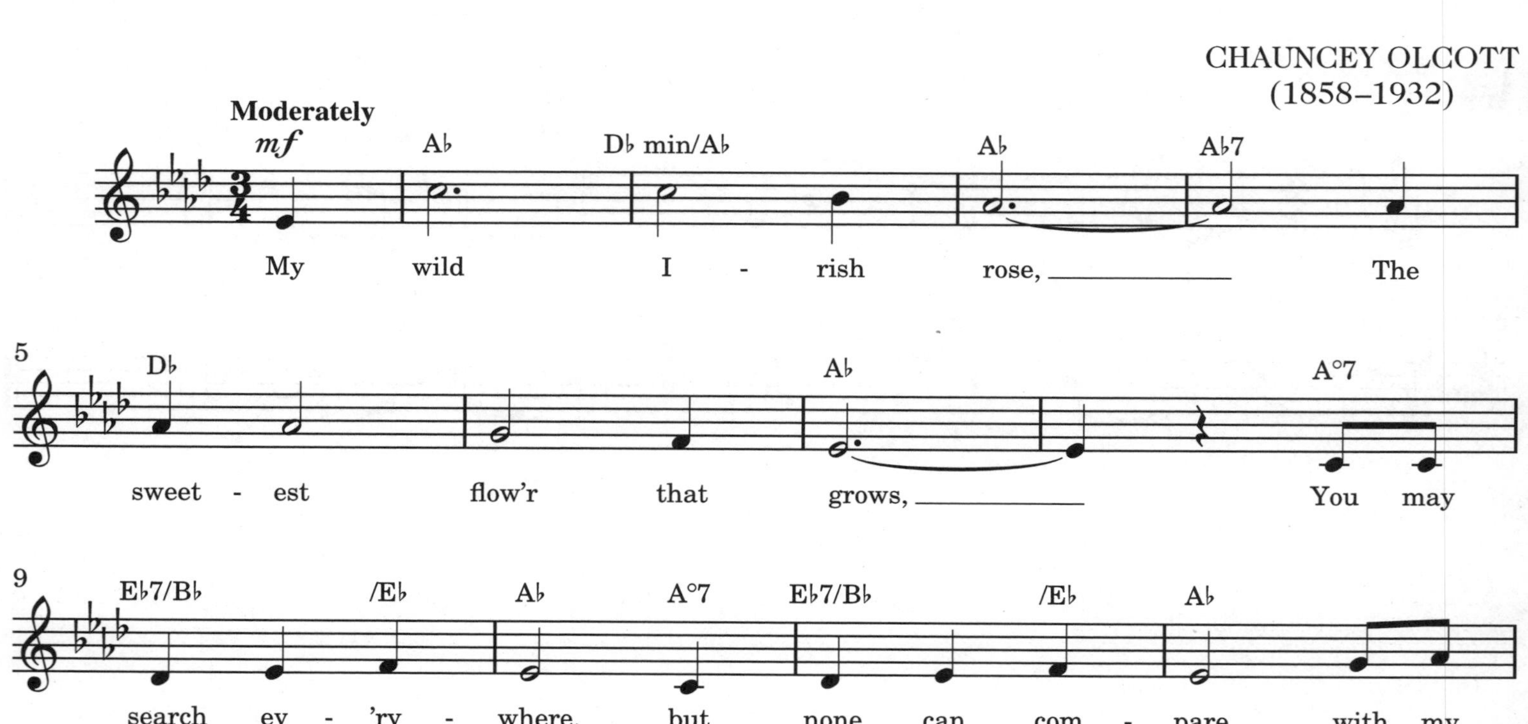

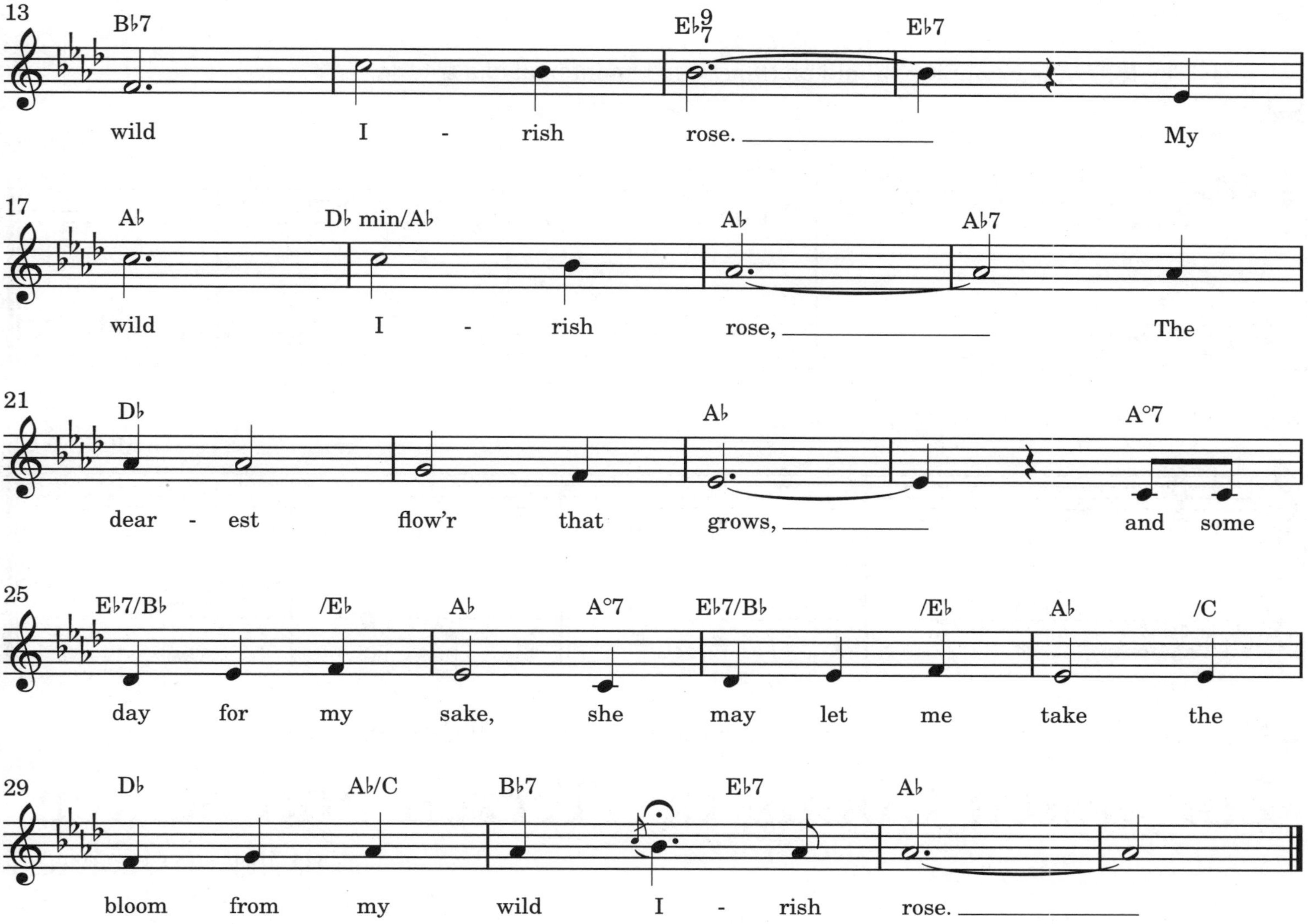

13
B♭7
wild I - rish
E♭9/7
rose.
E♭7
My
17
A♭
wild
D♭ min/A♭
I - rish
A♭
rose,
A♭7
The
21
D♭
dear - est flow'r that
A♭
grows,
A°7
and some
25
E♭7/B♭ /E♭
day for my
A♭ A°7
sake, she
E♭7/B♭ /E♭
may let me
A♭ /C
take the
29
D♭ A♭/C
bloom from my
B♭7 E♭7
wild I - rish
A♭
rose.

4. Accompany in keyboard style.

Eddie's Tune

MARTHA HILLEY

Stirringly
mf
I vi ii 4/2 V6 V6/4 I6 V4/3 I V6/5/IV
6
IV iv ♯ii♯6/♯4/3 I6/4 V7 ♭VI ♯ii♯6/♯4/3 I6/4 V7 I

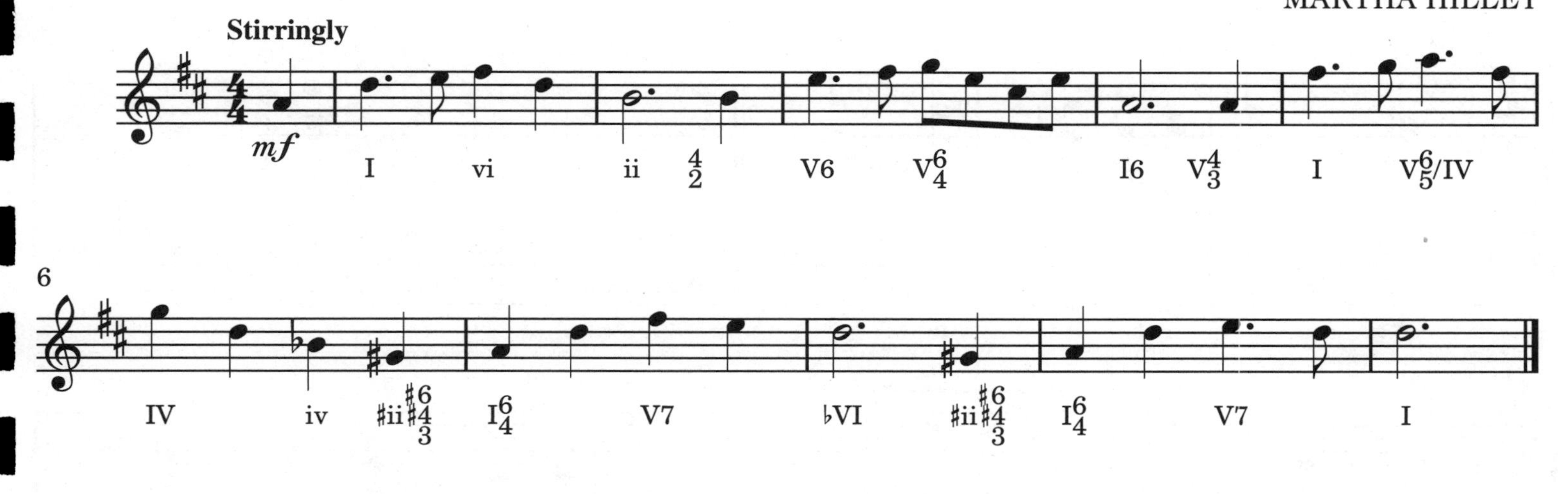

Go to the PDM Web site for additional help with items 2, 3, and 4.

TRANSPOSITION

1. The following examples should be transposed an interval of a tritone.

a. Transpose *up* to B♭ major.

C. MORENUS

b. Transpose *up* to D major.

C. MORENUS

2. Transpose Türk's *Zur ersten Übung der Terzen und Sexten* to C major and B♭ major.

Zur ersten Übung der Terzen und Sexten

DANIEL GOTTLOB TÜRK
(1756–1813)

Andantino

mp

6

12

Go to the PDM Web site for an extensive tutorial on the Türk piece.

3. Play this excerpt as an ensemble: Part I—clarinet, Part 2—violins I and II, and Part 3—viola and cello. Then play all string parts together as a classmate plays the clarinet. Compare the key signatures. How does a clarinet in A transpose?

Quintet in A Major

(Excerpt)

WOLFGANG AMADEUS MOZART, K. 58
(1756–1791)

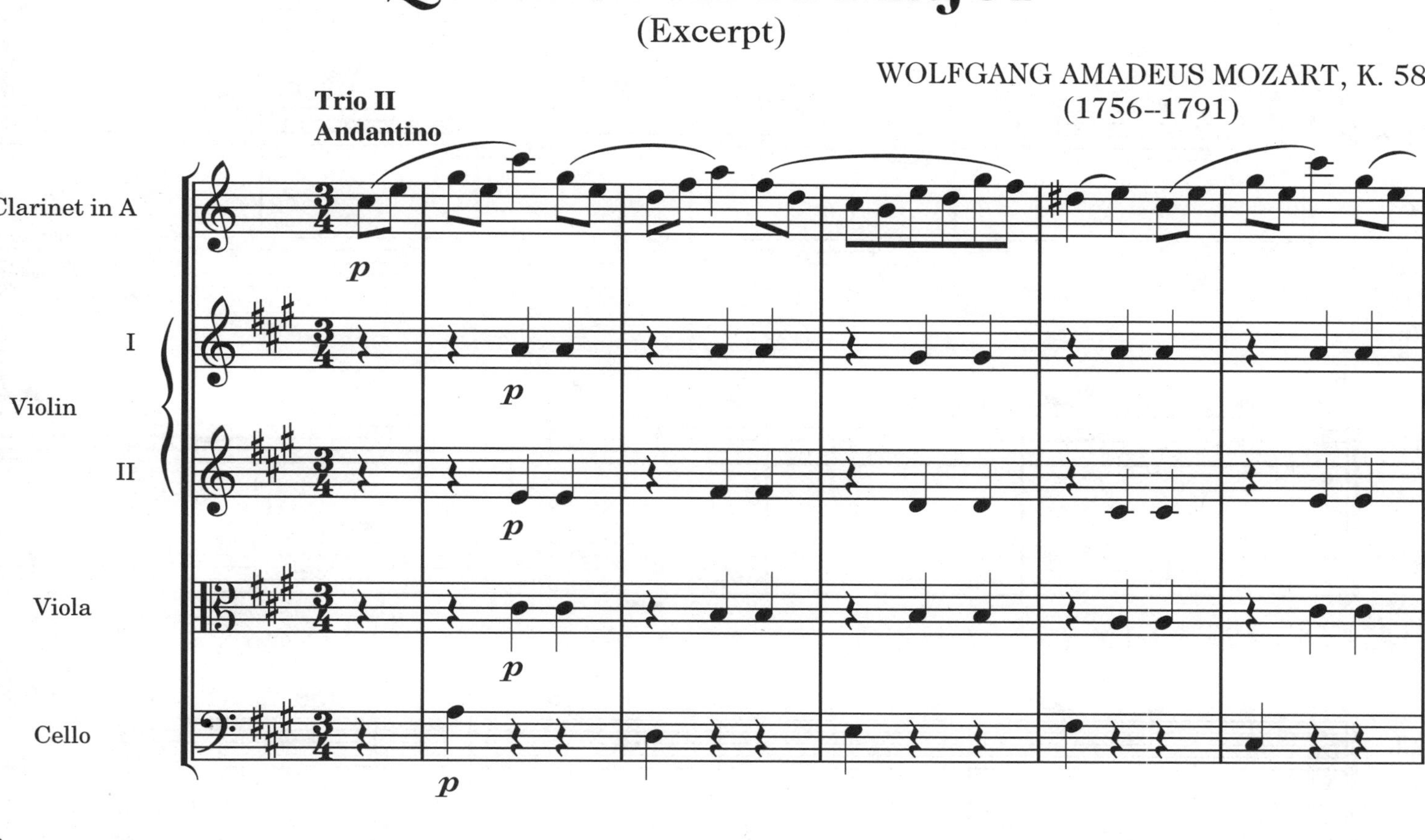

4. Return to the "Chorale Style" reading in Chapters 11, 12, and 13 (pages 283, 312, and 341) and do a key signature transposition (i.e., if the excerpt is in A, play it in A♭. If in E♭, play it in E, etc.).

5. In what key will you think? Choose a partner and perform. Switch parts and perform again. Try playing both parts.

Duo II

(Excerpt)

FRANÇOIS DEVIENNE, Op. 21, No. 2
(1759–1803)

IMPROVISATION

1. Improvise three choruses of blues in F.
    - Chorus 1: RH non-root 13th and 9th chords with LH walking bass
    - Chorus 2: LH non-root 13th and 9th chords with RH blues scale melody
    - Chorus 3: RH non-root 13th and 9th chords with LH walking bass

Go to the PDM Web site for more help with blues improvisation.

2. Develop the following fragments into 16-bar segments to use with basic movement by 7-year-old children.

3. Return to the *Ballad* progression on page 314. Using the recorded background as a stylistic guide, place 7th chords in your left hand as you improvise in the right hand. The melodic improvisation should consist of chord tones, passing tones, neighbor tones, etc. Remember, simplicity is a strong characteristic. Background 1 contains more of the harmonic content while background 2 is more sparse. Therefore, your improvisational style for the two should probably differ.

COMPOSITION

1. Discuss the compositional techniques used in II. Write a short work "in the style" of the Schuman. What characteristics should you include?

ENSEMBLE

1. You will notice that Part 1 is blank—improvisation on B♭ blues scale is Part 1. There are several ways to perform this ensemble:

   - Trio: Part 1 improvises; Part 2; Part 3
   - Duet: Part 1 improvises: Parts 2 and 3 played as one
   - Duet: Part 1 improvises; Part 2 omitted; Part 3
   - Tradin' 12s: Play as trio and on each repeat move to next part

Red Rover, It's Over!

MARTHA HILLEY

(This page has been left blank to eliminate a difficult page turn.)

1. Enjoy!

Latin Journey

ARLETTA O'HEARN

With a Latin Feel (♩ = 116)

mp

pedal ad lib.

mf

mp
mp
cresc.
mf
mp
pedal ad lib.
cresc.

2. The composer states that the second half of this etude is great for accompanying another instrumentalist who improvises in a C blues scale. Invite a classmate to join you!

Jazz Blues Etude

JOHN FUNKHOUSER

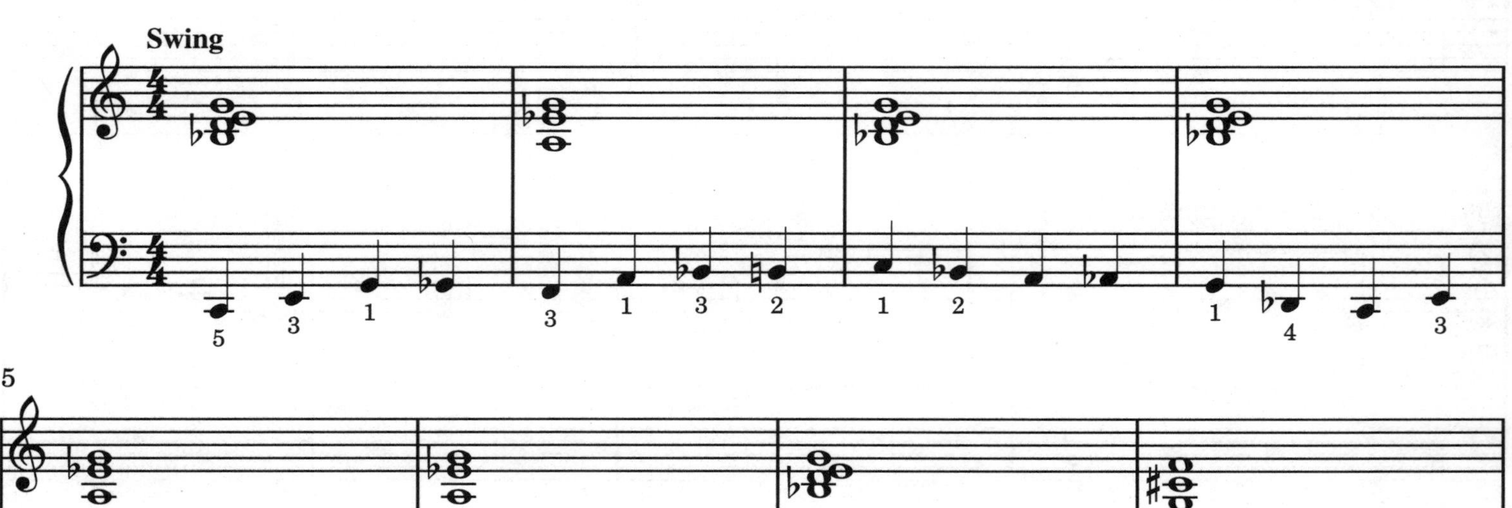

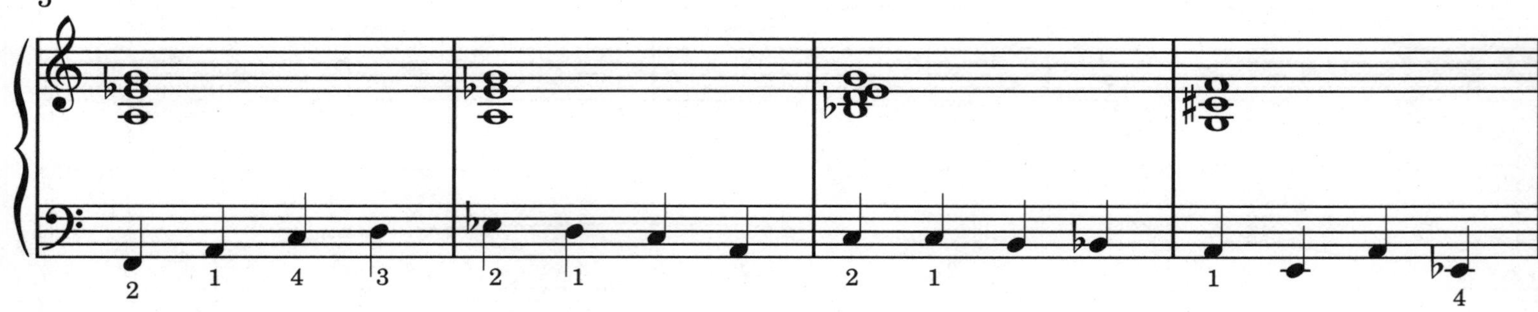

16
19
22
1.
25
2.

3. Play twice. On the repeat, sing as you play.

The Water Is Wide

British Isles Folk Song
Arr. Lynn Freeman Olson

16
20
mf
24
p
28
rit.
mf

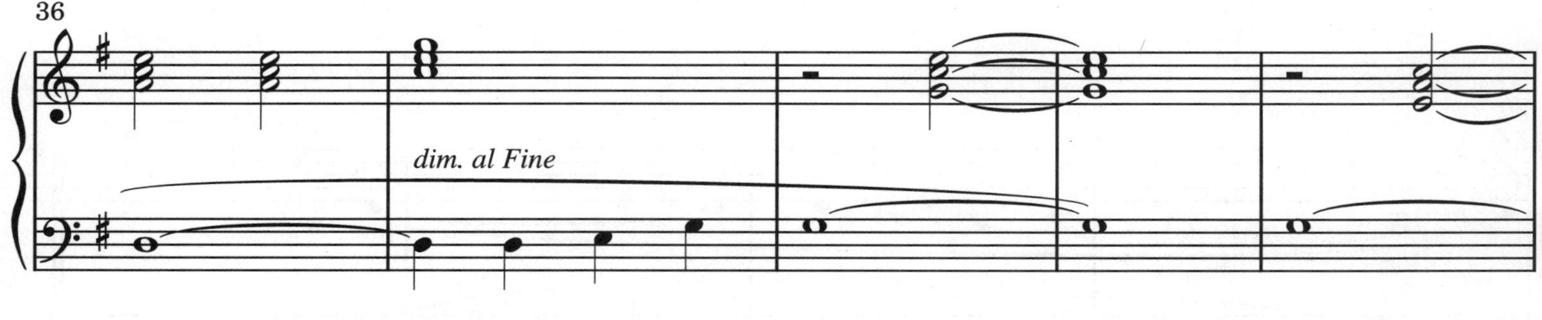

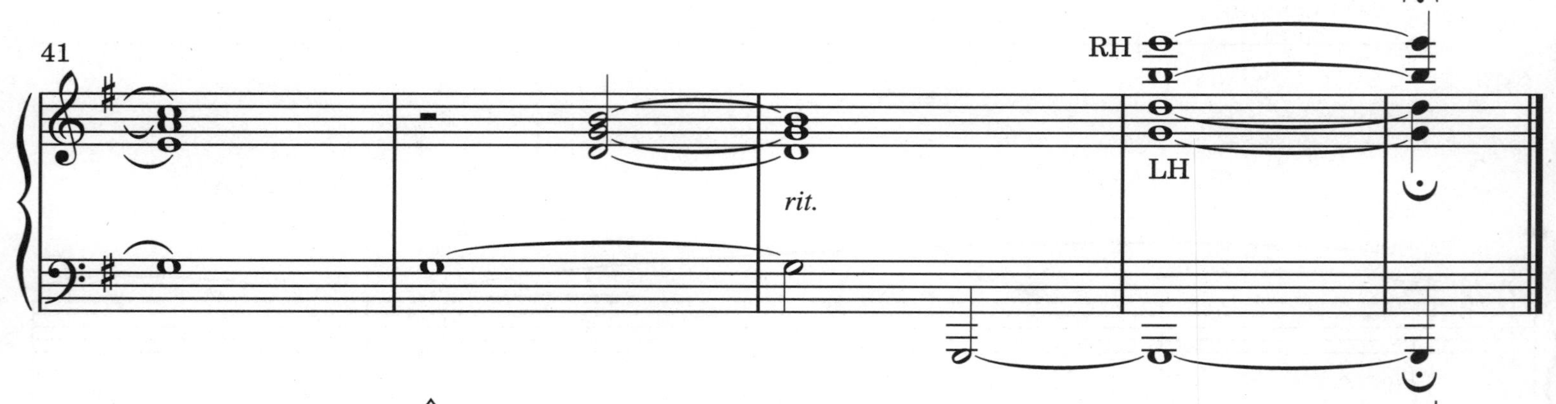

The water is wide, yet I must go.
Oh, would that I had wings to fly!
Is there a boat that will carry two?
Then both may go, my love and I.

A ship that sails out on the sea
Is loaded deep, deep as she can be,
Yet not so deep as the love I'm in—
I know not if I sink or swim.

Appendix A, B, and C from previous editions are now found on the PDM Web site.

Glossary

A bene placito at the pleasure of the performer
A tempo return to original tempo
Accelerando (accel.) gradually faster
Ad libitum (ad lib.) at your pleasure
Adagietto rather slow
Adagio slow
Adagissimo very slow
Agitato restless
Al fine to the end
Alla marcia in a march style
allargando getting broader
Allegretto slightly less than Allegro
Allegro in a lively manner
Andantamente smooth
Andante a moderate tempo; leaning toward slower
Andantino moderately slow
Appoggiatura nonchord tone occurring on a strong beat
Ardito in a spirited manner
Authentic cadence dominant to tonic

Behaglich easily
Bewegt in an agitated manner
Breit broad, stately
Brioso vigorously

Cantabile to make the music "sing"
Cédez to go slower
Celere swiftly
Cesura (//) a complete break in sound
Chorale style 4-part texture, usually voiced "two and two"
Coda ending of a passage or piece
Come sopra same as above
Comodo at a relaxed or leisurely pace
Con brio with spirit
Con forza with force
Con moto with motion
Con riposo in a calm, tranquil manner
Continuo bass line with figures to indicate harmonies to be played on a keyboard instrument
Crescendo (cresc.) gradually louder

Da Capo (D.C.) from the beginning
Dal Segno (D.S.) from the sign
Deciso decidedly
Decrescendo (decresc.) gradually softer
Diatonic pertaining to the key
Diminuendo (dim.) gradually softer
Dolce sweetly
Dolente sorrowful

Einfach simply
Espressivo (espr.) expressively
Etude a study; exercise or composition with a particular technical problem presented

Feuerig with fire

Gavotte a dance from the French usually written in 4 and beginning with a strongly accented third beat
Gemächlich leisurely
Geschwindt quickly
Getragen slow; sustained
Giocoso playful
Giustamente with exact precision
Grazia graceful

Hemiola rhythmic relation of three notes in the time of two

Intimo from the heart
Invention contrapuntal writing; a short piece usually consisting of a theme (subject) and a counter-theme (countersubject)

keyboard style in harmonization, "3 & 1" voicing; melody is the highest sounding voice and determines the shape of the right-hand chord
Kräftig strong

Langsam slow
Larghetto slow; not quite as slow as Largo

Largo slow; in a broad manner
Leading tone 7th degree of the scale
Lebhaft animated
Legato in a smooth, connected manner
Leger line short line used to extend above and below the normal five-line staff
Leggero (leggiero) lightly
Leichtlich lightly
Lento very slow
Lesto lively
Liscio smoothly
Loco play as written
Luftig light
Lunga sometimes used in conjunction with a fermata; long
Lustig happy; merry
Luttoso mournful

Ma non troppo but not too much
Maestoso stately
Marcato emphasized
Mässig moderately; may be used with other terms (i.e., mässig langsam—moderately slow)
Meno Allegro not so fast
Mesto melancholy
Mezza voce half voice
Misterioso creating a mood of mystery
Mit viel Kraft with much force
Moderato at a moderate speed
Modes in early music history, the collective name for scales
Molto much
Morbido soft, tender
mordent in Baroque ornamentation, refers to an alteration of the written note with the note immediately below it
Morendo gradually dying away
Mosso motion
Motif subject
Munter lively

Neighbor tone upper or lower second of a harmonic tone that returns to original harmonic tone
Nicht zu schnell not too fast

Pastorale an instrumental piece depicting a feel for rural scenes
Pensoso pensive
Pesante heavy
Piacevole pleasant; free from strong accents
Piangevole mournful
Piú more
Pizzicato plucking a string
Poco little
Poco a poco little by little
Portato indicates a nonlegato tone; not as short as staccato
Posato dignified
Preciso with marked precision
Prestamente rapidly
Prestissimo the fastest possible

Rallentando (rall.) gradually slower
Retenu to hold back
Risentito vigorous
Risoluto in a resolute manner
Ritardando (rit.) gradually slower
Robusto boldly
Rondeau a genre of music popular in French monophonic songs of the 13th century
Rondo a particular form of instrumental music which uses a recurring theme
Roulade as a florid vocal phrase
Rubato as a means of expression, to extend the duration of one note at the expense of another
Ruhig calm

Scat syllables used to verbalize blues and jazz rhythms
Scherzando in a light hearted fashion
Scherzo a composition in a lively tempo
Schwungvoll in a swinging fashion
Scorrendo flowing
Semplice simple
Sempre always
Sentito with emotion
Senza without
Sequence a compositional technique employing transposition of a motive to different scale degrees; the transposition may be literal or diatonic
Serioso grave
Sforzando (sfz) giving a strong accent
Simile (sim.) in a similar manner
Smorzando (smorz.) dying away
Sostenuto usually equivalent to slowing the tempo
Staccato detached; usually an upward motion
Stretto typically in contrapuntal music, to overlap the subject in two or more voices
Subito suddenly
Svegliato animated

Tempo I original tempo
Tempo primo first tempo
Tonal center the tone or harmony that represents the tonic of a given key
Tritone augmented 4th or diminished 5th
Troppo too much

Un poco a little

Vistamente animatedly
Vite fast

Vivace quite fast
Vivacetto less lively than vivace
Vivo very lively

Wiegand swaying, rocking

Zierlich delicately, gracefully
Zeitmass tempo

Index of Titles

Index of Composers